A View from the Deckplates

Two Decades Aboard Destroyers during the Cold War (1950-1970)

By

George J. Chambers
Senior Chief Firecontrolman
United States Navy (Retired)

from Roger Byrd for my 75th Birthday

ISBN: 1-4184-0962-6 (e-book)
ISBN: 1-4184-0963-4 (Paperback)

Library of Congress Control Number: 2003099417

This book is printed on acid free paper.

Printed in the United States of America
Bloomington, IN

1stBooks - rev. 04/28/04

A navy ship is today—as it always has been—a small bit of America upon the sea. It sails everywhere, defending the Flag, or just showing it, building goodwill for our nation...

—Allan R. Bosworth
Captain, U.S.N., Retired

CONTENTS

ACKNOWLEDGEMENT

My thanks and my appreciation are extended to the many different web sites where sailors have posted insights and comments that have served to refresh my memory. In addition to various web sites, I have consulted books addressing naval history and naval lore. Those that Ihave found to be most useful are listed in the bibliography. I would like to acknowledge the staff of the National Archives and Record Administration, College Park, Maryland, who assisted me in researching the deck logs of the six ships that I served in. I would also like to thank my ex-shipmates who have provided me with their memoirs. Of special note is the assistance provided to me by Ms. Julie Lecher, Reference Librarian, Naval War College, Newport, Rhode Island. Also, a special thank you must go to my wife Jackie who provided the inspiration to research and write this book and who provided encouragement, research assistance, and proofreading during the writing process. Without her this work would never have happened.

PROLOGUE

The beginning of the second half of the Twentieth Century was very tumultuous for America. World War II (WW II) had been over for several years, Harry S. Truman was president and America and most of the world community was looking forward to years of peace. However, the military draft was still in effect. On 24 October 1945, the United Nations (UN) was born in San Francisco. Shortly thereafter, on 5 March 1946, Winston Churchill declared that "an iron curtain has come down across [Europe]." Then on 24 June 1948, the Soviet Union blockaded Berlin and the U.S. Air Force began the Berlin Airlift in order to save the people of democratic West Berlin from starving. The State of Israel was also created in 1948. Then, in August 1948 a California Congressman, Richard M. Nixon, exposed the presence of communist infiltration within the U.S. Government in the Alger Hiss case.

In 1949 Communist Chinese forces under Chairman Mao Tse-tung drove the Nationalist Chinese forces under Generalissmo Ch'ang Ki Shek out of Mainland China. Under threat of invasion by the mainland communists Ch'ang's Kuomintang government and nationalist forces established themselves on the island of Taiwan (formally Formosa). Also in 1949 the Union of Soviet Socialist Republics (USSR) exploded their first atomic bomb, thereby joining the club of world atomic powers. The threat of a shooting war between the United States and the Communist USSR seemed imminent. In response, the *North Atlantic Treaty Organization* (NATO) was formed. It consisted of the United States and 14 other Western countries. On

25 June 1950, President Harry S. Truman had ordered the "neutralization of the Straits of Formosa." The U.S. 7th Fleet[1] then established a naval blockade in the Straits.

My desire to serve in the U.S. Navy was probably influenced by where I grew up. Long Island, New York has always been associated with the sea. It was on the eastern end of the island where the first English settlement in New York was established in 1639. As a youngster, before WW II, my best buddy, Ray, and I had our own "yacht"—a dilapidated, rotten hulk of a fishing boat that was beached near where we lived. During this period we lived near Jamaica Bay, in an area that is now part of John F. Kennedy International Airport. Later, I constantly heard stories about the trans-Atlantic convoys and ships being torpedoed by Nazi submarines right outside of New York Harbor and off the Rockaways. Neighbors would periodically exhibit souvenirs that had washed ashore. Still later, three neighbors and my uncle joined the Navy, at least two of whom served in destroyers. When I was about 15, without our parent's knowledge, Ray and I went into the City and took the test for the Merchant Marine. We both passed with high scores but veterans with veteran's preference points[2] kept us from being called.

It was under these conditions that a 17-year old high school dropout, totally unsophisticated in the liberal arts, embarked on a twenty-year career in the U.S. Navy. This is the story of that career, primarily served aboard destroyer-type ships. It is autobiographical in nature with selective milestones in history inserted in italics to keep the story in the context of world events.

Although some dates may not be accurate and some events may be out of time-sequence, all are factual to the best of my memory as I did not maintain a diary or had any letters or notes to refer to.

NOTE: Items and events in the text that do not directly pertain to one of the six ships that I served in are in *italics*. Due to limited space in this book I've limited these comments, however they do provide a context for naval operations during the time period in which I served.

CHAPTER 1: First Enlistment, February 1950

*Any man who may be asked in this century what he did
to make his life worthwhile...can respond with a good
deal of pride and satisfaction, 'I served in the United
States Navy.*

—President John F. Kennedy
Annapolis, MD, 1963

On Tuesday, November 22, 1949, I turned seventeen. Since I
thought that I needed to wait one day to be "official," the next day I
went to the Navy Recruiting Office at 90 Church Street in downtown
New York City to enlist. I was given the screening test and received a
grade of 100%. Shortly thereafter the recruiters found that the test
had been compromised and informed me that I had to retake the test
using another version. I received a grade of 100% on that version
also and as a result my father had to have an interview with the recruiters. Apparently he satisfied them that I was not involved with the
compromised tests and I was accepted. I never did find out what this
situation was all about.

Originally, my swearing-in was scheduled for Monday, 30
January 1950, so on Saturday night my friends held a farewell party.
When I reported on Monday the Navy had a draft of 115 recruits
planned, but that morning the quota was cut to 100 and I was number
102. The recruiter told me not to worry about it as "normally not eve-

rybody passes the final physical." This time they all did and I had to return home and remained in my room for two days before I went out and faced my friends and local merchants. I was quite embarrassed and frustrated over this situation and having to continually answer the same question, "I *thought* you *were* going in the Navy?"

The following week, on 1 February, I was finally sworn into the U.S. Navy. The next test that I took was the famous "Eddy Test," a test designed to measure aptitude for electronics training. My marks on that were high enough to qualify me for my first Navy rating: EFSR (Electronics Field Seaman Recruit).[1]

After completion of the enlistment ceremonies culminated by the Oath of Allegiance to the United States, about fifty other recruits and myself were sent to Hoboken, NJ, where we boarded a train for the Great Lakes Naval Training Center, located 40 miles north of Chicago. Except for a weekend train trip to Washington, DC with my mother this was the furthest that I'd ever been away from home. We spent the days being awed by sights that "city boys" didn't get to see very often, such as herds of cows in the fields. For most of us this was also our first trip where we slept in Pullman cars. Little did we realize that these sleeping compartments would provide our last privacy for 16 weeks!

Basic Training

Our draft of recruits arrived at the Great Lakes railroad station at about 3 A.M. in freezing cold weather. There was no one there to greet us or to tell us where to go. Here we were tired, cold and just a little disillusioned. We thought that we were special for entering the service of our country, but we soon realized that we were just another bunch of new recruits. Finally someone located a posted notice that advised us to go down the hill, under the railroad bridge to a "camp" (this was Camp Dewey, Downs, or Porter). When we arrived at camp we were asked If we were hungry to which we all replied with an emphatic, "Yes." We were escorted to a messhall where we were fed eggs and beans. Nothing ever tasted so good! We were to discover that this was the Navy's traditional Wednesday and Friday breakfast. Finally we were led to a barracks where we tried to settle down, but like most young men of our age in a new, strange environment we were full of excitement. Apparently we were making a lot of noise as a Chief (at that time most of us had no idea what a "Chief" was, but we were about to learn quickly) came in and warned us that if we did not settle down we would be out on the "grinder."[2] Of course we did not know what that was either, but we did settle down. At least we did until we were rudely awakened by shouts of "reveille, reveille, hit the deck" and the loud "clatter, clatter, clatter" noise made by a Coke bottle being run around the inside of a corrugated trash can.

The next day our recruit training company was formed as Company 14. Our company commander was Chief Torpedoman M. J. Duerr. His assistant was a First Class Boatswains Mate (BM1) J. J. Nooner ["Boats"]. The first order of business was getting a close cropped haircut. This served two purposes: one was to eliminate any head lice, and the other was to make us all equal in appearance. The haircut was followed by us receiving our issue of working uniforms (dress uniforms would come later). We also received a set of two dog tags on a chain to wear around our necks. These had our name, service number, religion, and blood type stamped into them. We were somewhat shocked and had our first dose of reality of the possibility of death when we were told the notch in one corner of the tags was there to facilitate jamming it between our teeth in case we were killed. Boot camp was run-of-the-mill except for the fact there was a coal miners' strike that winter and the training center was running low on coal.[3] For several weeks we had little heat and the messhalls in the camps were closed. We had to march over to "mainside" for all our meals for a period of time. These meals were served in the messhall and were equivalent to what one would get in any fast-food restaurant.

Company 14 was a typical company formed of boys and young men most of whom were from New York, New Jersey, or Connecticut. They ranged in age from barely 17 up to the mid-20s.

Educationally, we had high-school dropouts, high school graduates, and a few with some college credits. We also started training with two recruits who had prior military service. Our days consisted of drilling, small arms firing, gas mask drill, and classes in Naval History, Navy Traditions, Seamanship, Military Law, and Fire Fighting. In our "free time" we wrote letters home, did a little male bonding (essentially telling lies about our success with the ladies and in sports), and studied our *Blue Jacket's Manual*, which theoretically contained everything that we needed to know in order to become good sailors. We also had calisthenics and competitive track exercises where I anchored our company's 100-yard relay team as I was quite fast at that time. We competed against the other recruit companies and frequently won.

Our barracks were two-story "H"-shaped wooden buildings. Recruit companies were quartered in each wing. The washrooms, heads (toilets), and heated clothes drying rooms were located in the cross arm. Company 14 was in the lower-left segment. The living compartment (room) was divided into halves with two wooden tables in the middle. This area was known as the "quarterdeck" and was where "official" functions were held. There was a 4-inch metal pipe running down the center of each wing on which we hung our seabags. Running down either side of the pipe were rows of wooden, two-tier bunk beds.

Our daily uniform was dungarees, blue chambray shirts, and pea coats. We also had to wear leggings, canvas wraps around our lower legs. These identified us as new recruits. Some individuals had problems getting the hang of putting their leggings on properly with the lacing hooks on the outside. They would lace them inside and when they tried to walk the hooks would tangle. The recruit company occupying the other segment had been in training for several weeks; therefore, they qualified as "old salts" and were not required to wear leggings. The absence of leggings was one of two signs that one wasn't a "new recruit." The other was the length of our hair. Their words of advice were to be respected. They also shared critical information, often more legendary than factual, such as when they warned us "the cooks put saltpeter in the food." We did not know whether to believe them or not.

All of our clothing was supposed to be stowed in our seabags. There was a special "Navy Way" of how this was to be done. Periodically we would have seabag inspection where all of our gear was to be properly cleaned, rolled, tied off with clothes stops, and laid out on our blankets. If our gear was rolled properly, the Navy Way, it would all fit into the seabag. Hence the well-known expression, "If the Navy wanted you to have a wife, she'd come in your seabag."

In the evenings we had to hold "field day"[4] in the barracks and wash our bedding and clothing. One day I had to go to the dentist and have a tooth extracted and that night I bled on my pillowcase. I washed it but there was a faint outline left that could be seen if the light was just right. Apparently the light was right when the barracks was inspected as "Boats" Nooner found it marked with a large red circle indicating a demerit. If a Boot accumulated an excessive number of demerits, he would be put back into another company and, therefore, have his training period extended.

These were the closings days of the era of the so-called "Rocks and Shoals," the *Articles for the Government of the Navy*[5] that had been the rule of law for over a hundred years. In 1950 Congress enacted the *Uniform Code of Military Justice* (UCMJ), which replaced the Rocks and Shoals and which became effective on 31 May 1951 and govern the military to this day.[6] The *Articles* were much more Draconian than the UCMJ and no sailor wanted to run afoul of them.

When Boats found the marked pillow, he bought it to the quarterdeck where we were all sitting on the deck listening to Chief Duerr. He then proceeded to slap me in the face with the pillow, a physical assault that undoubtedly would not occur in today's Navy. My reaction from the blow caused me to rock back on my heels, banging my head against the wooden bunk, and then rocking forward. This resulted in me stomping Boats instep. As a result of this perceived transgression, I was designated Barracks Master at Arms (MAA), responsible for ensuring the barracks was ready for inspection after the company left for morning drill or classes. After performing this duty I then had to race to join the company for the days scheduled activity. The companies would compete for award flags in different categories: scholarship, drill, barracks cleanliness, and other activities. The company with the flag for Overall Performance was entitled to "head of the line" privileges at the messhall.

At about 4 A.M. one morning, after we had held field day and secured the barracks for the night, a rival company commander came in. He rousted us out of our racks (beds) and had us stand at attention while he inspected the barracks. He said the barracks was a mess, kicked over the butt kits, and left. Apparently this was his way of giving his company "an edge up." We were up for the rest of the night cleaning up. When Chief Duerr arrived and saw the deck was still wet we told him what happened. We know that he had "words" with the other Chief out behind the barracks and we never had problems with him again.

During our fifth week (or was it the sixth week?) our company took its turn at "service week." During service week we served as "mess cooks": working in the messhall setting up, serving meals, cleaning up, assisting in food preparation (e.g., peeling potatoes), and performing other typical chores. We also worked in the scullery where we cleaned serving trays and washed pots and pans.

One of the most exciting times was when we had fire-fighting training. There was a mock-up of a ship's engine room that would be filled with oil and set afire. We then had to attack the blaze and put it out using the equipment and techniques that we had been taught. Generally there would be several recruits manning a fire hose and we all had to take our turns at the different positions. On occasion one of the recruits would get scared and drop his part of the hose and run. This would put the nozzleman in a position where he had to really fight the nozzle to keep the spray between the hose team and the fire.

One of the most demanding episodes of our training was the time when we took our GCTs—General Classification Tests (or apti-

6

tude tests). These tests were given in a large classroom much like those in civilian schools. The main difference was that the proctors were senior petty officer drill instructors. We were commanded to not look anywhere but at our test papers, not to either side or up. If our pencil points broke we were to hold the pencil in the air while keeping our eyes on the desk. Being new boots, we weren't exactly sure what the consequences would really be if we violated these orders, but we didn't "test" the outcome.

For the first eight weeks, our only form of recreation was a movie shown in the drill hall on Saturday nights. During one show I lost my wallet from the back pocket of my dungarees. It had everything in it, including my address book, and it was never found. This loss was destined to play havoc when I went home on "boot leave" at the end of training as I no longer had those very important telephone numbers. After about our fourth week, a new company of "boots" (by now we were "old salts") moved aboard on the second deck. Their arrival provided some diversion as we "old salts" taught them the ways of the navy. These ways were what we had learned from the companies that went before us.

We also had to watch quite a few WW II era venereal disease (VD) movies and these were old, scratchy, and generally of poor quality. These typically warned that even "the girl next door" could be carrying VD. After these movies many jokes would be told about plans to meet the "girls in the white socks."

After our eighth week of training, we were allowed 12-hours of liberty. A few friends and I went into Milwaukee. That afternoon we met some girls and I asked one if we could meet later. She said "Yes, meet me outside of the Ruff." Later I waited on the designated corner and finally asked someone where I'd find the "Ruff." He pointed across the street to a place called the "Roof." This was my introduction to regional dialects—I only knew "New Yorkeese." Eventually we did meet, but by then my liberty time was just about up and it was time to return to camp.

Not everything was drilling, classes, and occasional fun. We also had to learn to stand military watches. After we were well versed in the *Eleven Rules for Sentries,* we would stand clothes line watch. These were two-hour watches where we would "guard" the outside clothes lines, weather permitting. If the weather was snowing or too cold we would stand watch by the clothes drying room in the barracks. As we matured in our training we also got to stand watches at the main gate. During these watches the Officer of the Day (OOD) would come around and challenge us on the *Eleven Rules*. Woe be to the recruit who could not answer the challenges correctly, as he would receive demerits.

When I was about 15 my friend Ray and I had visited the Chrysler Building in New York City. A radar antenna had been installed on the top and it was feeding images of the City to a PPI (Plan Position Indicator) scope in the lobby. This was one of the first public demonstrations of radar following World War II. I was fascinated as the revolving sweep painted an image of the City and I became determined to learn how radar worked. One day Boats Nooner told me that I had to report to sickbay for a hearing test. I asked why and was told it was to qualify me for Sonar School. I then asked what would happen if I failed and was told, "Then you won't be able to go to Sonar School." Needless to say I failed, as I wanted RADAR and not SONAR. Besides, I had no idea what they meant by such things as "tone" or "pitch."

At graduation as the companies passed in review, for some unknown reason, the band dropped the beat just as Company 14 was approaching the reviewing stand. Instead of having the company change step to match the band, Chief Duerr started calling cadence in the original step. As a result of our not breaking step, we were rewarded with an extra week "boot" leave. At this time I was advanced to EFSA (Electronics Field Seaman Apprentice).

The train trip home following "boots" was by way of Buffalo to Albany and then down to Grand Central Station in New York City. When the train stopped for awhile in Buffalo, some of us managed to visit a liquor store in the station. I remember that I bought a pint of

Southern Comfort—don't ask me why I picked this. I guess it was popular when I left home.

After the train left Albany, I got to talking with a young lady. She was cold so I loaned her my pea jacket to wrap around her. I found out that she was from France and her grandparents were seated right behind us so we had to maintain proper decorum at all times.

I was so over-trained that while I was home on leave I'd wash out my socks, skivvies[7] and white hat every night and hang them on a line in our kitchen.

Radarman and Combat Information Center Schools, Norfolk, Virginia

After completing "boots," I was sent to Radarman Class-A and Combat Information Center (CIC)[8] schools in Norfolk, Virginia. When I reported into the Norfolk Receiving Station (RecSta) after boot leave I met a buddy from boot camp and we decided to take a bus downtown. When the bus came, following our habit from back home of guys gravitating to the back of the bus, we went to the rear of the bus and sat down. We were busily talking away and after a few minutes we realized that the bus wasn't moving. Next we heard someone call out "Are you guys just going to sit there?" When we looked up we saw the driver glaring at us through his rearview mirror and both the white and black passengers were also staring at us. For both of us this was our first direct encounter with racial segregation. We decided that discretion was the better part of valor and moved forward.

For a young sailor, downtown Norfolk consisted mostly of East Main Street. This was nothing but bars, bars, bars; B-girls; uniform shops; and the Gaiety Theatre, a burlesque house. There wasn't much for a 17-year old to do. For one period of time my buddy from home, who was stationed aboard the USS ROOSEVELT CVA-42, was in port and would pick me up in the ship's jeep. We'd go to the amusement park or clubs where they didn't observe the 21-year old drinking age.

> *On 25 June 1950, the Korean War broke out when North Korean troops, members of the North Korean People's Army (NKPA) reinforced by Russian-made tanks, invaded South Korea. President Harry S Truman appealed to the United Nations (UN) to take "police action." This was the first time in its brief four-year history that the UN requested member nations to provide military aid and authorized armed intervention against a Communist aggressor nation. Truman then extended all enlistments and draftees for one year* [as I still had three plus years on my current enlistment this action did not impact me].

The Radarman School was in an isolated facility about a mile from the Naval Station and we had to walk about ½ mile to the mess-shall. My main memory of my time at the school was the sailor in an adjacent bunk who had a radio that only received one station. At reveille he would turn it on and it seemed that they were always playing "Good Night Irene," a song that was popular at the time. Another memory was standing nighttime security-fire watches. There was a deactivated air traffic control tower that was about five stories high. We carried a typical night watchman's time clock and had to climb to the top of the tower in the dark to turn a key in the clock. The only light that we had came from a two-cell flashlight. The problem was that the tower was infested with giant roaches (they called them "water bugs") that would squish under our feet as we made the climb to the top and back down.

One highlight on my "growth curve" as a sailor was being able to buy "tailored" Seafarer brand dungarees with bell-bottoms. These would replace the standard, loose-fitting, navy issued dungarees. Another learning experience was about the policy of the Navy occasionally being paid in $2.00 bills. The Navy would periodically do this in order to flood the marketplace with them, thereby showing the local populace how much they depended on the Navy's presence.

I completed these schools and was designated a RDSA (Radarman Seaman Apprentice[9]) on 8 September 1950, and was assigned to USS SOUTHERLAND DDR-743, a radar picket destroyer based in San Diego, California.[10] These orders excited me and I looked forward to my first ship as I had a fascination with destroyers. This was perhaps developed from WW II movies and sea stories told by friends and neighbors. Upon detachment I was placed in charge of a draft of eight sailors, all going to San Diego by train.

Our first stop was Chicago where we had chits to transfer by taxi from one railroad station to another. However, as we had several hours to kill, we sold the chits to a cab driver for about 75-cents on the dollar. We then had something to eat (a hot dog) and saw the downtown area before walking to the other station. When we boarded the San Diego-bound train, the porters assigned us all to lower berths in the Pullman car. The next day a bunch of Marine reservists recalled for the Korean War boarded the train. That evening, when we returned to the Pullman car, we found that the Marines, who outranked us, had commandeered our berths. At some point a young lady boarded the train and she would sit primly looking out of a window. What drew the attention of these young sailors was the fact that she wore a sheer blouse without a slip, only her bra. None of us from the East Coast had every seen anything like this. At another stop a recalled lieutenant commander boarded the train and we all became friendly. When we stopped in Albuquerque he left the train and returned with two cases of beer that he shared with us.

First Visit to San Diego

We arrived at the San Diego railroad station on a Saturday. I still remember how impressed I was with the Spanish-style station building and the ballpark right down the street, the home of the San Diego Padres of the Pacific Coast League. In 1950, San Diego was a much smaller town than it is today. The main street, Broadway, was mostly naval clothing shops, locker clubs, and bars.

When I reported to the Naval Receiving Station (RecSta) at 32nd Street, I found that SOUTHERLAND was already in WestPac (the Western Pacific). My main memory of my time in San Diego was participating in a "drumming out" ceremony [remember, this was before the days of the UCMJ]. One morning all hands at the RecSta were ordered to fall out in dress uniforms. After we were formed in ranks on the grinder, Marine guards marched in six prisoners. Their charges and dishonorable discharge sentences were read and then all insignia were removed from their uniforms and they were given a suit of civilian clothing. We were all then ordered to about face thus turning our backs on the prisoners and they were escorted out of the main gate. This left a lasting impression on me, as it was my first true-to-life experience with having to pay serious consequences for ones actions.

First Transit to WestPac, 1950

After a few days I was shipped to Treasure Island in San Francisco Bay and then transferred to USNS GENERAL DANIEL I. SULTAN for transport out to SOUTHERLAND. The cruise across the Pacific to Yokosuka, Japan took sixteen days with a brief stop in Hawaii. Up until this time, the largest ship I had every been aboard was the Statue of Liberty ferry in New York Harbor. Fortunately I didn't get seasick. As we entered Pearl Harbor we were all shocked into silence as "Attention to Port" was announced on the ship's public address system. That's when we had our first view of the hulk of the battleship USS ARIZONA, BB-39, that had been sunk on 7 December 1941.[11] At that time the memorial that now covers the ship had not been built. This "rendering of honors" would be repeated during each subsequent visit to Pearl Harbor. This trip also provided me my first experience in crossing the International Date Line when, as a "landlubber," I was initiated into *King Neptune's Realm of the Golden Dragon*. While aboard GENERAL DANIEL I. SULTAN I got into a craps game with some other transient sailors, one was a BM1 who was also heading to a ship out of Japan. I happened to win all of his money, about $50. Although I did not know it at the time, this would cause me several days of anxiety after I arrived in Japan.

Most our time was spent in utter boredom as we didn't have any assigned duties. However, there are three other things that I remember about this trip. One was playing cards with nurses on the deck. We couldn't fraternize, as they were officers, but someone spread a blanket on the deck under the line separating us "swabbies" from the nurses. This became our card table and "seats" were highly sought after. Another was when a young Air Force private looked at the blue water off the Islands and wanted to get a bottle full to send home! The third thing that I remember was that most of the troops got sea sick at one time or another.

When I arrived in Yokosuka I kept hearing stories about "running the gauntlet" outside the main gate. I decided to see what it was all about. Well, outside the gate there were literally hundreds of prostitutes who would grab at the sailors as they tried to walk through the crowd. I finally made my way through the crowd of "ladies" to the Enlisted Men's (EM) Club. After having dinner and a few beers, I made my way back through the crowd to the base.

The next morning I went to the messhall for breakfast and saw what I thought was containers of milk on the table. This was a welcomed sight as the GENERAL DANIEL I. SULTAN had run out of fresh milk about two days out of Pearl Harbor. I poured myself a glass and took a big gulp. That's when I found out that it was buttermilk. I had never had buttermilk and almost gagged. Later that day I went to the cafeteria for lunch and had the biggest prawns I' ha ever seen. They must have been at least 6-inches long and were wonderful.

One of the "must do" things for a young sailor on his first visit to the Orient was to get embroidered dragons sown inside his dress blue jumper cuffs. Ostensibly, this was to show the folk back home (read "young ladies") that he wasn't a "Boot" but a true Asiatic sailor. Of course, I got mine.

During this period Japan was still an occupied country and, under the direction of General Douglas A. MacArthur, was trying to recover from the ravages of WWII. Inflation was running at a high rate, but the exchange rate for Japanese money was frozen at 360 yen to a U.S. dollar. However, higher exchange rates were available on the black market if a sailor wanted to risk getting caught. In an effort to stem the rise in inflation, we were prohibited from taking American "greenbacks" ashore, instead we had to use military script, or "funny money."[12] On paydays, the paymaster would post long lists of names and the amount of money each individual had coming ("on the books"). We would then fill out a pay chit for the amount that we wanted to draw from what we had coming to us. The paymaster was surrounded by several armed guards and was a real stickler for accuracy in the filled-out paychits. Anything that looked like a strike over was rejected and the individual had to fill out a new chit and go to the end of the line. On one particular payday when I checked the list and noticed that the name that followed mine "Robert Chambers." As I'd never met anyone else named Chambers other then my family, I was looking forward to meeting him while in the pay line. As it turned out he was African-American and not a relative.

A few days after arriving in Yokosuka I was sent south to Sasebo, on the southern island of Kyushu. There were several of us going to Sasebo, but I was the only one going to SOUTHERLAND. We traveled on a pre-World War II Japanese train with Japanese versions of Pullman cars. This trip took about two nights and three days. During the day we sat and watched the countryside go by, read, and played card games. Sleeping accommodations in that Pullman berth was quite an experience as it couldn't have been over five-foot long and I am just shy of six feet tall! Each morning my body suffered from muscle stiffness and other aches and pains.

14

CHAPTER 2: A Legacy of Destroyers

Before discussing life aboard a destroyer (DD), it will be useful to briefly discuss the history of DDs from their origin to the current time. This will help to understand and appreciate the love that destroyermen have for their ships. Perhaps no one had a greater appreciation for destroyers and destroyermen[1] than World War II hero Admiral Arleigh Burke[2] who said:

> [D]estroyermen have always been a proud people. They have been the elite. They have to be proud people and they have to be specially selected, for destroyer life is a rugged one. It takes physical stamina to stand up under the rigors of a tossing DD. It takes even more spiritual stamina to keep going with enthusiasm when you are tired and feel that you and your ship are being used as a workhorse. It is true that many people take destroyers for granted and that is all the more reason why destroyermen can be proud of their accomplishments.
>
> Admiral Arleigh A. Burke
> U. S. Navy[3]

Destroyers have traditionally been named for naval heroes and leaders, including deceased Secretaries of the Navy, Admirals, and inventors. Whatever the assignment, whatever the situation, destroyers are ready to respond to John Paul Jones' request to *"Give me a strong ship and the men to sail her, for I intend to go in harm's way."* Ever since the War of 1812 when the frigate USS CONSTITUTION ("Old Ironsides," Captain Isaac Hull, commanding) engaged and sunk HMS GUERRIERE, the American Navy has "owned" the Atlantic Ocean. Following WW II, the American Navy has also "owned" the Pacific Ocean and the adjacent seas. The modern destroyers continue to assist in enforcing this ownership.

It has long been a tradition for sailors to refer to their ships as if they were female. In that context, the modern DD is a "lady" who has grown from infancy (the "motor-torpedo boats" used by European nations at the end of the 19th Century) to adolescence during the period between World War I (WW I) and WW II, to maturity during WW II. Their infancy period was started by USS BAINBRIDGE, DD-1, and her sister ships. These were called "torpedo-boat destroyers." Next came the HOPKINS-class ships that were true "destroyers." The adolescence period was exemplified by the WW I "four-stackers" or "flush-deckers" developed by the US Navy that fought throughout the Atlantic and Pacific during WW II. Due to their thin steel hulls and lack of armor plating they were affectionately called "tin cans" by their crews and divisively by others. The bar of performance for destroyermen was set high by Commander Joseph K. Taussig right after the U.S. entered WW I. Taussig and his squadron of six destroyers[4] left Boston for Ireland on 24 April 1917. They arrived in Queenstown on 4 May after battling North Atlantic spring storms and gales for ten days. When they arrived, Vice Admiral Sir Lewis Bayly, British Commander in Chief of the Coasts of Ireland, asked Taussig when his squadron would be ready for patrol duty, Taussig replied, "We are ready now, sir, as soon as we finish refueling." These six DDs immediately left on patrol to hunt German U-boats.[5]

Then destroyers lived through the growing pains exemplified by seven DDs of Destroyer Squadron Eleven (DesRon 11) running aground off Santa Barbara, California in September 1923.

16

At the beginning of WW II, fifty DDs of the CALDWELL, WICKES and CLEMSON classes, built in the early 1920s,[6] were transferred to the English Commonwealth and renamed as TOWN class. This transfer was under the lend lease program of "Destroyers for Bases." On 4 September 1941, USS GREER, DD-145, was attacked in the North Atlantic by a German submarine. Then on 17 October USS KEARNY, DD-432, was torpedoed by a German submarine resulting in 11 destroyermen being killed and 22 others injured. Five weeks before the infamous attack on Pearl Harbor, USS REUBEN JAMES, DD-245, while on neutrality patrol in the North Atlantic was sunk by a German torpedo with the loss of 115 destroyermen.

On 6 December 1941, USS WARD, DD-139, detected a miniature Japanese submarine outside Pearl Harbor and sunk it with depth charges. On 20 January 1942, USS EDSALL, DD-219, sank the first full-sized Japanese submarine[7] and on 12 April USS ROPER, DD-147 sunk the first German U. Boat in the Atlantic. When the United States entered WW II, destroyers advanced to young adulthood during the Battle of the Atlantic, the Battle of the Aleutian Islands, the War in the Pacific, and *Operation Overlord* on 6 June 1944, where thirty DDs participated.

At the start of the war most of the Navy's destroyers were old, having been built in the mid-1930s. These included the CLEMSON, PORTER, MAHAN, BAGLEY, BENHAM and BENSON classes. However, they immediately started making their presence known. On the night of 24 January 1942, USS JOHN D. FORD, DD-228; USS PARROTT, DD-218; USS PAUL JONES, DD-230; and USS POPE, DD-225 (later sunk), surprised a Japanese invasion force off Balikpapan, Borneo, and sank 4 of 12 transports and a patrol boat. This action became known as the *Battle of Makassar Strait.*[8] Then on 18 April 1942, LT COL James H. Doolittle conducted his famous B-25 raid on Tokyo, flying off the deck of USS HORNET, CV-8. What is less well known is that there were other ships in company with HORNET, including eight destroyers.[9]

17

On 8 October 1942, destroyers took a beating during the *Battle of Cape Esperance* where USS DUNCAN, DD-485 was hit by gunfire from Japanese ships and later sunk. USS BUCHANAN, DD-484; USS FARENHOLT, DD-491; USS LAFFEY, DD-459; and USS MCCALLA, DD-488, were also damaged. LAFFEY was later torpedoed and sunk. Destroyers suffered perhaps their worst defeat at the 4th *Battle of Salvo Island* in November 1942 when nine were hit and badly damaged and three were sunk.[10] They then covered themselves with glory through the actions of Captain Arleigh A. "31 Knot" Burke and his "Little Beavers" of DesRon 23 during the classic *Battle of Cape St. George*. On 26 March 1943, the *Battle of Komanadorskis* occurred in the Aleutian Islands. Destroyers that took part in this action were USS BAILEY, DD-492; USS COGHLAN, DD-606; USS DALE, DD-353 and USS MONAGHAN, DD-354 (later sunk). The destroyer fleet suffered severe losses during *Typhoon Cobra* of December 1944 when USS HULL, DD-350; USS MONAGHAN; and USS SPENCE, DD-512, capsized in the Philippine Sea. Eventually destroyers came of age with the arrival of the FLETCHERS in 1942, followed by the ALLEN M. SUMNERS and GEARING classes starting in 1944.

The destroyers rose again to glory during the *Battle of Okinawa* in March 1945. However, during this battle nine destroyers were lost: USS BUSH, DD-529; USS CALLAGHAN, DD-792; USS COLHOUN, DD-801; USS DREXLER, DD-741; USS HALLIGAN, DD-584; USS LITTLE, DD-803; USS LONGSHAW, DD-559; USS LUCE, DD-522; USS MANNERT L. ABELE, DD-733; USS MORRISON, DD-560; USS PRINGLE, DD-477; USS TWIGG, DD-591; and USS WILLIAM D. PORTER, DD-579. During the war in the Pacific, destroyers also learned the tactics necessary for them to operate effectively with the fast carrier task forces.

Finally, at the end of the war in the Pacific, USS SOUTHERLAND, DD-743,[11] became the first man-of-war to enter Tokyo Bay, right after the minesweeper, USS REVENGE, AM-110. On 28 August she anchored off the Imperial Japanese Naval Base at Yokosuka. Then USS LANSDOWNE, DD-486, carried out the duty of ferrying Japanese dignitaries from Yokohama to USS MISSOURI, BB-63, for the signing of the surrender documents. Overall, seventy-one destroyers were lost during WW II.

Destroyers next distinguished themselves on 13 September 1950, prior to the amphibious landing at Inchon during the Korean War. DesRon 9, consisting of USS MANSFIELD, DD-728, USS DEHAVEN, DD-727; USS LYMAN K. SWENSON, DD-729; and USS COLLETT, DD-730, augmented by USS GURKE, DD-783, and USS HENDERSON, DD-785, from DesRon 5, earned the sobriquet of "*The Sitting Ducks.*"[12] These ships, under the command of RADM John Higgins, steamed up the "Flying Fish Channel" and anchored off Wolmi Do in order to draw North Korean gunfire, thereby exposing their positions. At that, the cruisers present could destroy them. Only one American was killed during this operation, LTJG David H. Swenson, who was hit by shrapnel aboard LYMAN K. SWENSON. Later, SOUTHERLAND relieved COLLETT after she had been hit nine times by enemy gunfire. GURKE was also hit twice.

After the BENSONS and FLETCHERS came the SUMNERS and their 14-foot longer twin sisters, the GEARINGS. These were followed by the "mature" post-war MITSCHERS and FOREST SHERMANS and then by guided missile destroyers of the CHARLES F. ADAMS, the FARRAGUT (or COONTZ) classes (later reclassified MITSCHERS) and the SPRUANCE and KIDD classes. This ongoing growth in destroyer capabilities was driven by the ever increasing capabilities of aircraft and submarines, first by the Japanese and Germans and then by the Soviets. The DD have assumed dowager status with the development of the modern Aegis-equipped destroyer of the ARLEIGH BURKE class.

Destroyers have always taken a back seat to the *Grande Dames* of the fleet, the so-called capital ships: the aircraft carriers, the battleships, and the cruisers. However, these "major combatants" seldom, if ever, go anywhere without their destroyer escorts or screens. Destroyers also present commanders with a tactical advantage in that they can go places that the larger ships cannot go. Their smaller size also is an advantage to their crews when it comes to liberty ports: as frequently they can moor alongside a pier instead of anchoring out.

In the mid-to-late 1930s the Navy built the PORTER and SOMERS classes of DDs that were known as "destroyer squadron leaders." These ships had more anti-aircraft weaponry (eight 5"/38 caliber guns in four twin mounts)[13] than the conventional "flush deck" DDs and were designed to lead and protect those DDs into and during torpedo attacks. Light cruisers had normally performed this role, but a 1930 international treaty limited their numbers.[14] The designation, "destroyer leader" was not used again until the mid-1950s when the MITSCHER class destroyer leaders (DL) were commissioned. These had originally been classified as DD. Next came the FARRAGUT and LEAHY class destroyer-leaders, guided missile (DLG). Ships of these classes ware later redesignated as guided missile cruisers (CG). As we move into the 21st Century, the future of DDs in the US Navy is up to the ARLEIGH BURKE and the under-development ZUMWALT, DD (X), classes.

The legacy of always being ready to respond immediately to any emergency has been passed down from generation to generation of those sailors who call themselves "destroyermen." This legacy had been drummed into me by Chief Duerr during boot camp, through movies, and by friends. It was with this legacy in mind that I proceeded to WestPac to report aboard my first destroyer, USS SOUTHERLAND.

CHAPTER 3: USS SOUTHERLAND: WestPac Cruise 1

When we arrived in Sasebo, I was assigned aboard a fleet oiler, USS CIMMARON, AO-22,[1] for the next leg of my journey to catch SOUTHERLAND on duty in the Sea of Japan. It turned out that the BM1 from the craps game aboard GENERAL DANIEL I.

SULTAN was in charge of the inter-ship transfer station aboard CIMMARON. This type of transfer is made via a highline² at sea with the two ships steaming adjacent to each other and about sixty feet apart. For the several days that it took us to meet up with SOUTHERLAND'S Task Group, "Boats" kept telling me how I was going to get dunked. On 16 November, just prior to my eighteenth birthday, I was finally transferred from CIMMARON to SOUTHERLAND riding in a "breeches buoy"³ dangling from the high line. My fears of getting dunked turned out to be unfounded as both ships kept the lines as taut as a frozen rope.

However, this transfer took place at a very unfortunate time of day for me. After I was lowered from the high line to the portside weather deck of SOUTHERLAND, someone escorted me below to what turned out to be the engineering division's berthing space. No sooner had we gone below when GQ (General Quarters) was sounded, a Klaxon and a voice on the ship's general announcing system commanding, "General Quarters, General Quarters, All Hands Man Your Battle Stations." Next I heard the slamming of hatches and doors as Condition Zebra was set.⁴ I had no idea what to do or where to go.⁵ As I remember, I waited in the dark berthing compartment until GQ was over. At that time it was customary for ships operating off the coast of Korea to go to GQ for both dawn and dusk alerts, when the threat of enemy air attack was greatest. Eventually everything got straightened out and I took my place in the Operations, or "O" Division. At this time I was one or two weeks from my 18th birthday. Up until now Hollywood had provided my only concept of a sea war. I was to learn that the Navy "owned" the sea and was unchallenged by the North Koreans.⁶ However, attacks by MiGs or submarines were always a potential threat as were floating mines and shelling from shore batteries.

On board a Gearing-class destroyer the Combat Information Center, or CIC, was located one deck below the bridge and pilot-house. While on watch in CIC we would rotate stations from monitoring the surface search radar displays to plotting the air situation on vertical Plexiglas plotting boards where we would plot information

22

and write backward on the back of the boards. This allowed the information to be read correctly from the front. Watch tasks also included monitoring the air search radar displays and telephone talker on the Captain's battle circuit and plotting surface and submarine contacts on the DRT (Dead Reckoning Tracer). In order to enhance viewing the radar scopes, except for a few small desk-type lamps, CIC was kept in constant darkness from the time the sea detail was set prior to getting underway until we returned to port and the sea detail was secured. At that time we would all commence holding a field day in CIC.

One of the major responsibilities of CIC was to keep the OOD (Officer of the Deck) informed of the position of our ship in relation to all other ships in the formation. Then whenever the formation changed course, we had to inform the OOD of a course and speed to our new station, on a particular bearing and specific distance relative to the formation guide that was normally an aircraft carrier.

SOUTHERLAND'S History

USS SOUTHERLAND, DD-743, was built by Bath Iron Works, Bath, Maine and was commissioned on 22 December 1944. She was named for Admiral William Henry Hudson Southerland who had an illustrious Navy career in the early 20th Century. He served in four destroyers (BIDDLE, DD-151; BARRY, DD-2; DALE, DD-4 and STOCKTON, DD-73). He was commanding officer of DALE and his last fleet assignment was as Commander, Pacific Fleet. By 24 April 1945, SOUTHERLAND had completed her shakedown training and headed for the Pacific Theater of operations. Over the next several months she operated with the fast carrier task forces and conducted shore bombardment against the Japanese homeland.

After the war, SOUTHERLAND operated out of San Diego and on 19 March 1949, she was redesignated DDR-743. During an overhaul period in the San Francisco Naval Shipyard (SFNSY) in the spring of 1950, SOUTHERLAND'S commanding officer committed suicide by shooting himself in the head in his washroom.[7] On 10 May CDR Homer E. Conrad, USN, assumed the duties of commanding officer. SOUTHERLAND was operating in Hawaiian waters when the Korean War started in June 1950. In September, she participated in the landings at Inchon and was slightly damaged by counterbattery fire after relieving COLLETT, one of the so-called "Sitting Ducks" that had been hit earlier by North Korean gun fire.

Life Aboard a Destroyer

In order to appreciate what life aboard a destroyer at sea is like, one has to understand a destroyer's principle mission: screening fast aircraft carriers from both air and submarine attack. Normally a carrier is escorted by four, or more, destroyers stationed in an arc out in front of the carrier by several thousand yards. This is referred to as a "bent line screen." The lateral displacement of the destroyers on the arc depends on the number of destroyers present. From this position the destroyer's sonar is able to detect any submarines that may be lying in wait along the line of advance.

When the carrier prepares to conduct flight operations, she turns into the wind and increases speed so that a steady, strong wind blows down the flight deck providing lift for launching or recovering aircraft. The course that the carrier assumes may or may not be optimal for the much smaller destroyers. When the course is changed, the destroyers execute a procedure known as "reorienting the screen." While doing this, each destroyer must race across the ocean to new screening stations, typically many thousands of yards away, in order to keep them out in front of the carrier. This frequently means that each destroyer must race across the ocean at high speed[8] without regard to sea and wind conditions to reach their new stations. These operations can take place at anytime and on a moment's notice. Therefore, the sailors aboard the destroyers must constantly be on the alert for heavy rolling and pitching.

In addition to screening stations, destroyers are assigned to "plane guard" stations. These stations are typically off the port side of the carrier and about 1,000 yards behind the carrier on the starboard side. Again, this typically requires the destroyers to race across the ocean without regard to sea and wind conditions.

Arguably, the most strenuous work a typical destroyer's crew engages in is replenishment at sea (RAS). A destroyer is essentially a small, self-sustaining city with limited storage space for fuel, ammunition, foodstuff and other necessities of life. When operating at the high-speeds demanded during operations with aircraft carriers, a destroyer must take on fuel about every three to four days.[9] Enough food and other human needs commodities had to be carried on board for the 16 officers and 300+ enlisted men who served in SOUTHERLAND. During the Korean War period the Navy used three different types of replenishment ships: oilers or tankers for fuel, ammunition ships, and stores ships for food and other items such as mail. In addition, destroyers could replenish from an aircraft carrier when required.

When conducting RAS, the supplying ship would steam on a constant course and speed and the receiving destroyer would steam on a parallel course and speed about 80-100 feet adjacent to the supplying ship. Frequently there would be receiving ships on both sides of the supplying ship. When refueling, highlines would be strung between the two ships and hoses would be manually drawn across from the tanker to the destroyer's fuel inlets. At that time destroyers did not have power winches. When taking aboard ammunition or stores, the same procedure would be used except that the goods would arrive at the destroyer's limited deck space and would have to be immediately struck below. These operations required that the entire crew that was off-watch lend a hand. Since the Korean War, the Navy has developed more advanced methods of RAS, such as the use of helicopters that aren't as demanding on the crew. However, stores still have to be expeditiously struck below. These replenishment operations are carried out during the day, during the night, in all kinds of weather unless the seas are too rough to allow such operations.

Typical off-watch hours at sea were spent cleaning assigned spaces (e.g., berthing compartments, heads, passageways, etcetera) chipping rust and re-painting, writing letters, and eating and sleeping whenever possible. In the evenings, after dusk alert, a movie would be shown on the messdeck and many of the off-watch crew would sacrifice other activities in order to watch it. This routine was periodically interrupted by the need to refuel and to load stores from replenishment ships, to strike them below and to man the lines on high-line transfer stations rigged between the ships. Within this schedule we also had to find time to complete required correspondence courses and to study for advancement in rating exams. Our dirty clothing was sent to the laundry, on a weekly basis, in big canvas sacks and when it was returned we also had to find time to sort it and deliver it to the owner's bunk (bed).

The Radar Gang's living compartment was in the after part of the ship, one deck below the main deck and under the sickbay. We slept in three-high bunks or "racks" (metal frames with canvas laced between them). These were suspended from the overhead by chains. Each rack also had a set of straps that we could use to strap ourselves in when the seas were extremely rough. Under each set of racks were the lockers where we stowed all of our personal belongings, including uniforms. These lockers were approximately two feet wide, three feet deep and about ten inches high. When at sea and engaged in high-tempo operations, the living compartments were dark most of the time as sailors tried to catch some sleep. There were red emergency lights, but for the most part the bulbs would be unscrewed so that the sailors in the nearby bunks would not be disturbed. Periodically there would be disturbances as messengers woke up the ongoing watch standers. Alarm clocks were not allowed as no one would have been able to sleet uninterrupted.

Normally, weather and light conditions permitting, the crew would line up for chow call on the portside weather deck and file down one deck to the cafeteria-style serving line. From there they would go to the next compartment forward, the mess deck. The mess deck consisted of a series of ten-man tables with fold-up benches attached. There was a lip around the edge of each table to keep items from rolling off. When it was dark or sea and weather conditions did not permit access to the weather deck, the crew would line up in an inside fore and aft passageway.[10] Those who were going on watch had head-of-the-line privileges. These conditions lead to short tempers after we were at sea for a few weeks. Comments such as "Watch where you're stepping" and "You don't have the watch" were frequently heard. On some ships senior petty officers also had head-of-the-line privileges.

The quality of our meals mostly depended on three factors: the skill of the duty cook, how long we had been at sea (as that would determine what was available to the cooks), and weather conditions. Breakfast would consist of either fresh or canned fruit, hot or cold cereal, and, on a rotating basis, either eggs and sausages, corned beef hash, Navy baked beans, ground beef in a tomato sauce on toast, or creamed chipped beef on toast. Lunch and dinner would be about the same as one would find on the menu of any of the major chain restaurants.

Another situation that caused short tempers was water hours. The ship's evaporators made all of our fresh water, but the needs of the ship's boilers for water to generate steam to drive the turbines came first. If the evaporators couldn't make enough water to feed the boilers, the water to the showers would be shut off except for brief periods during which everyone who wanted a shower had to "get in, wet down, shut off, soap-up, rinse off, and get out." Some individuals found it difficult to adhere to this regimen and would take extended showers until they got caught, either by the duty water tender (a Boilerman, BT) or the MAA.[11]

In the early 1950s, destroyers did not have teletype capabilities and the only world news we got at sea was when a radioman (RM) had the time to copy the BBC Morse code news broadcast by hand. This would then be duplicated on a mimeograph machine and a limited number of copies would be distributed on the mess deck. Of course, this was also before photocopies or satellites.

No matter how long we had been at sea or how intense the tempo of operations, nothing could restore the crew's morale like mail call.[12] Typically mail would be put aboard a replenishment ship or another destroyer that was scheduled to meet our ship. However, this was frequently unsuccessful as our assignment would be changed and we would not connect with the transporting ship. That ship would then transfer the mail to another ship that had a higher likelihood of catching up with us. Eventually we would get mail, but sometimes we would get later post-marked mail well before earlier post-marked mail. When mail was received aboard, the postal clerk (or whomever was assigned as a "postal clerk") would sort it and the division leading petty officers would pick it up for their divisions and distribute it.

An important inport activity, particularly when overseas in a Navy facility, is having medical or dental problems attended to. Destroyers normally had a hospital corpsman aboard who was prepared to take care of emergency situations and stabilize them as the situation demanded. If the situation required the services of a physician, the crewman had to be transferred.

A close second to mail call for restoring morale was liberty call, when we would get to leave the ship for a few hours. While moored out in the harbor in Yokosuka, we frequently had to decide whether or not it was worth it to wait for a boat and then endure a long, cold ride into fleet landing (the boat landing used by all the ships moored in the harbor). Frequently it wasn't. If we did go ashore, on return we would have to wait in long serpentine queues, separated by railings, for our boat to arrive to return us to the ship. There would be hundreds of cold, somewhat inebriated sailors all waiting for their particular boat to be called. Then there would be a long, cold ride back out to the ship. Once aboard, we had to pass through a "pro-station." At this station was a jar of silver nitrate and a syringe in a jar of alcohol. The drill was for a sailor who had "indulged" to flush his penis with the silver nitrate and put the bulb back in the alcohol. By the time the night was over the silver nitrate and the alcohol would be mixed together and blood-curdling screams would be heard. Eventually this practice was stopped. There was another associated humiliating routine in which we all had to participate. About a week after leaving a port, all of the crew had to undergo a so-called "short arm inspection" where we would line up and have our genitals inspected by a corpsman. This usually happened prior to going through the pay line. If a sailor was trying to hide signs of verneral disease (VD) he could not get paid.

Another good morale booster was what was known as "Rope Yarn Sunday." [13] This was typically a Wednesday afternoon when all unnecessary ships work would be suspended for the afternoon. Ostensibly, this time was to mend clothing, shine shoes, write letters, or to take care of other personal concerns. In practice, it frequently meant a time to catch up on sleep.

On occasion, we would be moored outboard of one of the larger ships such as a destroyer tender or a battleship. This would cause problems for the "tin can" sailors as we did not have the facilities to be as squared away (haircuts, uniforms neat and cleaned) as the watch officer on the large ship would like, so they would send our sailors back to the ship. On other occasions we would encounter the same type of problems when officers from the large ships were stationed at fleet landing.

Inport time for RDs was devoted to holding field day in CIC and other assigned spaces. The radar gang also had responsibility for the torpedo deck (it was still called that even though DDRs no longer carried torpedoes) and several other topside areas. Keeping these areas in ship-shape condition required frequent scraping of rust and old paint and repainting. RDs were also responsible for holding preventative maintenance on assigned electronic equipment: radars, display scopes, the TACAN system, [14] and other equipment. This task mostly consisted of cleaning the equipment, cleaning air filters, and checking and replacing vacuum tubes as needed.

Life Aboard SOUTHERLAND

One of my earliest learning experiences was when I was assigned as bridge talker on the bridge JA sound-powered telephone circuit—the Captain's battle circuit. I was given a message from CIC, "TBQ" ("Tare Baker Queen" in the phonetics of that time) that I knew meant to re-orient the screen. I relayed the message in decoded form to the Captain and OOD. After SOUTHERLAND gained her new station, the Captain proceeded to chew me out, and inform me in no uncertain terms, that my task was ONLY to relay exactly what was said and NOT to interpret the messages. After I was relieved, I found out that standard procedure was for the OOD to look-up and decode each and every message in the appropriate code book, each and every time. It was definitely not the responsibility of a seaman apprentice.

After I was aboard for awhile I was assigned my turn as a messcook. This duty consisted of assisting the ship's cooks, mostly peeling potatoes or mixing powered eggs; working in the scullery; carrying food from the galley to the messdeck; and cleaning the messdecks. One incident that stands out is when another messcook, a radioman striker,[15] and Iwere carrying a large tureen with about four gallons of hot chili from the galley to the messdeck, one deck below the galley. I was on the downside of the ladder (staircase) holding my end of the tureen high as we descended the ladder when suddenly my fellow messcook called out "I can't hold it any longer" and let go of his end. As I was near the bottom of the ladder I managed to jump backwards and thus avoided getting burned by the falling hot chili; however, it was lost, all over the deck. We then spent the next fifteen minutes cleaning up the mess while the ship's cooks hustled to put together something to replace the lost chili. I believe that the off-coming watch ate cold sandwiches.

Over the next few weeks after I reported onboard, SOUTHERLAND performed various duties in support *of Fast Carrier Task Force 77 (TF 77)*[16] that was conducting air strikes against tactical positions and supply lines of the North Korea forces. These duties were mostly plane guard and carrier-screening operations, providing cover for minesweepers and conducting various shore bombardment missions. On 26 October 1950, Communist Chinese People's Liberation Army troops poured across the Yalu River from Manchuria and changed the complexion of the war. The United Nations' X Corps, consisting of the 1st Marine Division, the Army's 3rd & 7th Infantry Divisions; and three South Korean Army divisions, were badly outnumbered and dangerously overextended. On 3 November, General O.P. Smith issued orders for the Marines to "advance to the rear" or to "attack in another direction." Later in the month we were ordered to standby the coast near Hungnan and be prepared to take aboard Marines and X Corps personnel returning from the Chosin (Changjin) Reservoir, south of the Yalu River. After being at GQ for many hours, we were ordered to stand down and resume Condition Three,[17] a normal wartime watch standing condition where only about one third of the ship's stations are manned.

Our normal at-sea routine was really quite boring: stand watch, eat, clean passageways and other assigned spaces, sleep, and then back on watch. Of course we also had to battle the effects of salt water, which meant chipping paint, applying a base coat of zinc chromate and then painting with haze gray, weather permitting. This was a never-ending task.

While at sea in the Sea of Japan floating mines were a constant threat. Whenever possible we kept a lookout posted on the ship's bow. When a mine was spotted it would be either blown up or sunk by gunfire.[18]

Perhaps the worst part of duty in the Sea of Japan was the extreme cold in the wintertime. In addition to the occasional snowstorms, the spray would freeze and coat the ship in ice. Unless it was absolutely necessary, sailors would seldom go out on the weather decks. To complement the mines and the cold, MiG 15s were introduced into the North Korean arsenal posing a potential threat to the fleet; although we were constantly on the alert, I am unaware of any ever approaching Task Force 77 (*TF 77)*. The following chart illustrates how a "fleet" is organized:

31

Fleet	7th Fleet, 6th Fleet, etc.
↓	↓
Task Force (TF) _____	TF 77
↓	↓
Task Group (TG)_____	TG 77.1
↓	↓
Task Unit (TU) _____	TU 77.1.1
↓	↓
Task Element (TE) _____	TE 77.1.1.1

While on station with TF 77, CIC was normally dark and quiet, except for the crackling sounds made by the several voice radio circuits that were being monitored. In one corner, the surface search radar operator would be monitoring his PPI scope for any signs of surface contacts. In the opposite corner, the air search radar operator would be monitoring his PPI scope for any air contacts and providing position updates to the plotter behind the Plexiglas air plot board. The voice-radio operator on the "Screen Common" circuit would be monitoring his earphones and logging all traffic. The sound powered (SP) telephone talkers on the Captain's Battle (JA) and the Weapons Control and lookout (JC) circuits would be standing alert for any reports. In addition, the JA talker would be constantly monitoring the range and bearing to the formation guide and reporting any deviations from the assigned station to the CIC Watch Officer stationed in the middle of CIC. The CIC supervisor would be performing multiple duties including monitoring the PriTac (Primary Tactical) voice-radio circuit and logging all transmissions; monitoring the overall performance of the team; ensuring that all code and authentication plans were up to date; that all status boards were current; and ensuring that team members were relieved or rotated as appropriate. The CIC Watch Officer would be monitoring all internal and external activity and the ship's position in relation to the assigned station and recommending courses of action to the Officer of the Deck (OOD). He would also keep the OOD informed of all other activities including the air, surface and sub-surface picture.

One evening we were anchored in an unknown place (perhaps Wonsan Harbor or near Ch'ongjin[19]) and when we were getting underway I had the sea-detail watch on the fantail. The night was extremely foggy to the point that I could not see the after 5" gun mount (Mount 53) from my station. At one point I could sense, rather than see, something moving in the fog astern of us and off to starboard. I reported this to the bridge and CIC, who reported they had nothing on radar. A few minutes later I saw the bow of USS SAINT PAUL, CA-73, coming through the fog and crossing about twenty feet abaft[20] of us, inside the minimum range of the radar. They were totally unaware we were there!

That fall, our commanding officer (CO) was CDR Homer E. Conrad, USN and our executive officer (XO)[21] was LCDR Manley C. Osborne. LT. May was our CIC officer. On Thanksgiving Day 1950 the following poem (author unknown) was printed inside the holiday menu:

> *Thanksgiving comes but once a year,*
> *So let's be thankful for all we have here;*
> *With taters high on the TP [torpedo] deck,*
> *And beans that haven't been eaten yet;*
> *The turkey is luscious and done to a turn-*
> *The gravy, thank God, has not been burnt;[sic]*
> *If you don't care for turkey, gravy and yams,*
> *There is plenty of SOUTHERLAND baked hams.*

Task Force 95[22] was charged with blockading Wonsan Harbor. This blockade would last until the end of the "Police Action" and would become the longest blockade in U.S. Navy history. Perhaps the bravest sailors that we encountered were those onboard the minesweepers. We would "ride shotgun" for them ostensibly to protect them from fire from North Korean shore batteries. Whenever they would come under fire, we would try to move in to provide counter battery fire. However, they would tell us to move out of the way as they were sweeping mines! Even when out in the open sea, floating mines were always a major concern. When one was spotted, destroyers would try to sink it by gunfire. On 21 November, SOUTHERLAND did sink a floating mine by rifle fire. We had anchored in Wonsan Harbor on 22 November as part of *TG 95.2*. As we were leaving Wonsan Harbor with the sea and anchor detail set, SOUTHERLAND's bow was inundated with a swell that washed one of our sailors under Mt. 51 (the forward 5" gun mount), badly injuring him. Our Chief Hospitalman (HMC) and his assistant (a HM3) attended to him in the wardroom providing the best medical care available. He was later transferred in a Stokes stretcher via highline to a larger ship that had doctors and surgeons aboard. Unfortunately, he did not survive his injuries and was buried at sea. It was some time later that we all aware this sailor had a twin brother who was also in the service.[23]

From the 25th to the 27th we again operated with TF 77, but from the 28th until 4 December we were in Sasebo. As we entered Sasebo Harbor we were glad to see the distinctive shape of a hill to the port side. This geographic mound had various names such as "Jane Russell Hill" and others less delicate. No matter what its name, when we saw it we knew that it was time to "stand down," at least for a short while.

Next we escorted USS PRINCETON, CV-37, out to TF 77. On 21 December, we sunk another mine.

On Monday, 25 December, Christmas Day everything changed. On that day there was the largest collection of U.S. Navy warships ever assembled at one time in the Sea of Japan. There were twenty-two warships—five aircraft carriers, a battleship, two cruisers,[24] and 14 destroyers all on station within a circle that twelve thousand yards in diameter! The weather was extremely cold and SOUTHERLAND and the other ships had snow on the decks; ice coated the lifelines, antenna, gun barrels, and other parts of the ship. However, it was not reminiscent of a "White Christmas." It was dark, dreary, gray and the best we could do was open a hatch, peek out, and shut it quickly. Later in the day our destroyer squadron (DesRon) commodore received a message asking if Destroyer Division (Des-Div) 51 was ready to carry out an assignment.

DesDiv 51 was ready, so that afternoon we were detached and ordered to proceed to Sasebo at top speed. When we arrived there, we proceeded to fuel and to load stores and ammunition for a 90-day deployment.[25] Two days later we sortied from Sasebo. At this time I was ashore on a working party picking up additional stores, including some 300 cases of beer. For some unknown reason the LCM (Landing Craft, Medium) that was supposed to ferry these stores from the pier out to SOUTHERLAND never showed up. While we were waiting, our motor whaleboat[26] came in and told us that we were ordered back to the ship immediately. When we looked out into the harbor we saw SOUTHERLAND making preparations to get underway. We threw as many boxes of toilet paper (a valuable commodity aboard a deployed ship) as possible into the whaleboat and raced out to the ship that was already standing out. We never did find out what happened to all that beer!

First Hong Kong Visit

Once at sea, on 27 December, we learned we were heading for Taiwan (Formosa) to assume Formosan Straits Barrier Patrol duties as part of TG 77.3. This was a naval patrol established in the straits between Taiwan and Mainland China to prevent the Chinese Communists from invading Taiwan and to ensure Taiwan was not used as a base for military operations against Mainland China.

Fortunately, SOUTHERLAND did not draw the first patrol. Instead, we proceeded to the British Crown Colony of Hong Kong where we made a brief port call. When we arrived, we moored to a buoy in Victoria Harbor where we were greeted by hundreds of Chinese boats, the so-called "bum boats,"[27] all trying to sell us their wares. Eventually, select merchants were allowed to board the ship and set out their wares on the fantail and other main deck areas. Mary Soo and her crew of girls in sampans also welcomed visiting ships.[28]

For the right to collect the ship's trash and garbage Mary and her girls would scrub down and paint the ships sides.

At that time it was not "legal" for a foreign warship to visit Hong Kong for more than 72 consecutive hours. If this was violated, Hong Kong could have been declared a base in support of the Korean War effort. Therefore, on New Year's Eve day we had to get underway and clear the harbor. While we were steaming out, we could visually observe Chinese aircraft flying to the north. Immediately after SOUTHERLAND crossed the 6-mile line and entered international waters, we were ordered back to port. We were allowed liberty in Victoria, Hong Kong, but Kowloon in the New Territories was off-limits. While there, and on subsequent visits, we toured the fishing village at Aberdeen, Tiger Balm Gardens, Victoria Peak, and the beach at Repluse Bay with the two huge statues of Chinese deities. The traditional New Year's midwatch deck log entry was written in rhyme by LT J.R. De Leonardis:

> *Now all you good men I pray lend me your ear,*
> *On this new day of a wonderful year.*
> *If you listen closely, I'll tell you the way,*
> *Our mighty ship SOUTHERLAND is moored in Hong*
>   *Kong Bay.*
>
> *To buoy Baker-3 with 90 feet of chain,*
> *We are riding easily, there's only a slight strain.*
> *We have boiler #2 in auxiliary use,*
> *While #2 generator furnishes electrical juice.*
>
> *SOPA is skipper of the tanker GUADALUPE,*
> *Which makes other ships here look just like a sloop.*
> *The weather is balmy, with stars in the sky,*
> *To be with our loved ones, is our low woeful cry.*
>
> *Along with the SOUTHERLAND, moored in this bay,*
> *Are ships of His Majesty's navy today.*
> *There also are merchantmen from far and near,*
> *Their nationalities vary, but their purpose is clear.*

However there's one happiness prevalent I see,
Because of the fact we're here, not at sea.
There's also one complaint, I can't help but say,
Who gave me the watch on this New Year's Day?

Hong Kong on New Year's Eve 1951 found me in the Hong Kong Hotel (long since torn down) at midnight where a very tall Scotsman in army uniform insisted that I had to stand up to sing "Old Lang Syne." I'd sit down and he would haul me back up by my jumper collar. Every New Year's Eve this incident comes clearly to my memory. I also vividly recall the menacing-looking figures that would be seen standing in doorways in the evening. I found out later that these were Gurkhas[29] hired to guard the premises. On 4 January 1951, we finally left Hong Kong and instead of joining the rest of our division in the Formosa Straits area, we headed southwest to the Malacan Straits, west of Malaysia.

Malacan Straits Patrol

When we left Hong Kong, we were on a supposed-to-be secret mission to intercept an American freighter that was suspected of carrying war goods to China. However, SOUTHERLAND never made the intercept as our "secret" mission had been published in a news magazine and the freighter changed course and went elsewhere.[30] One benefit from this diverted cruise was liberty in Singapore on our way back. On 10 January, we anchored in the "Man-of-War" anchorage in Keppel Harbor, Singapore Roads. At that time (January 1951) there were political problems in Singapore,[31] so our range of liberty was restricted to a few streets downtown and a British military club.

After we left Singapore on 12 January, on our way back to Hong Kong, we encountered a typhoon. A patrol frigate, USS ALBUQUEQUE, PF-7, that was in the region was having major problems dealing with the storm. She was running low on fuel and couldn't do any cooking or baking. Our cooks baked night and day in order to make enough bread for the crew of the frigate. After we made a rendezvous, we transferred fuel and foodstuffs including bread and ice cream.

Return to Hong Kong

We arrived back in Hong Kong early in the evening of 16 January. One of our sister ships, GURKE, was in port and already on liberty. When some of our sailors went to their favorite dance hall, they found GURKE sailors dancing with "their girls." These ladies promptly left the GURKE sailors to welcome ours back and a Hollywood-style donnybrook broke out that required the SP (Shore Patrol) and local police to break it up. We left Hong Kong on 21 January enroute to the Taiwan Straits.

Taiwan Straits Patrol

When SOUTHERLAND arrived in the Taiwan Straits on 22 January, we relieved HENDERSON, one of our sister ships and assumed the patrol. When we were relieved in turn by HENDERSON, we steamed into Keelung Harbor[32] where we were assigned a mooring with our bow to Buoy A and our stern to Buoy B. Only there was only 100-yards (300 feet) between them! This would have been OK except for the fact that SOUTHERLAND was 396 feet, 6 inches long! I was doing the backup position plotting on the DRT in CIC and for some reason I measured the distance between the buoys and realized that we wouldn't fit. About that time the Captain came into CIC and I tried to make someone aware of the problem but, being one of the junior sailors, I was ignored until I yelled, "Will someone listen to me?" Just in time I made the Captain aware of this discrepancy so that we could request a different mooring assignment, thereby avoiding an embarrassing situation. While inport we refueled from USS KASKASKIA, AO-27, and then relieved HENDERSON on patrol.

While we were in port in Keelung in February, several ship-mates decided to go to Taipei for a visit. Apparently they had a bottle of spirits that they dropped and broke. Being good Americans they decided that this "fallen soldier" needed to have a Christian burial and they proceeded with a burial ceremony. This activity drew a crowd of Chinese, one of whom laughed. A fight ensued, the police came and broke up the fight. Our sailors were arrested and the Chinese who laughed wound up in the hospital with some broken bones. The Chinese government reported this incident to Washington. Word was then relayed from Washington, via Commander Naval Forces Far East (COMNAVFE) in Tokyo and Commander Seventh Fleet (COMSEVEN) down to us that the Chinese considered SOUTHERLAND and her crew to be persona non-gratis and we had to leave port. Thereafter, either the Pescadores station seaplane tender or USS NAVASOTA AO-106, normally based in Keelung had to refuel us at sea until our division was relieved and we returned to Sasebo on 9 February.

Sea of Japan Operations.

After a tender availability period alongside USS PRAIRIE, AD-15[33] and a brief drydocking in Sasebo, we returned to the Sea of Japan and continued to perform typical destroyer duties: screening and plane guard duty with *TF 77*, shore bombardment with *TF 95*, etcetera. for the next several months. During that time SOUTHERLAND operated from Pusan to Wonsan to Ch'ongjin, North Korea, an ice-free port on the Sea of Japan. One incident that I deemed particularly interesting was the time when we steamed into Wonson Harbor and moored alongside USS MISSOURI BB-63. While there we detected communist MiGs to the north on our radar and we went to GQ—the "Mighty Mo" did not, but continued her normal routine apparently totally unconcerned about the threat of MiGs. Nothing developed from this detection of MiGs. We then left Wonsan and rejoined TF 77.

On 4 March, LCDR David A Merrill, USN, relieved Mr. Osborne as XO. Mr. Osborne detached to become CO USS TWINING, DD-540.

On 10 March, a Navy aircraft was shot down and crashed close to the coastline. The pilot managed to get out safely, but was stranded near the top of a hill. His flightmates managed to keep the North Koreans from ascending the hill by strafing and dropping napalm while they waited for a rescue helicopter to arrive. By the time it got dark the rescue helo still had not shown up and we never did learn the fate of that pilot. During the day SOUTHERLAND rendered as much assistance as possible, including shooting at a concrete bridge in the town of Konjapoo, in order to prevent NKPA troops from reaching the pilot.

Homeward Bound

On 19 March, DesDiv 51 was relieved of duties in the WestPac and we returned Stateside via Guam and Hawaii. The mood aboard a ship "homeward bound" is totally different from when it was "outbound." While homeward bound the watch is normally relaxed from Condition Three to Condition Four and drills and exercises are frequently suspended. Weather permitting, movies are shown topside, either on the fantail or on the torpedo deck. Later, after the movie, it is nice to go topside and, if the moon is out, to listen to the water as the ship surges through it and watch as the moonglow highlights the phosphorescence along the sides. As the ship gets closer and closer to CONUS (Continental Limits of the U.S.), sleeping becomes a problem: the crew develops "Channel Fever." The symptoms of this disease are the ability to smell CONUS while still several days at sea, a heightened impatience to see loved ones, and a sudden awareness of the status of uniforms, shined shoes, and personal appearance. Also, when returning from WestPac, the crew becomes more interested in the sun rising over the eastern horizon, or if returning from Europe, the sun setting over the western horizon.

CHAPTER 4: USS SOUTHERLAND: San Diego and Hawaii, 1951

After refueling stops in Guam where we moored at Zero Pier, Apra Harbor, and Pearl Harbor, SOUTHERLAND and the other ships of DesDiv 51 moored in a nest[1] to Buoy 25, in San Diego Harbor on 7 April. The next several months of 1951 were spent in and out of San Diego conducting refresher-training exercises such as damage control, collision drills, fire fighting drills, gunnery exercises, anti-submarine warfare (ASW) exercises, man overboard drills, and honing our skills on the other daily routines.

San Diego Liberty

Being underage and without a car limited what I could do on liberty in San Diego. However, I did manage to explore quite a bit and visited the ballpark, the zoo, and several different movie houses. A favorite hangout was the Trianon Ballroom on Broadway that was somewhere between 11th and 13th Street. We would go there and listen to the big bands and those who could would dance with the hostesses (I believe that it was something like ten cents a dance). I tried this a few times, but having no prior dancing experience, I mostly made a fool of myself. Another hangout was the USO downtown where the coffee and dancing were free. Frequently, SOUTHERLAND would moor at a buoy off the foot of Broadway where we had to catch a water taxi to Navy Pier to go ashore. There was a donut shop at Navy Pier and it was traditional for a radarman coming off liberty to bring a box of donuts to CIC, making the Broadway mooring point a favorable location.

One of our favorite pastimes in San Diego was having beach parties while on liberty. As I did not have a car, I had to depend on a shipmate for transportation. Somehow there were always different girls there. Someone would bring a watermelon and we'd cut the end off, scoop out the pits and fill it with vodka or whatever else was available (most of us were underage). This was then buried in the sand to keep it cool. The party would go on until the shore patrol broke it up shortly after dark. To my knowledge, no one every got in trouble at these parties. This might be a good place to mention that I seldom had trouble getting a beer in San Diego even though I was under age twenty-one. However, I didn't push this too often for fear of getting in trouble.

On 12 May 1951, the United States detonated the first H-bomb on Eniwetok in the Marshall Islands. On 10 July 1951, peace negotiations began in Kaesong and on 23 August the communists broke off the talks. Then on 25 October they resumed at Panmunjon. These talks would continue until July 1953, mostly centered around the issue of prisoners of war (POW). The main question was should POWs be repatriated on a voluntary basis or not.

From 14 through 17 May we conducted hunter-killer exercises with USS SEGUNDO, SS-398 in the San Diego Operational Area (OpArea). These ongoing ASW exercises were conducted to hone and perfect our ability to respond to the growing threat of Communist Russia's submarine force. They also gave our submariners an opportunity to develop their skills.

During our stay in San Diego I was sent for a one-week training course at the Fleet Anti-Air Warfare Training Center (FAAWTC) on Point Loma. While there we had to watch radarscopes with different color displays: green, blue, white-on-black, orange, as well as other combinations, and report on our perceptions and reactions to each. This was a human factors experiment to determine which color would be easier on the eyes and which would best display weak or faint targets. My personal vote was for white target information on a gray background. I returned to SOUTHERLAND on 25 May. We continued underway training exercises throughout June.

Military Justice

Earlier I discussed the fact that when I joined the Navy we were governed by *The Articles for the Government* of the Navy, the so-called "Rocks and Shoals." These told sailors how they could go astray and what their punishment could be for certain offenses. As examples of what a sailor could expect under the "Rocks and Shoals" the following results of courts martial were entered into SOUTHERLAND's deck log on 8 June 1951:

1. Charge: absence over leave and absence without leave from proper authority: Sentence: solitary confinement on bread and water for a period of thirty (30) days, with a full ration every third day, and to lose $40.00 per month of his pay for a period of four (4) months. The period in solitary was reduced to 15 days.

2. Charge: willful disobedience of a lawful order, absence over leave and absence without leave from proper authority. Sentence: solitary confinement on bread and water for a period of thirty (30) days, with a full ration every third day, and to perform extra police duty[2] for a period of thirty (30) days, and to lose $45.00 per month for a period of five (5) months. Period of confinement reduced to twelve (12) days.

3. Charge: abusive, obscene, and threatening language towards his superior officer. Sentence: reduction to the next inferior rating and to perform extra police duties for a period of sixty (60) days.

On 12 June, USS WALKE, DD- 723, struck a mine in the Sea of Japan. The destroyer was badly damage, but managed to steam to Sasebo where it was repaired. As a result of hitting the mine, 26 destroyermen were killed and 40 others were wounded. This turned out to be the single greatest combat loss suffered by the Navy during the Korean War.[3]

Hawaiian Operations

On 9 July DesDiv 51, in company with JUNEAU, departed San Diego for underway training in the Hawaiian OpArea. On 25 July we left Pearl Harbor and returned to San Diego. An aircraft carrier, USS PRINCETON, was also returning stateside from Hawaii at the same time that we were. The carrier was ordered to have DesDiv 51 escort her and to refuel us as needed in order that DesDiv 51 could maintain the carrier's speed. All the ships in the division were able to keep up the grueling pace set by the carrier (approximately 30 knots) except for GURKE, who fell behind. From 29 August until 17 September, we were moored alongside USS PRAIRIE, AD-15, in San Diego harbor. PRAIRIE had returned from WestPac on 3 August.

On 22 July, Admiral Forrest Sherman, USN, Chief of Naval Operations (CNO) passed away. The DD-963 class of destroyers were named in his honor.

Around this time I took the shipboard exam and was advanced to RDSN. While inport I hitchhiked to Long Beach to visit the famed *Pike* with its roller coaster, tattoo parlors, carnival atmosphere, and girls, girls, girls. To me, it was a smaller version of Coney Island. Of course, with limited funds and no transportation it was not as much fun as it could have been. On yet another trip, this time to Los Angeles, I was sitting in the balcony of a movie house when I felt a rumbling and remember saying to myself, "There goes the subway." Only there wasn't any subway! That's when I heard a couple a few seats away say, "Oh, we must be having an earthquake." Welcome to Southern California!

On another occasion, one of my shipmates decided that I had to learn to drink Tequila so we went south to Tijuana, Mexico. There was a bar that claimed to be "the longest bar in the world." Instead of a foot rail it had a trough running the length of the bar. My shipmate bought me a shot of Tequila; I tasted it, spit it out, and dumped the remainder in the trough. That was the wrong thing to do as my shipmate blew his top. He told me that if I didn't want it that I should have given it to him. Eventually things quieted down and we enjoyed the rest of the evening.

My shipmates and I frequented bullfights as well where most of the spectators were either American sailors on liberty or American coeds looking for a day of drinking and carrying on. Bullfights in Mexico, at least in Tijuana in the early 1950s, were different from those that I would experience in Spain or Portugal in later years. In Mexico, it was customary for the matador to kill the bull.

One of my buddies from Richmond Hill had joined the Marine Corps and was stationed at Camp Pendleton. I had a postal address for him so one Saturday I decided that I would hitchhike up to Pendleton for a visit. In those days it was relatively safe to hitchhike and people would stop and give a serviceman a ride. When I got to Oceanside I stopped a Marine and asked how to get to "Tent Camp No. X." He looked at me like I had two heads and told me that it was way back in the mountains and that I couldn't just walk there. He also told me that there were no telephones out there so that ended my attempted visit and I hitchhiked back to San Diego.

During this period I learned first-hand about weather conditions in Southern California. During the day, when the temperatures were in the 70s or 80s our uniform of the day was dress whites, and when the temperatures dropped into the low 50s in the evenings, we would wear our pea coats over our white cotton uniforms in order to stay warm!

A good part of our time in the States was spent in and out of San Diego Harbor. Typically, we would leave on Monday conduct ASW exercises all week, practice shore bombardment at San Clemente Island, or conduct anti-aircraft firing drills for our 5" and 40-mm gun crews. All of these external exercises involved CIC and the radar gang; therefore, we spent 12 to14 hours a day in CIC. In between these external drills, we also had to participate in internal drills such as man-overboard, abandon ship, collision, fire, etcetera. While in port we would spend our day cleaning our spaces, shining the brass turn-buckles on the lifelines on the 0-1 deck, and redoing the cotton cord work on the ladder outside CIC that led to the bridge.[4] On 7 September LT May (he was commissioned lieutenant on 8 August) was detached with orders to USS MERGANSER, AMS-26, and LT Norman B. Alverson assumed the duties of CIC Officer.

On 8 September 1951, the United States signed a Peace Treaty with Japan. Under the terms of this treaty the US would retain a military presence on Japanese land for the defense of Japan.

On 17 September, SOUTHERLAND departed San Diego enroute to Mare Island, California, to off-load ammunition before going into the San Francisco Naval Shipyard (SFNSY) for overhaul and drydocking. SOUTHERLAND was moored in the SFNSY on 3 October when Bobby Thompson hit a home run off the Brooklyn Dodger's Ralph Branca to win the 1951 National League baseball pennant for the New York Giants. At the time I had the inport voice radio monitoring watch in CIC and heard the famous announcement: "The Giants win the pennant! The Giants win the pennant! The Giants win the pennant!" Being an anti-Dodger fan, this was like music to my ears! Then, in March, I took the high school GED (General Educational Development) test given by USAFI (U.S. Armed Forces Institute, University of Wisconsin) and passed with high scores.

In November I took thirty days leave and a shipmate and myself tried to catch military aircraft hops back east. This trip started with us hitch hiking to March Air Force Base to try to catch a hop to

Albuquerque, New Mexico. If there was space available on a flight, we could book it at no cost. There were no flights scheduled for the next several days so we started hitchhiking. First we took a bus to the edge of town where we waited. Before long a highway patrolman came along and asked where we were heading. He told us that he would check back just before dark and if we were still there he would have to take us back into town. Fortunately we caught a ride to the other side of the mountains. While waiting in a coffee shop, an Air Force guy came in who had just picked up his Pontiac from a shop where he had it "souped up." He was going to Oklahoma City and offered the three of us a ride.

The next morning, a Sunday, we stopped in Amarillo, Texas, for coffee. The young, buxom, blonde waitress tried to convince me to stay and spend my leave with her. I refused her invitation, as I did not think this would be a smart move since I knew nothing about her or the area—and, being from New York, I was naturally skeptical. I also did not have any money. The next day we arrived in Oklahoma City. I do not recall how I completed the remainder of the trip.

On 9 December, SOUTHERLAND left the shipyard and went to the Naval ammunition Depot (NAD) at Port Chicago to on-load ammunition after completion of shipyard overhaul and then returned to San Diego. We were in San Diego on New Year's Eve, but for some unknown reason the deck log was not written in prose.

WestPac Cruise 2

On 4 January 1952, DesDiv 51 left San Diego for another tour in WestPac. Accompanying us were USS JOHN A. BOLE, DD-755; USS LOFBERG, DD-759; USS BUCK, DD-761; and USS JOHN W.THOMASON, DD-760. On the way out we stopped over in Pearl Harbor where we conducted ASW exercises and shore bombardment exercises off Kahoolawe Island.[5] During ASW exercises sonarmen

(SO) search for, classify, and track submarine contacts while the bridge and CIC teams practice engagement techniques.

Liberty in Honolulu was extremely expensive for someone on a seaman's pay. Hotel Street was the street where all the tattoo parlors, clip joints, and beer gardens were located. There was also a YMCA facility. Hotel Street was subsequently made prominent in the movie *From Here to Eternity,* starring Burt Lancaster and Frank Sinatra. About the only place that we could afford to eat was at Fort De Russy on Waikiki Beach, the Armed Forces facility located next to the Royal Hawaiian Hotel. Fort De Russy was also a good entrée when meeting young tourists, as the price of a steak dinner was reasonable and much cheaper than in the civilian sector. Fifty years later this facility is still operational. Waikiki's shark barrier reef and the individual who sat on the beach all day weaving hats figure prominently in my memory.

While in Pearl Harbor, the ship's MAA discovered two of our sailors "engaged in immoral acts." They were transferred to the Rec-Sta, Pearl Harbor for safekeeping and further disposition.

On the next leg of this deployment we had a humorous situation that is typical of life aboard a destroyer. When we left Hawaii on 31 January, we were joined by a Canadian destroyer escort, HMCS NOOTKA DDE-213,[6] with her dual Squid ASW weapons[7] mounted abaft the superstructure. We were scheduled to rendezvous with an aircraft carrier, USS BATAAN, CVL-29, that was also bound for WestPac. When we joined up, the captain of the carrier sent our division screening station orders. However, DesRon 5's commodore, Captain J.L. Melgaard, was the second senior captain in the Pacific Fleet, junior only to the Chief of Staff for CINCPACFLT (Commander in Chief, Pacific Fleet). He replied to BATAAN's screening order "Negative, proceed to station 1000 yards astern of me." Bear in mind that it takes a lot to maneuver an aircraft carrier as compared to a destroyer. In reply BATAAN stated "Roger, wait, out." We could just picture the OOD (Officer of the Deck) aboard the carrier checking published lineal numbers[8] of the respective captains. When they found out that their captain was junior to ComDesRon 5 they replied, "Roger, proceeding to station."[9] However, before BATAAN could move, ComDesRon 5 negated his order, ordered the carrier to resume course and speed, and ordered DesDiv 51 and NOOTKA to the appropriate screening stations. This was more than a "power play," although I'm sure there was some of that involved. In the military, the senior person present is always accountable for anything that happens and the Commodore was just setting the record straight.

Between Hawaii and Midway Island we encountered a typhoon and we were in it for several days. At one point the carrier requested to know how the "small boys" (destroyers) were riding in the storm. NOOTKA replied, "Like a submarine." We finally cleared the storm and stopped at Midway to refuel, arriving on a Sunday morning. This presented problems as ComDesRon 5 wanted his crews to have a few hours shore leave. The clubs being located across from the chapel where Sunday morning services were in progress caused the problem. The commanding officer of the base at Midway at first refused to allow the clubs to open during church services, but somehow our Commodore convinced him that it would be prudent to allow them to open for the few hours that we would be in port. While we were at Midway we had some time to observe the "gooney birds" (albatross). They are beautiful birds while in the air or on the ground but their landings and takeoffs are hysterical; they are clumsy birds who always make crash landings and never look like they'll get airborne as they run along for takeoff.

When we left Midway on 31 January an embarked passenger, a sailor being transferred to another ship, apparently decided that he didn't want to go to WestPac so he jumped over the side and he was picked up by a NavSta boat.

On 20 January 1952, General Dwight David Eisenhower took the oath of office as president and Richard M. Nixon, became vice president. On 7 February, the reign of Elizabeth II of England began.

On 11 February we arrived in Yokosuka and nested alongside USS HAMUL, AD-20. Every deployment is similar in nature, characterized by carrier screening operations, plane guard and night shore bombardment against enemy transport facilities, boats, troop concentrations, and gun emplacements. Unlike the previous deployment, during this cruise, we spent a significant amount of time on the west coast of Korea, in the both the Yellow Sea and Korea Bay. We spent time operating with both smaller American and British aircraft carriers. These operations also included performing Search & Rescue (SAR) missions for downed pilots. These were frequently conducted offshore from the section of northwest Korea known as "MiG Alley." On 14 February, SOUTHERLAND departed Yokosuka for the Korean OpArea via the Inland Sea and the Shimonoseki Straits, between Honshu and Kyushu. This was an extremely busy time in CIC: there were hundreds of vessels of all sizes that had to be tracked, their courses and speeds determined. We also had to inform the OOD of their closest point of approach so that he could adjust our course and speed as required to avoid a collision.

We again joined the Task Group 95.1 (*TG 95.10* off the west coast of Korea on 16 February. Also present were USS BAIRKO, CVE-115, British destroyers HMS COSSACK and HMS CHARITY and USS MARSHALL, DD-676. On one occasion we had to go among the islands in Korea Bay, near the northwest corner of Korea to rescue a downed English pilot.

On 19 February, we were steaming independently on anti-invasion patrol south of Yuk To Island when we fired our 5" guns against enemy troops and boat areas. On the 27th we were on patrol between Mamap To Island and Changsan Got Point.

On 1and 2 March, in the Cho-do area on the Korean West Coast, the enemy was reported to be massing for an attack on Re- do. Night illuminating and interdiction fire was believed to be holding off the enemy.

On 4 March, we were on anti-invasion patrol between Sunwj Do Island and Mamap To Island, east of Kirin Do Island. On 5 March, after refueling from the Royal Fleet Auxiliary (RFA) WAVE BARON, A242, we were detached and proceeded to Yokosuka via the Van Diemen Straits (Osumi Kaikyo), south of Kyushu. Later in March, we were engaged in ASW training exercises with USS BATAAN off Okinawa. Upon completion of these exercises, SOUTHERLAND moored in Buckner Bay Beach on the east end of the island for some much needed R&R (Rest & Recreation) for the crew. After participating in a beach party on White Beach, some of us decided to climb up to the top of the so-called "Suicide Cliff" where many Okinawan civilians and Japanese soldiers jumped off to commit suicide near the end of WW II. As we fought our way through the plush undergrowth I stepped out and there was nothing under my foot but air! Fortunately I was able to grab on to a branch to keep from falling. Two of my shipmates grabbed my arms and helped me back to safe ground.

While deployed, timely mail delivery was a constant problem. Normally this didn't bother me, but on one occasion it did. I was sent a Christmas "care" package from home and Heaven only knows where it was before it caught up with me while we were in Buckner Bay. Anyway, when I opened it, amongst other items, was a large Hebrew National salami. Several shipmates gathered around for the ceremonial "cutting of the salami." They were sorry that they did, as it was more than ripe. I think I broke a speed record getting it topside and over the side.

After we left Okinawa on 31 March, we rendezvoused with USS SAINT PAUL, CA-73, in the Van Diemen Straits and escorted her into the East China Sea and then north through the Sea of Japan to the TF 77 OpArea. The next day USS ROCHESTER, CA-124, joined up. We then spent several days conducting interdiction and harassing fire prior to rejoining TF 77 on 7 April. The 13th of April, Easter Sunday, was spent at GQ while we engaged in shore bombardment around Ch'ongjin. On 17 April, we again transited the Van Diemen Straits enroute to Yokosuka.

I was advanced to RD3 on the 16th of April; however, as a result of a shortage of non-rated personnel on-board, I was still assigned to working parties. The major advantage that this bought me, in addition to a few extra dollars, was admission to the various Petty Officer Clubs. This meant that whenever we were in Yokosuka, I no longer had to fight my way to the Enlisted Men's club in town. Two days after I sewed on my "crow," (my rating badge) we were in Yokosuka, again nested alongside HAMUL, and I was a member of a working party onboard a LCM that we used to ferry supplies from a stores ship to SOUTHERLAND. After we loaded supplies from the stores ship I asked the coxswain if I could drive the LCM (with twin diesel engines). Reluctantly he agreed—I promptly rammed the bow into the side of the stores ship with a loud bang that echoed over the harbor. Fortunately, no one was hurt. This happened on the opposite side from the ship's quarterdeck so their OOD did not respond. The LCM was not damaged and the coxswain did not report the incident. That was my last attempt at driving a LCM. DesDiv 51 departed Yokosuka on the 25th and joined JUNEAU and PRINCETON and then conducted training exercises around Okinawa.

On 26 April, USS HOBSON, DD-464, was run over by USS WASP, CV-18, resulting in the death of 176 destroyermen. Then on 28 April the Allied occupation of Japan ended and Japan recovered its own sovereignty.

On 13 May, CDR Otis A. Wesche, USN, was transferred via highline from USS CUNNINGHAM, DD-752, as relief for Captain Conrad. CDR Conrad was transferred three days later via highline to USS EVANS, DD-754, with orders to report to CNO. Like most skippers, Captain Wesche had his quirks. His main one was that whenever he entered CIC woe be to the watchstander who had to move more than 16-inches in order to be at his assigned watch station. During that period the commanding officer's GQ station was on the ship's bridge. However, Captain Wesche would frequently come down to CIC in order to get a better understanding of the tactical situation as it existed. With the introduction of computerized CIC and communications in the 1960s, the captain's GQ station was changed to CIC and the XO was stationed on the bridge.

On 22 May we again went to the Van Diemen Straits to escort USS IOWA, BB-61, to the TF 77 OpArea. Then on 28 May we escorted JUNEAU.

Sometime in May, while operating with *TF 77*, one of the aircraft carriers arrived on station after a stateside overhaul. Apparently she had a problem with her new catapults as three aircraft in a row couldn't gain altitude and were catapulted directly into the water. Although the planes were lost, all three pilots were rescued.

During this inport period I had a problem with one of my wisdom teeth so I reported to the base dental clinic. The dentist examined me and decided the tooth had to be pulled. This was in the upper left side of my jaw. The dental clinic was in an old wooden building and the dental chair was in front of a steam radiator against an outside wall. As the dentist tugged on my tooth, my body became more and more rigid and my feet came off the footrest and pushed against the radiator. After one particularly strong tug on the tooth I kicked the radiator right through the wall!

During the first week of June we made several visits into Wonsan Harbor before being detached on the 5th. We then proceeded to Sasebo where we nested alongside USS DIXIE, AD-14. Later in June, we once again performed Formosa Straits patrol duty. Several times we refueled from USS MANATEE, AO-58 in Takao (Koa Hsiung), Formosa. On 28 June, SOUTHERLAND was again in Hong Kong for a brief port call. On the 4th of July our new XO, LCDR Kenneth P. Hill, USNR, relieved LCDR Merrill who was detached on the 13th with orders to the 11 Naval District.

On 10 July SOUTHERLAND rejoined *TG 95.2* on bombardment patrol in Wonsan Harbor. From the 11th to the 13th we patrolled off Yang Do Island, in the vicinity of Songjin, and between Nan Do Island and the Korean mainland. On the 14th, SOUTHERLAND was in the vicinity of Kojo when we were hit four times by shells from Communist shore batteries. As we were patrolling, several of our crewmembers saw the North Koreans removing camouflage from in front of caves and rolling out their guns. Eight enlisted men suffered minor injuries. SOUTHERLAND silenced five of the seven "Red" batteries and was back in action two hours after receiving hits. My GQ station was in the ECM (Electronic Countermeasures[10]) Room directly under the after tripod radar mast. At the time we had many crates of potatoes stored on the weather deck directly under the mast. One of the "Red" shells landed in the potatoes, but fortunately did not explode. It did cause the light bulbs in the ECM Room to shatter raining glass down upon my head. In the middle of delivering counter-battery fire and taking evasive action, we had a steering casualty! When I returned to my normal watch station in CIC, I overheard the embarked Army liaison officer remark (jokingly, I hope), "Well I've got my [rotation] points, now I have to get my sergeant's." At that time Army personnel had to accumulate "points" earned in a combat situation in order to rotate home.[11]

On the 18th, we were scheduled to rendezvous with a Netherlands's destroyer PIET HEIM, D-805, in the vicinity of Ch'ongjin to conduct night operations in amongst some offshore islands. The North Koreans would use these islands as bases for guerrilla operations and as radar sites. On the 21st, we were once again in the Ch'ongjin area to meet HMS ST. BRIDES BAY, F-600 in the Yang Do Islands area. That evening, when we picked up a contact on our surface search radar, I tried to establish voice radio contact without success. After several attempts and as the target came closer, Captain Wesche ordered that we light it up by firing a star shell over it. When the star shell went off, we received an urgent radio message from the ship, "SOUTHERLAND, are you illuminating me?" in a thick English accent. Yes, it was the ship with which we were supposed to operate.

On 22 July, we were relieved by USS JOHN R. PIERCE, DD-753, and headed for Sasebo. On the 25th, DesDiv 51 left Sasebo after a refueling stop and stopped in Yokosuka before returning stateside, via Midway and Pearl Harbor.

CHAPTER 5: USS SOUTHERLAND: San Francisco and San Diego, 1952

SOUTHERLAND and the other ships of DesDiv 51 arrived back in San Diego on 10 August and moored downtown at the Broadway Pier. After we moored, LTJG Edward R. Judy reported aboard. Mr. Judy eventually assumed the duties of CIC Officer. Although I served under several outstanding officers during my naval career, I consider Mr. Judy one of the two best leaders. The other would be Captain Robert O. Welander, commanding officer of USS FOX, DLG-33. Both these officers provided the inspiration, support, and encouragement that causes one to strive to be the best that they could be.

One example of Mr. Judy's leadership style was the night that we missed changing authentication codes at midnight, local time. The CIC Watch officer thought that they were changed at midnight GMT (Greenwich Mean Time). However, I knew that they changed at midnight local time and deferred to the Watch Officer's direction to use the old codes. When our authentication was denied, Captain Wesche had Mr. Judy paged to the bridge. After he got the codes straightened out he told me that he'd see me in his stateroom in the morning. At that meeting he chewed me out for not doing what I knew was right and informed me that part of my job was to train junior officers.

Once we returned to San Diego we lost many of our experienced crew, especially those who completed their "Truman Year" extensions and their reserve time. In the words of James A. Fields, Jr., who discussed the personnel problems caused by the rapid mobilization for the Korean War:..."[I]n some areas famine was endemic: certain rates were short throughout the war; with the release of reservists in 1952, the shortage of reliable and experienced petty officers became increasingly acute...in those critical specialties—yeoman, radarman, radioman, and electrician's and machinist's mate—in which the armed forces were competing directly with American industry."[1]

One Sunday morning while moored in a nest alongside USS HAMUL, AD-20, a couple of signalmen on our bridge spotted a foxy looking lady waiting on Spanish Landing. This is a landing for officer's boats running between San Diego and North Island Naval Air Station across the bay. Using signal lights they exchanged comments about her "architecture" with sailors on another ship. Little did they know that she was a captain's wife and that she could read signal light. This was made clear to them during a "conference" with our executive officer on Monday morning.

Hunter's Point Naval Shipyard, San Francisco

On 27 August SOUTHERLAND left San Diego enroute to NAD, Mare Island to unload ammunition prior to entering Hunter's Point Naval Shipyard, San Francisco. We spent a good part of the fall and winter in the shipyard being upgraded to a DDR II configuration including receiving extensive superstructure, new antiaircraft guns, new radars and sonar modifications.[2] Our steel superstructure was replaced by aluminum one.[3] This was to lighten the weight of the ship above the waterline, thereby improving sea-keeping characteristics.[4] The Operations Department berthing compartment had been relocated to the forward area of the ship, directly under the mess deck. This compartment also provided access to the sonar shack. A newer model was replacing our old QHB-A sonar. This required cutting a hole in the ship's side so we had to vacate our living compartment and we had to sleep aboard a floating barracks barge (a huge floating dormitory) that was not heated. Many a night we would sleep with a mattress under us and a mattress over us.

Time in a shipyard for overhaul is a very demanding time for the crew as all normal routine is interrupted. In addition, there are typically various holes cut in the ship, and doors and hatches are left open, letting cold winds blow throughout. The decks and passageways are cluttered with air hoses for paint and metal chipping guns, gas hoses for metal cutting torches, and electrical cables for welding and lighting. Dust is flying everywhere and the stench of burning metal permeates the entire ship. There was little of no concern about the hazards of asbestos or other environmental issues at that time.

Junior rated personnel who are not standing security watches or chipping paint and repainting are kept busy standing fire watches to ensure that a yard worker does not accidentally start a fire while cutting or welding. If the ship is in dry dock, these fire watches can be long and boring as the only breaks come when the yard worker takes one. There are also extra security watches for spaces that would normally be off-limits and locked. Also during this time, areas of the ship that are normally not accessible must be chipped and repainted. Engineering personnel are kept busy cleaning bilges and rebricking the boilers. By the end of the day most of the crew look like they just came out of a coal mine. If an individual is fortunate enough to have liberty that afternoon, he only wants to get cleaned up and go ashore. However, he's now faced with a cold water shower!

This period did provide a chance for several of us to go to Palo Alto to watch the Stanford—USC football game. Stanford's quarterback was Bob Mathias, decathlete star of the 1952 Helsinki Olympics.

One of our sonarmen had a girlfriend who would call the quarterdeck and ask for him. When the Petty Officer of the Watch told her that he wasn't aboard she would ask to talk to whoever was available. When we found out that the sonarman was going to marry this girl we did everything that we could to talk him out of it including arranging visits with the chaplain. Nothing worked and he did marry her. However, during our next WestPac cruise he did not get a single letter from her. One of my collateral duties was picking up the mail for our division and distributing it. It was tough to have to tell him, "Sorry, nothing for you" after each mail call.

While in Hunter's Point in order to improve my social life I decided that I needed to learn how to dance so I signed up for lessons at Arthur Murray's. I must have been a quick learner because the more lessons I paid for the better I got (or so I was told). This never seemed to be the case outside of the studio.

One afternoon while in the shipyard at Hunter's Point, I was Petty Officer of the Watch on the quarterdeck when one of our newest Naval Academy ensigns told me that he was expecting his wife aboard for dinner and "ordered" me to inform him when she arrived. When she showed up, I sent the Messenger of the Watch to notify the ensign. Meanwhile, I thought that I detected a New York accent so I asked her where she was from. It turned out she, too, was from Richmond Hill and we knew some of the same people and had many experiences in common. When the ensign approached the quarter-deck, he was quite putout that I had the audacity to talk to HIS wife and let me know so in no uncertain terms. Remember, in those days there were still vestiges of the old "Rocks and Shoals," and enlisted men did not fraternize with officers wives, even casually. Eventually he became a fine naval officer.

One day I went to my cleaning station, a passageway between the wardroom and the wardroom pantry. When I got there, I heard an irate voice coming from the wardroom (there was a small serving port in the bulkhead where the stewards could pass food from the pantry into the wardroom and it was open). It was the Captain dressing down a junior officer and making disparaging remarks about his wife. When the Captain screamed, "And keep that &*%$# the $%@# off my ship," I decided that I'd clean the passageway at another time and left.

While in the shipyard, I took advantage of the opportunity to have a cavity in a front tooth repaired. The dental clinic dentist examined it and told me that he thought that he could save it, but that it would take some work. After I told him that I'd prefer not to lose the tooth, he got started. I was in the chair over an hour when an inspection party came by. I could hear my dentist arguing with them about why he was taking so much time with one patient. He argued right back saying that the tooth was worth saving and that he was going to do it. He finally finished after about three hours and I've never had another problem with that tooth.

In October, I took thirty days leave and caught hops back to New York. This trip started with a hop from March Air Force Base to Albuquerque. From there I was offered a ride on a twin-engine B-25 Mitchell bomber[5] that was scheduled to go to Dallas, Texas. A few other hitchhikers and myself rode in the unheated area behind the pilots and we were cold even with our pea coats on. All we had to sit on were canvas bucket seats. When the plane arrived in Dallas airspace, the pilot was informed that he did not have clearance to land in Dallas so he flew on to Shreveport, Louisiana.

While waiting for another hop, we went into town and when we returned the CQ (Air Force term for person in Charge of Quarters) asked if we had has anything to eat and informed us the messhall was serving dinner. While waiting in the chow line, an Air Force MP came in carrying a sub-machine gun and asked if we'd mind waiting over by the wall for a few minutes. Who were we to argue? So we went over by the wall. Then they marched in about twenty guarded Air force prisoners, fed them, thanked us for our cooperation, and left.

The next morning I caught a hop to Mobile, Alabama and from there to Westover, Massachusetts. This flight was aboard a huge Air Force plane that was carrying a single large crate that they were delivering somewhere in Southeast Asia. There were two crews aboard and they treated us like honored guests—providing us coffee and making places for us to sleep. From Westover, there were no flights going any closer to New York so I went out on the highway and started thumbing. By now it was about 10 P.M. and cold.

Before long a car stopped and offered me a ride. A short distance down the road the driver told me to look in the glove compartment as he had some pictures that I might enjoy. When I had them out, he put his hand on my knee. At that I told him that he had his choice of either removing his land or to start losing teeth. He pulled over to the side of the road and I got out, about half a mile from the nearest street lamp. Before long a 18-wheeler came along and stopped. When I told the driver that I was trying to get to New York, he told me that I was in luck since that was where he was going. After a long, bumpy ride we arrived in downtown New York at about 9 A.M. on Sunday morning. The nearest subway station was closed so I had to walk about a mile to find one that was open. This entire trip took from Friday afternoon until Sunday afternoon!

While home on leave in New York I received a telegram with orders to report to the Naval Station on Treasure Island, California, at the expiration of my leave. When I reported SOUTHERLAND was not in port so I was assigned mess cook duty and all that I had to wear was my dress blues! No one seemed to care, but it surely was not comfortable. After a few days SOUTHERLAND returned from sea and I reported aboard.

San Diego

SOUTHERLAND left Hunter's Point on 4 December. After loading ammunition at Port Chicago, we returned to San Diego. On the 11th, a Chief Radarman reported aboard. This chief had been taken prisoner as a seaman during WW II and had little practical experience either as a sailor, a Chief, or a radarman. On the 12th LT Richard L. Ploss reported onboard as relief for the XO.

On 1 January 1953, ENS E. L. Box wrote this deck log entry:

As we start this New Year it is our fate,
To be moored to buoy number twenty eight.
In San Diego Harbor riding well, Ten fathoms of port
*   anchor chain, there is no swell*
Number One generator is producing juice,
Number Two boiler is ready for use.
The USS HENDERSON (DD 785) is moored along-
*   side,*
Six 6" manila lines hold her while she rides.
Units of the pacific Fleet are on our beam.
Present also are local and district craft in this New
*   Year's dream.*
SOPA is ComAirPac, U.S. Naval Air Station,
Located in Coronado, California, much to our elation.

The next several months of 1953 were spent in and out of San Diego conducting refresher-training exercises. This was a particularly trying time since Captain Wesche insisted on always having the "first team," those team members with the most experience, on duty in CIC at all times when an exercise was in progress.

On another occasion we were conducting gunnery exercises. As part of these exercises, one of my responsibilities was to ensure the sound powered telephone circuits were all correctly connected. Before we started, I saw someone in khaki bending over by the sound-powered telephone switching box and did not think anything of it. When the Captain ordered the 40-mm guns to "commence firing," nothing happened. He summoned me to the bridge and wanted an explanation of why the bridge could not communicate with the gun mounts. I then remembered the individual by the telephone switching box. Meanwhile, the CO was chasing me around the bridge scream-ing "When I order open fire, I want those guns to go 'Bang, Bang, Bang'." When I returned to CIC, I straightened out the phone circuits and the exercise proceeded normally. It was not my place to question why a Chief did whatever he did, but in the future I made sure to

61

check and recheck the circuit setup. For the next several months SOUTHERLAND's main duties consisted of participating in the Navy's patrolling and blockading mission.

On 2 February 1953, President Eisenhower lifted the 7th Fleet's blockade of Taiwan. In his State of the Union address, he stated that it was ludicrous to require the 7th Fleet to serve as a defensive arm of Communist China. On 27 July 1953, the Paris Peace Talks that had begun in July 1951 finally resulted in the signing of the Korean War Armistice. A demilitarized zone (DMZ) was established at the 38th parallel dividing North and South Korea. This DMZ is still manned by UN peacekeepers.

One Saturday, while back in San Diego, Captain Wesche held personnel inspection. Our division was all lined up in ranks on the main deck near the portside quarterdeck in our best dress blue uniforms, when a radioman striker in our division failed to answer muster. A runner was quickly dispatched below to find him, but was unsuccessful. About that time we saw him on the pier approaching the ship in civilian clothing, obviously having been "out on the town." Our Division Officer (DO) told him to get below, get changed, and back into ranks before the CO reached our division. This scheme proved successful up to a point. When the CO inspected the division, he decided to inspect socks. We had to pull up our left pant leg and raise our foot. Unfortunately the radioman striker had forgotten to change his socks and was wearing international orange socks! This cost him a loss of liberty for several days and he was restricted to the ship. Sometime later, while returning to San Diego after being at sea for a few days, this same sailor made disparaging sexual remarks to the OOD. The next day, following Captain's Mast, he was on his way to the brig at North Island for three days on bread and water.

During our stay in San Diego I was again sent to FAAWTC on Point Loma. Only this time it was for training as an air controller. Navy fighter planes would take off from North Island Air Station and were vectored out over the ocean. From that point, control of the aircraft would be turned over to the students (under direct supervision).

We would have the pilots perform all various maneuvers: climbing, diving, turning, intercepting other aircraft, etcetera. Then we would direct them into making dummy bombing and strafing runs on the beaches of Point Loma. After our training time was up we would vector the aircraft back to North Island.

Soviet Premier Josef Stalin died in Moscow on 5 March 1953, after suffering a brain hemorrhage on the 1ˢᵗ. He was succeeded by Georgi Malenkov, who was succeeded by Nikolai Bulganin. Eventually Nikita Khrushchev took over in Russia as General Secretary of the Soviet Communist Party. Khrushchev was deposed in 1964 and was replaced by Leonid L. Brezhnev.

From constantly watching radar screens, I had begun to notice problems with my eyesight and on 15 March I received my first pair of eyeglasses at the Balboa Naval Hospital. The next day I was advanced to RD2 and was the leading petty officer of the radar gang consisting of 18 sailors. The senior petty officer in our division was a 1st Class ET (Electronics Technician) who was a genius at diagnosing problems in the electronic equipment, but had absolutely no administrative or leadership skills. Our division officer gave him his choice of abdicating his right of seniority or being reduced in rank. He abdicated and I was appointed Division Leading Petty Officer. This was my first experience at being responsible for 36 men (RDs, ETs, and RMs), most of whom were older than me. One of the tasks that I inherited was updating the navigation charts in CIC in accordance with received *Notice to Mariners*. Because we never knew where the ship might be ordered to go, all of our charts had to be kept current.

WestPac Cruise 3

SOUTHERLAND's third deployment of the Korean War commenced on 21 March 1953 when DesDiv 51, accompanied by USS LERAY WILSON, DE-414, again left San Diego bound for Pearl Harbor. While on liberty in Hawaii, several of us went to a club on Waikiki Beach, the *Queen's Surf*.[6] We couldn't afford more than one of the fancy Hawaiian drinks with the little umbrellas so we were nursing one when all of a sudden another round showed up. A party of civilians who were a few tables away realized our plight and bought us several rounds.

We departed Pearl Harbor on 4 April, enroute to Midway Island. Shortly after we left Hawaii, I was holding plain language radio checks with the other ships in DesDiv 51 when the ship we were scheduled to relieve called and asked where we were. Using secure coding, I told them our position, which was a disappointment to them. They were sure that we were already in WestPac and would be relieving them early (this confusion was due to atmospheric conditions that cause what are known as "skip waves" where radio signals "skip" across the atmosphere).

On Easter Sunday, 5 April 1953, our CO was still CDR Wesche and our new XO was LT Richard L. Ploss, USN who had relieved LCDR Hill when he finished his tour.

Again during this cruise we spent a lot of time with *TG 95.1* in the Yellow Sea on the west coast of Korea operating with the British aircraft carrier HMS GLORY, CVL-62, and the cruiser HMS NEWCASTLE, CA-76. These operations also included performing SAR missions for downed pilots.

Early in April, while operating the ECM gear, I detected Communist firecontrol radar signals. This radar then "locked on" to SOUTHERLAND and started to track us. We took some evasive action and nothing further came of this incident. However, over the next few days we detected several other radars. As our RFD equipment was WWII vintage and could only determine a broad direction (e.g., SE, NW, etc.), we devised a plan to determine exactly where those radars were located. We had a WWII height finding radar (an SP) mounted on the after tripod mast that did not function most of the time; however, it operated in the same frequency band as the North Korean radars. I convinced the "powers-that-be" that if we could hook the antenna from the height finder to the ECM receiving equipment then perhaps I could get accurate bearings on the Communist's radars. SOUTHERLAND's ETs (Electronic Technicians) made this hook-up and it worked. This entailed them stringing several hundred feet of coax cable from the radar antenna to the front-end of the ECM receiver. Over the next several days SOUTHERLAND steamed up and down the coast while we took cross-bearings on the radar sites.

Eventually I plotted all the information that we collected on "Irish Linen" (a wax impregnated linen) chart of Western Korea and the various bearings intersected exactly where one would pick to setup a radar. About six or eight sites were identified. We requested permission to shell these identified sites, but permission was denied. These radars were being used by the North Koreans for GCI (ground-controlled intercept). It was better to know where they were in the event that an operation might take place in that particular area. At that time they could be destroyed. We sent the map into military headquarters in Tokyo. A few weeks later, several guests arrived aboard including "brass" and high-ranking civilians. These gentlemen had my map, only by now it had been classified TOP SECRET. The "brass" wanted to know more about the map, how the information was collected, how the map was made, etcetera. There was just one problem—I was the only one who knew the details and I was not cleared for TOP SECRET! Utilizing a little subterfuge, we managed to provide answers to all the brass' questions.

On 4 May, we searched for a downed pilot without success. Then we rejoined TU 95.1.1 on 8 May and operatcd with USS BATAAN, CVL 29. Then on the 9th we were once again on anti-invasion patrol between Changsan Got and Maha To. On the 10th and 11th we were engaged in bombardment of Che Do. These islands were being used as staging areas by the NKPA for attacks on the mainland. On the 16th we were relieved by USS HIGBEE, DDR-806, and headed to Yokosuka via the Shimonoseki Straits. In Yokosuka, we nested alongside USS FRONTIER, AD-25. Then we were in drydock for a few days. On 23 May, LTJG Judy was transferred for discharge and LTJG R.W. Brown assumed the duties of CIC officer.

While we were in Yokosuka, I had an opportunity to accompany several other shipmates to an R & R (Rest & Recreation) facility, the Fuji View Hotel, on Mt. Fuji. Each morning there would be ten of us around a big round table for breakfast. The waitress would give each of us menus with each individual item numbered, then she would go around the table and we each would give her our order by its number: 2, 5, 6, 11, etcetera. The waitress would constantly nod, but not write anything down. When our food arrived at the table, each of us got exactly what we'd ordered!

One day three other sailors and myself decided to take a sail boat out on the lake. After a while a slight squall came up and we found out that none of us were proficient sailboat sailors. It took some time, but eventually we made it back to the pier without incident.

Back in Yokosuka, a couple of shipmates and myself were out celebrating when we saw a shiny, new model jeep parked outside a bar. We decided that we had to check it out and climbed aboard. None too soon, we got back down as two Marine MPs, including a major, exited an adjacent bar and went to their jeep. A few seconds earlier and we would have been in serious trouble.

We departed Yokosuka on 2 June and conducted ASW exercises with USS POINT CRUZ, CVE-119, in the Okinawa OpArea. On 15 June, we rejoined TU 95.1.1, and operated with USS BAIRKO, CVE-115, and HMS OCEAN, CVL-68, off the west coast of Korea. From 27 June until 8 July we were in Sasebo undergoing upkeep alongside DIXIE before returning to the west coast of Korea.

Of particular note was the rescue of a downed English pilot on 15 July. This pilot was able to ditch his plane in the vicinity of his carrier, HMS OCEAN. The carrier wanted to rescue the pilot by helicopter, but apparently did not have experience with helicopter rescues. The rescuer on the ladder did not drop into the water to assist the downed pilot who was obviously injured and in no condition to help himself. Our motor whaleboat was in the water and in the area, but was ordered to stay away from under the downwash from the helicopter's rotors. When our coxswain saw the severe condition of the pilot, he decided to ignore orders and go in and pick up the pilot, which he did. When they got the pilot onboard SOUTHERLAND, we discovered that he was the same pilot we had rescued the previous year. Artificial respiration and other attempts to save his life were performed by a surgeon transferred from HMS OCEAN, using the wardroom table as a hospital bed. Unfortunately none of our efforts were successful and he died. We transferred his body to HMS OCEAN where he was buried at sea that evening following flight operations.[7] During this ceremony we steamed close alongside the carrier and manned the rail. It was an emotional event for those of us who had previously rescued him successfully.

On 19 July, we detached and proceeded to Buckner Bay. From there we went to Hong Kong for R&R. While in Hong Kong, I had a blue gabardine suit made to fit me in three days. At the time I was quite pleased with my first suit since grade school graduation, and tailor made no less. When I went home to New York on leave I got caught in a rain storm and my suit shrunk to a size that would fit a young teenager! I also had a white uniform made out of sharkskin material. These uniforms were not "regulation," but were more practical than regulation cotton whites (or so I thought). The Shore Patrol could send a sailor back to his ship for wearing them. Also, if we had to cross over a large "chicken sh _ _ " ship, the OOD would refuse to allow us to cross his quarterdeck and would send us back to our ship. I was wearing this uniform in Honolulu when I was caught in a rain-squall. I boarded a bus and was strap hanging when several young ladies seated in front of me started giggling and making motions towards me. That is when I realized that the U.S. Navy was smarter than I was—as my uniform was transparent when wet!

One of my shipmates that I particularly remember, Billie D., was from Alabama. He had two girlfriends back home, Reba Faye and Emma Mae. We heard a lot about these girls and his problems with them. At times he would stand for hours on the deck under the after tri-pod mast just staring out over the water and cogitating on his two ladies. After a while he would say "God damn," turn on his heel, and go about his routine business.

This sailor must have lived under a black cloud. One evening in Sasebo he was in a bar having a drink and minding his own business when a fight started. He had just made 3rd class petty officer so he decided that it was best for him to leave the club. He was going out the door, the shore patrol was coming in and arrested him. There were witnesses who affirmed that he was not involved in the fight. When he went before Captain's Mast the CO dismissed the charges; however, he appeared before the Mast still wearing his seaman's stripes. The Captain said that seeing as he could not appear in proper uniform, he could stay seaman.

On 27 July, an armistice was signed that ended the Korean War. A DMZ (De-Militarized Zone) was established at the 38th parallel dividing the Korean peninsula.

After leaving Hong Kong on 27 July, we proceeded to the Taiwan Straits for patrol duty. On 2 August, we entered Kaohsiung where we refueled from USS PLATTE, AO-22. While there, I was assigned shore patrol duty, tasked with ensuring all sailors returned to the ship by 2200. At that hour the SP detail searched the town, looking for recalcitrant sailors. After completing our duty, we were allowed liberty afterwards. During this period we also conducted training for personnel of the Nationalist Chinese Navy. One day we had several South Korean officers aboard and I was asked to teach them small arms. I demonstrated a .45-caliber automatic pistol and asked if there were any questions. At that one of them reached under his jacket and drew his .45 and cocked it, all with one hand. Class dismissed.

On the 8th we returned to patrol duty.

Then, on the 15th, DesDiv 51 went to Lingayan Gulf in the Philippines to avoid a typhoon. While there we refueled from KASKASKIA on the 16th. We were steaming in the Philippine Sea when we hit something with a cable attached floating in the water. The cable wrapped around one of our screws. We anchored in Subic Bay where the XO went into the water and dislodged the cable. When this was accomplished we again got underway.

One evening when we were steaming in the Philippine Sea and I was on watch in CIC, we heard a SAR in progress in the Sea of Japan thousands of miles north of us. Due to atmospheric conditions the downed pilot and the SAR team could not communicate; however, I could hear both of them loud and clear. I requested and received permission to try to establish communications with them, which I did. For the next several hours I coordinated the SAR. About 2 AM the next morning I asked to be relieved, but Captain Wesche ordered me to stay on watch for as long as we could maintain radio contact. We were able to continue to assist until about 5 AM when I was relieved after thirteen hours on watch. We never did learn the outcome of this mission since we lost radio contact as the morning warmed up.

From the Philippine Sea we went to Yokosuka for tender availability alongside FRONTIER, arriving there on the 20th.

We again joined TF 77 off the east coast of Korea on 5 September. One night, while patrolling off the coast with *TG 95.2*, we received word via radio to be ready to support a Marine Forward Observer's (FO, a "spotter") request for a gunfire support mission at first light the following day. That morning we attempted to establish radio contact with no luck. Eventually Captain Wesche decided that I would have to go ashore and act as a gun fire spotter. I had been trained in shipboard procedures for gunfire support, but NOT the shore-based spotter's role. We put our motor whaleboat into the water and when we got a little way out from the ship I held a radio check with SOUTHERLAND. At that time the Marine FO heard me and inquired if we were ready to support his fire mission. I answered YES and returned onboard, much to my relief.

On another occasion a Marine FO contacted us and requested an immediate fire mission. When I plotted his coordinates and the target's coordinates I saw that they were about 15 meters apart. When I requested confirmation, the spotter replied "Are you ready to provide a fire mission or not?" We did from about 11,000 yards out and were thanked, and informed "Mission accomplished." We never found out who or what was so close to the front of his position.

One night, another FO requested a fire mission on some buildings that he identified as barracks. When I inquired if they were occupied he replied "Yes, are you ready to fire?" I relayed the coordinate information to gun plot and when we were ready we opened fire. After a few rounds the FO reported "Target destroyed." The fact that we were blasting barracks containing sleeping soldiers instead of active positions upset me, but we moved on to other targets of opportunity and I was able to put this in the back of my mind.

During the night, while patrolling off the coast, we would keep up a steady harassing and interdiction fire[8] from our 5" guns to try to prevent the North Koreans from re-building the railroads and tunnels that had been shelled during the day. In order to prevent the North Koreans from getting used to a firing rhythm, we would roll dice in CIC and whatever number came up would be the number of minutes between rounds.

While operating with *TF 77,* one of my tasks was to assume radio control of attack aircraft (F-4U) after they had been launched from a carrier and vector them to their targets. One day an aircraft was badly shot-up shortly after he went "feet dry" (meaning he was over land). I vectored the pilot back to the carrier; however, he had reported that his aircraft was dirty (e.g., still had all the bombs, napham and ammunition on board). We tried to get him to drop the munitions, but he was unable to do so due to the condition of the airplane. Normal procedure was for us to control the aircraft until it was near the carrier and then transfer control to their on-board controllers. However, by the time this aircraft made it back, the pilot was in bad physical and mental condition. I was directed to continue control until the Landing Signals Officer (LSO) on the flight deck could visually assess the situation. It was decided they would try to land the aircraft, as they did not think that the pilot could survive a water landing. When the LSO took radio control, he talked to the pilot in the most calming manner imaginable, convincing him that everything was going to be OK. The flight deck was cleared, the aircraft was landed safely, and the pilot was saved.

One night while steaming in formation with *TF 77*, the Junior Officer of the Deck (JOOD) decided, on his own volition, to test the alertness of the CIC watch team. He did this by telling the bridge sound-powered telephone talker to report "Man Overboard" to CIC. I was the CIC Supervisor of the Watch at the time and protocol called for me to alert TF 77, via radio, of the situation, which I did. Unfortunately, the JOOD had not informed the OOD of his plan to conduct this drill. The Captain was in his sea cabin at the time and when he heard my report go out over the radio. Immediately, he was out on the bridge asking the OOD what was happening. Needless to say, the OOD had no idea, as the first that he heard was my report. In the meanwhile, *CTF 77* was calling to ask us what our intentions were— were we going to maneuver to pick up our man or not? Eventually things got squared away. The JOOD learned a valuable lesson and was restricted to his stateroom (put in "hack") for two weeks.

On 20 August 1953, the USSR exploded its first H-bomb.

Because we were short-handed, while underway the radar gang was standing exceptionally long CIC watches. The junior rated personnel were standing six hours on and six hours off. The senior personnel were standing eight hours on and six hours off. For the most part, the crew was sustaining themselves on cigarettes and coffee. A new CIC watch officer who did not understand the pace of our daily routine, demanded the smoking lamp be out in CIC when he was on watch. In an effort to maintain the morale of the radar team, checked with the CIC Officer who told me the smoking lamp wasn't out unless he ordered it so. I then negotiated with the new watch officer that when he had the watch, the radarman would be allowed to step outside of CIC whenever they wanted a cigarette, providing the operational situation permitted.

On 28 September, we anchored off Sodo Island. From there, we were relieved from duty and set our course for Yokosuka via the Shimonoseki Straits.

Miscellaneous Incidents Out of Time Sequence

On one tour, after we left Pearl Harbor bound for WestPac, one of our sailors went out on deck on the fantail and removed his clothing. He folded them neatly and stacked them up. The stern watch of the 01 deck watched this happening and wondered what was going on. When the sailor jumped overboard the watch knew what was going on and reported "Man Overboard." However, when the albatrosses started pecking at his head, our sailor decided he did not want to die and instead, wanted back on board. Fortunately, we were able to recover him. On a return trip back to the States we stopped at Guam. When this same sailor saw the welcoming party on the pier, he ran and hid. When questioned why, he replied, "My mother has sent them to put me in a nunnery." He was sent away under guard and we never saw him again.

On another trip, our Log Room Yeoman (Engineering Office clerk) locked himself in the Log Room and hung himself. The next morning his body was discovered. He may have been the same individual who the MPs (Military Police) chased back to the ship for improper sexual conduct.

During one visit to Sasebo, we were put on six section liberty instead of the normal three section.[9] The military and Japanese governments had decided that they had to clean up the town and had driven most of the "Hospitality girls" out of town (I never did find out where they went). Most of the bars were also closed. Most of the crew would visit the large Navy Exchange in town and shop for dishes, cameras, and other items. Many of us used a visit to the exchange as an excuse to get off the ship for a few hours.

Return to San Diego and Discharge

On 3 October, SOUTHERLAND left WestPac and returned to San Diego via Midway Island, Pearl Harbor, and the Naval Weapons Station (NWS), Seal Beach, California. One day, while on watch in CIC, my Division Officer asked if I was going to reenlist. My answer was "No, I can easily make $90 a week on the outside!" At this time I had about seven weeks left on my enlistment. In retrospect I have no idea why I wanted to leave the Navy at that time.

After we left Pearl Harbor, we proceeded to the Weapons Station where ammunition was offloaded.[10] On our way down to San Diego, we were ordered to expedite our arrival for a welcoming ceremony at the foot of Broadway. This was quite a ride, doing flank speed (in excess of 27 knots!) in the sea swell off the California coast!

DesDiv 51 arrived back in San Diego on 19 October. Once back in San Diego several radarmen and myself went into the U.S. Grant Hotel downtown for a few drinks. While we were there, the police came in and were checking ID cards. They checked the other three, who were all over 21, but did not believe their IDs were valid and told them to leave. I was still about a month shy of my 21st birthday, but my ID was not even checked! A couple of weeks later I was discharged. When I shouldered my seabag and left SOUTHERLAND for the last time, I felt that I was leaving my home and family. She had been my home for the past three years, and I could not understand how the radar team would continue to perform without me. Then I remembered what someone had told me: "The only irreplaceable people are in the graveyard." With that thought in mind I headed for the airport and my flight back to New York. I was going to take the civilian work force by storm and earn my fortune!

<u>Note</u>

After I was detached from SOUTHERLAND, she continued to make periodic WestPac cruises operating with the 7th Fleet as well as other assignments. In November 1963, she had her first tour off the coast of Vietnam. After a major overhaul in 1964, she was redesignated back to DD-743. For the next several years she performed typical destroyer duties including additional tours in Vietnam. In 1981 she was stricken from the Navy Register and designated for disposal as a target ship. On 2 August 1997, SOUTHERLAND was sunk by airborne test ordnance fired off the coast of Central California. She had been the first to anchor in Tokyo Bay at the end of WWII and the last of the ships present that day to lower their ensign. Ships, like people can be award medals and citations. During her career SOUTHERLAND earned nineteen battle stars: one in WWII, eight during the Korean conflict and ten during Vietnam. She also was awarded a Presidential Unit citation for her role in the Inchon invasion during the Korean War.

CHAPTER 6: A Legacy of Destroyer Escorts

At the start of WW II Germany's submarine fleet was causing havoc with America's attempts to supply the British Isles by sea. The Navy Department decided that what was needed to protect the convoys was a destroyer-type ship capable of detecting and destroying submarines. This led to the development of destroyer-escorts (DEs), ships that were more maneuverable than destroyers and that had a much tighter turning radius. DEs were also smaller, varying in length from 290 to 308 feet.

The new DEs were equipped with the latest in sonar and ASW weapons. Some were equipped with air search radar and anti-aircraft weapons. There were several different types developed: some with 3"/50 caliber dual purpose guns as their main battery and some with 5"/38 caliber, dual purpose guns. Some carried torpedo tubes and some did not. All had combat information centers (CIC). Although the DEs were not as heavily armed as their big sister destroyers, they performed many of the same tasks such as shore bombardment. They also served as scout ships, and even engaging large enemy ships using both guns and torpedoes.

Beyond a doubt, the most illustrious action by a DE was that of USS ENGLAND, DE-635. During the two week period of 19thru 31 May 1944, ENGLAND, with the assistance of USS RABY, DE-698 and USS GEORGE, DE-697:

[U]tilizing to the full all available weapons and equipment [she] skillfully coordinated her attacks with other
vessels and with cooperating aircraft, striking boldly
and with exceptional precision at the [Japanese] enemy, In a sustained series of attacks, she destroyed six
hostile [submarines] within twelve days effecting this
devastating blow to enemy operations during a particularly crucial period and disrupting attempts by the enemy to supply or evacuate key units.[1]

On 9 May 1945, ENGLAND was severely damaged by a
Japanese kamikaze attack and sustained casualties of more than 20
men killed, 10 missing, and 25 wounded.

The finest hour in the glorious history of the DEs came on 25
October 1944, during "The Second Battle of the Philippine Sea," otherwise known as "The Battle of Leyte Gulf." One engagement during
this battle was "the Battle of Samar" or as it is frequently called, "The
Greatest Sea Battle Ever Fought." During this battle, ships of Task
Unit (TU) 77.4.3, know as "Taffy III"[2] from their voice radio call
sign, engaged Admiral Takeo Hurita's heavy surface force attempting
to enter Leyte Gulf and attack the Allied transports and beachhead.
This Japanese force consisted of four battleships and six heavy cruisers. Although "outgunned and outmanned, the [units of Taffy III] did
the only thing they could do in the face of such overwhelming odds
and firepower—they attacked." In a little over two hours the Japanese
broke off their attack and retired. American loses consisted of one
destroyer escort, USS SAMUEL B. ROBERTS, DE-413; two destroyers, USS HOEL, DD-533 and USS JOHNSON, DD-557; and
one escort carrier USS GAMBIER BAY, CVE-73 and 1,100 sailors
either dead or missing.

Perhaps the only black mark in the DEs logbook is what has
come to be known as "The Arnheiter Affair." On 31 March 1966,
LCDR Marcus Aurelius Arnheiter was commanding officer of USS
VANCE, DER-387 (an Edsall-class DE). After three months in command and while operating off the coast of Vietnam, Captain Arnheiter

and VANCE were ordered to Manila where Arnheiter was relived of command. He was charged with "a gross lack of judgment and an inability to lead people." These charges were the result of Arnheiter endangering VANCE in violation of operational orders and reports that he was conducting religious services in violation of some crew-members personal beliefs.[3]

In all, there were six different classes of DEs built. [4] Perhaps the main difference between classes of DEs was the types of power plants installed. There were at least four different types of power plants, but basically they were either steam turbines or diesel engines. They also differed by their main armament: some had 5" guns and some had 3" guns. I served in two different classes, a *Buckley*-class, USS WILLIAM T. POWELL, DER-213, and an *Edsall*-class, USS CHAMBERS, DER-391. WILLIAM T. POWELL was steam-driven, whereas CHAMBERS was diesel-driven.

In 1975, the Navy redesignated all existing DEs as Frigates (FF) and discontinued the name "destroyer escort" and the designation DE.[5]

CHAPTER 7: USS WILLIAM T. POWELL, DER-213:
Philadelphia, Pennsylvania, 1954

I was honorably discharged at San Diego on 30 October 1953, and returned home to Richmond Hill. During the time that I was a "civilian," I had problems adjusting to civilian life and missed the responsibility and excitement of CIC and the discipline of shipboard life. I could not relate to my peers and found that available civilian jobs did not offer the responsibilities and challenges that I faced in the Navy. So on 27 January 1954, I re-enlisted for another six-years as an RD2 and was assigned to temporary duty at the Brooklyn Navy Yard. After a short period of time there, I received orders to report aboard USS WILLIAM T. POWELL, DER-213,[1] a 4th Naval District[2] Naval Reserve Training (NRT) ship stationed in Philadelphia. There were two NRT ships in Philadelphia: WILLIAM T. POWELL and USS EARL K. OLSEN, DE-765. Normally these two ships operated in tandem. WILLIAM T. POWELL was out at sea when I reported into the shipyard where I was assigned courier guard duty. This duty required me to checkout a sidearm and escort an employee from the Navy Exchange to a bank downtown. Of course, in typical Navy fashion I had a 45-caliber automatic pistol, but no ammunition! Fortunately no untoward incidents occurred.

While waiting for my ship, another sailor and I drove to Baltimore to look up an old shipmate of his. When we got to Baltimore, we stopped into a pub to ask directions and to have a beer. Within minutes, the bartender set a second round in front of us. When we asked about it, he told us that "the guy down at the end of the bar bought it." We thanked him and were continuing our conversation when another round was set in front of us. The bartender said, "These are on that guy over there," pointing to the other end of the bar. It turned out that these two guys were friendly rivals who worked in a local electronics plant. After the first guy bought us a drink, the other was not going to let him get the better of him. Eventually we left leaving several bottles of beer on the bar.

WILLIAM T. POWELL'S History

USS WILLIAM T. POWELL, DE-213, was built by the Charleston Navy Yard and was commissioned on 28 March 1944, by Mrs. Elsie V. Powell, mother of Gunner's Mate 2 William T. Powell.

80

GM2 Powell was killed aboard USS SAN FRANCISCO, CA-38, when a Japanese twin-engine bomber crashed into his gun mount during the *Battle of the Solomon Islands* on 12 November 1942. She operated in the Atlantic Theater of Operations until May 1945, when she entered the shipyard for conversion to a radar picket ship. However, the war ended before she was redesignated. On 5 November 1948, she was assigned to the 4th Naval District, and homeported in the Philadelphia Naval Shipyard (PNSY). On 18 March 1949, she was finally redesignated as DER-213. She was decommissioned on 9 December 1949, and reactivated for reserve training duty on 28 November 1950.

Life Aboard WILLIAM T. POWELL

WILLIAM T. POWELL returned to the Philadelphia Naval Shipyard (PNSY) on 11 February and I reported aboard. At that time our commanding officer was CDR A.G. Hamilton, Jr., and the XO was LT Ernest King, Jr., son of retired Fleet Admiral Ernest J. King, who was CNO during WW II. The operations officer was LT H.G. Garfand and the CIC officer was LTJG R.W. Brotherson. At that time there were only two regular Navy radarman aboard, another RD2 and myself. WILLIAM T. POWELL was driven by steam turbines. She was essentially a smaller version of USS SOUTHERLAND except that all of our equipment was WW II vintage.

Our task, and that of our sister ship, EARL K. OLSEN, was to take naval reservists from the Fourth Naval District out for their annual two-week training cruises to enable them to complete their active duty training requirements. Normally we would leave Philadelphia on a Monday, spend the week at sea and then spend the weekend in ports such as Miami; Boston; Nassau, BWI; Havana, Cuba; or Kingston, Jamaica. The second week would be devoted to providing the reservists with additional training before we returned to Philadelphia on Friday.

Unfortunately for the reservists, their first couple of days would be lost for training as they were usually seasick. This was fortunate for the regular crew, as our commissary man was able to save on his food rations budget to be spent during our inport periods in Philadelphia when there were no reservists aboard. After the ship had been at sea for a few days and the reservists started getting their "sea legs," training could begin. This training frequently included "Sea Bat Indoctrination." The Sea Bat is a legendary creature of the deep that is rarely, if ever, caught and never while a ship is in port. When one is caught, it is bought aboard the fantail and a box is placed over it in order to protect it from sunlight and to protect crewmembers. A guard, generally a bos'n's mate armed with a broom or paddle, stands watch over it. An announcement is normally made over the ship's 1MC announcing system that a Sea Bat has been caught and everyone who has not seen one should lay to the fantail. Those new "boots" who have not seen one are permitted to bend over and take a peek under the box whereupon the bos'n's mate wields his broom to the boot's rear end and cries "See Bat?" Other reservists would be sent to the paint locker with orders to get "a bucket of dial tone." Another favorite trick was to send a "Boot" out looking for a bucket of "relative bearing grease." Later, a reservist would be stationed in the bow to keep a sharp watch for the "mail buoy." He would be informed that passing ships would drop off mail for us and we had to pick it up. There were other similar shenanigans.

Many reservists also lost training time due to the physical condition of the ship and its equipment. Most of the equipment in the ship was of WW II vintage. This included the electronics equipment as well as the engineering equipment. As a result, we had frequent breakdowns. Those reservists whose ratings involved repairing the various equipment did get a great deal of experience; however, the others would lose training time at sea.

Although I relate the humorous aspects of our reserve training task, at the time we all considered it serious business. We knew that in time of a national emergency, these would be the sailors who would augment the regular navy crews aboard ships. To my knowledge, no one had his qualifications checked off unless he demonstrated the requisite skills or knowledge. For the most part, the reservists stood watches, repaired equipment, chipped paint, and performed all the other tasks required on a ship at sea.

Kingston, Jamaica

My first reserve training cruise was to Kingston, Jamaica. We left the PNSY on 1 March and on the way down the Delaware River and through Chesapeake Bay, we had to anchor for several hours in the Newcastle Range due to high winds and low visibility. This was a routine situation for most cruises. When we arrived in Kingston on the 5th we moored at the Princess Street Pier. I was assigned shore patrol with a Jamaican detective unit. This evening provided me an opportunity to see what life was really like "beyond the waterfront." The people who lived there were dirt poor and lived in falling down shacks. Drugs, alcohol use, and fighting were rampant. On another day, four of us hired a driver with an old Cadillac touring car to show us the island. We asked him to wait while we went into a store to buy some rum, but he insisted on buying it where the locals shopped. It was much cheaper and not a "rip-off."

First we went to a rain forest and then to an outlying resort hotel where our driver "arranged" for us to use the pool. Who should we see sitting poolside? None other than a well know Hollywood-leading man with a thin mustache (we swore that he was Clark Gable) who was with his "daughter" (or was she his "niece"?). That evening, our driver took us further out into the countryside. When we asked where we were going he just said, "You'll see." Eventually we could hear Calypso music coming from ahead of us up the dark road. Finally the driver stopped and told us to wait in the car. We saw him duck into what appeared to be an entrance to a hut. In a few minutes he came back and escorted us inside the hut where native Jamaicans were enjoying their night out. We were made welcome and eventually a few of us even tried to do the limbo in our white uniforms!

During this visit we had an opportunity to see an English regiment relieving a Scottish one. The ceremony and the parade were exciting to watch with all the troops in full dress uniforms and the pomp and circumstances as only the Commonwealth can do it: precision marching, bagpipes, and regimental colors waving in the breeze. Jamaica had been an English colony for 307 years until the Union Jack came down for the last time on 6 August 1962, and Jamaicans had their independence. We left Kingston on the 7th enroute to Guantanamo Bay ("Gitmo") Naval Training Base off the southeastern coast of Cuba.[3]

Guantanamo Bay, Cuba

It was normal for us to stop in Gitmo as frequently as possible. My first visit came on 8 March, when we visited in company with EARL K. OLSEN. In order to get from the pier area to the exchange area, we had to ride in huge, open-sided "cattle cars." There were only two things for us do once off the ship. We could either go to the Navy Exchange and shop or go to the club and drink. The drink of choice was the local Cuban beer Hatuey, named after a legendary Cuban Indian chief who was the symbol of Cuban independence. On the label was a profile of Chief Hatuey. It was said that one had enough to drink when they could see Hatuey's two eyes. Sailors have been known to say something like, "Not only can I see two eyes, he's smiling at me!" On the return trips on the cattle cars there would frequently be fights as sailors stood up for the honor of their ship.

Whenever we stopped at Gitmo, the ship's officers would bring back supplies of tax-free liquor for the officer's club in Philadelphia in violation of Naval and Federal regulations. Ship's company would also bring back liquor and tax-free cigarettes. After one trip, an excess of tax-free cigarettes began showing up in town and there was an investigation. After that the practice of importing cigarettes and liquor was stopped. Once, before the practice was stopped, we were returning from a trip when we held a depth charge demonstration. During this demonstration depth charges would be released from the stern racks. They would be set to go off at sufficient depth so that the ship would be well clear of the explosion. However, one must have been defective as it went off about twenty feet abaft the fantail. The explosion lifted the ship up out of the water and shook it like a dog. The Captain ordered the XO to make a tour of the ship and to report any damage. Although the ship smelled like a distillery, the XO reported "No damage" and we continued on our way.

While we were operating out of Gitmo, an unfortunate event occurred aboard one of our sister ships. A first class firecontrolman was working on the firecontrol radar while wearing a T-shirt. He was standing on a chair to gain access to the top of the set and behind him was an open power panel. Apparently the ship rolled and he fell backwards into the live 440-volt circuits and was electrocuted.

Keystone Ship Engineering, Chester, PA

After we returned to Philadelphia from Gitmo, we had to go into the Keystone Ship Engineering Shipyard in Chester, south of Philadelphia, for drydocking. One of my shipmates found a shop that was selling "hoagies" (submarine sandwiches) for only thirty-five cents! That was cheap even at that time. Even after we returned to Philadelphia, someone would make a nightly run down to Chester to pick-up orders of these hoagies. It was not until later in the year that we learned that they were selling horsemeat!

While we were in the shipyard in Chester some of the crew began dating ladies who worked at the local Scott Paper Company plant. It was not unheard of for a sailor to drop his lady at the gate at the start of her shift and then pick up another lady coming off shift. We were to spend time in Keystone again in April, September, and December.

On Thursday night, 30 March, WILLIAM T. POWELL was transitting the Delaware River enroute to Nassau, BWI, when she collided with the 7,607-ton Moore-McCormack freighter

MORNACSPRUCE in Delaware Bay. WILLIAM T. POWELL suffered two sailors injured and a 10-foot square gash in her starboard side, aft. A propeller shaft was also extensively damaged.

Nassau, British West Indies

After a diver inspected our underwater hull and made minor repairs, WILLIAM T. POWELL and our sister ship EARL K. OLSEN continued on to Nassau where we moored to Prince George Wharf. One evening, several of us went to a fancy hotel where we were playing darts. One of the darts went out a window and while looking for it in the bushes the dart punctured my finger. The puncture was gushing and getting blood all over my white uniform so I went back to the ship and hung the uniform on my rack. Our berthing compartment was right outside sickbay and when the corpsman saw my bloody uniform the next morning, he was sure that someone was seriously hurt. I was not, but a stuck finger sure does bleed a lot!

For some not remembered reason, on 3 April I returned from liberty 40 minutes late. Fortunately all that I received at Captain's Mast on the 6th was a warning. This was the only time that I went "before the mast" in my Navy career. We departed Nassau on 5 April to return to Philadelphia.

In a speech given on 7 April 1954, President Eisenhower expressed his "Domino Principle," where he claimed that if the Communists took over Indochina, the entire island defense chain consisting of Japan, Formosa (Taiwan), and the Philippines might also fall to the Communists. As a resul, both Australia and New Zealand would be threatened. This speech had a major influence on events of the next twenty years, particularly involving Vietnam.

Havana, Cuba

From 13 thru 16 April, we were again in dry-dock at Keystone. Then on the 20th, WILLIAM T. POWELL, EARL K. OLSEN, USS COGSWELL, DD-651 and USS RIZZI, DE-537[4] conducted exercises in the Narragansett Bay OpArea. After these combined exercises, we returned to the PNSY on the 22nd. Next, along with EARL K. OLSEN, we paid a visit to Havana where we moored at the United Fruit Pier on the 30th. On several occasions our visits were punctuated by local residents warning us to get off the streets to avoid Castro's rebels who were coming into town. This was during the early stages of their efforts to overthrew Fulgencio Batista's extreme right-wing dictatorship. There would be a few tense minutes, sometimes with sporadic gunfire outside before we would be told, "All clear."

Perhaps what I enjoyed most during our visit to Havana was going to the National Capitol Building located in the heart of the city. This was a beautiful limestone building with granite steps. Inside it was lavishly decorated with marble, mahogany, and bronze. Imbedded in the center of the lobby floor was a huge gemstone (Was it a diamond?). A velvet rope to keep people away surrounded this stone. There must have been other security, but none of us ever saw any. In a side galley, to the left, was a portrait of President Roosevelt. He was sitting in a chair and his eyes gave you the sensation of following you wherever you moved. I had never seen anything like it.

One day several of us were at the beach engaged in water sports with some female tourists when I dove into a wave, missed the crest and slid over the coral cutting my face, chest, arms, and legs. When I got back to the ship, our Hospital Corpsman slathered me in salve and wrapped me in bandages. That afternoon the OOD, who was a young ensign. paged me to the quarterdeck to discuss a non-related problem. When he saw me wrapped up like a mummy he almost fainted.

We left Havana on 2 May and returned to the PNSY where we stayed until the 25th.

On 7 May, the People's Army of Vietnam under the leadership of Ho Chi Minh, defeated the French Army at Dien Bien Phu, Indochina. The French were unable to cope with the guerrilla tactics used by the insurgents. This was the end of France's rule in Indochina and led to the country being divided into North and South Vietnam.

Nassau, British West Indies, Second Visit

The last weekend in May found us and EARL K. OLSEN once again moored to Prince George Wharf, Nassau. A shipmate, I'll call him Mike, decided that I had to learn to drink martinis and he was going to buy them until I did. We went to a place that had a table on a small second floor balcony overlooking an alleyway. Mike ordered drinks and I raised mine toward my mouth, but instead of drinking it, I tossed it over my right shoulder into the alleyway. Mike was impressed that I "drank" mine so he ordered another. The same thing happened with that one. I eventually did learn to appreciate a good martini, but not until much later. We left Nassau on the 31st and returned to the PNSY.

Havana, 2nd Visit

The second weekend in June was again spent at the United Fruit Pier in Havana along with EARL K. OLSEN. On the way home we conducted ASW exercises with USS POMPON, SSR-267. We returned to the PNSY on the 25th.

Boston, Massachusetts and Hurricane Carol

During July and August, WILLIAM T. POWELL and EARL K. OLSEN spent time in the PNSY, the Narragansett OpArea, Boston and Provincetown, MA. The first time in Boston was the weekend of 16-19 July. On 2 August, while in the PNSY, we held open house for visitors. This was in connection with the release of the movie *Winds of War*, based on Herman Wouk's novel of the same name. Some of the publicity stills had been shot onboard WILLIAM T. POWELL some time before I reported onboard.

On the 10th and 11th of August we conducted ASW exercises with USS ROOKS, DD-804; USS HICKOX, DD-673; USS MILLER, DD-535; USS GATLING, DD-671; USS DORTCH, DD-670; and USS CORSAIR, SS-435, before visiting Boston from 13 thru 16 August. We returned to the PNSY on the 20th. On 31 August, WILLIAM T. POWELL and her sister ship again left Philadelphia bound for Boston. There had been reports of a hurricane developing in the Caribbean, but its track was predicted to take it inland, over North Carolina. However, like most hurricanes, this one was unpredictable and that evening we found ourselves right in the path of *Hurricane Carol*, the most destructive hurricane to strike southern New England since the *Great New England Hurricane of 1938*. Carol was packing sustained winds of 80 to100 mph and was generating waves in the 50 to70 foot range! Between 0800 and 0937 the barometer rose from 28.32 inches to 28.76 inches! During these conditions all personnel who were not absolutely necessary for the safe operation of the ship would retire to their bunks. Perhaps the most terrifying storm-related incident occurred was when EARL K. OLSEN, who was in front of us, broached in the trough of a wave. As we reached the crest of a following wave, we saw EARL K. OLSEN broached and without steerageway. Fortunately a collision was avoided and eventually EARL K. OLSEN was able to regain steerageway. When the storm abated, we spent the night anchored in Delaware Bay then returned to Philadelphia the next day.

On 9 September, we were once again in Keystone where on the 30th LT Ernest J. King, Jr., relieved CDR A.G. Hamilton as commanding officer. We then returned to Philadelphia on 14 October.

Later in September, I attended an experimental two-week Instructor Training Course given in the shipyard by a couple of professors from the University of Pennsylvania. This course was designed to upgrade instructor training from the model developed during WW

II. Over the weekend we were given a task to prepare a lesson plan as a homework assignment, which I did at home in New York. Unfortunately when I left home to return to the shipyard, I left my work on a kitchen cabinet. I was permitted to pick a lesson plan from a file and give that as my demonstration lesson. Fortunately there was a good one on shipboard fire safety, so I was able to make a reasonably fair presentation (and take a zero for preparation).

On 3 September, the Communist Chinese began an artillery bombardment of Quemoy and Matsu Islands. This led to what became known as The First Taiwan Straits Crisis. During this crisis, the U.S. seriously considered using atomic weapons to defend Taiwan. Shelling of the islands ceased on 1 May 1955, thereby ending the crisis. This crisis situation erupted again on 23 August 1958.

Fleet Exercises

During the third week of October, we were ordered to participate in a fleet training operation in the Virginia Capes OpArea. This required us to act in coordination with other destroyers on screening stations for fleet amphibious ships and supply transport ships. During this period we made brief stops in Norfolk and Morehead City, South Carolina. On the 19th and 20th we operated with USS KELLER, DE-419, conducting ASW searches in support of the sortie forces. During the majority of the time we operated with USS RIZZI, DE-537. Other ships involved included USS ROCKWELL, APA-230; USS LIBRA, AKA-12; and USS SANDBORN, APA-193. We had two problems while participating in these exercise: (1) we didn't have the speed[5] required to move from station to station expeditiously, and (2) nobody in CIC except myself knew the procedures for re-aligning the screen and changing stations as the formation changed course. It was CIC's responsibility to recommend a new course and speed to the OOD every time the Officer in Tactical Command (OTC) issued new maneuver orders. This recommendation had to come in a timely manner that did not leave time for "What do we do now?" We also had onboard a WW II vintage height finding radar that never worked and our air search radar frequently operated in less than optimal condition. After a week of apparent frustration on the part of the TF commander, we were relieved and returned to Philadelphia on 29 October.

On 30 September 1954, USS NAUTILUS, SSN-571, the world's first nuclear-powered submarine, was commissioned.

Naval Academy Visit

During football season, we went to Annapolis for the weekend and moored at Santee Pier on Friday, 5 November. Unfortunately, on that particular weekend, most of the brigade of midshipmen were at Durham, North Carolina, for the Navy-Duke game (Navy won 40-7). Our liberty time was curtailed, as we had to be aboard to "indoctrinate" the plebes[6] who were left behind. They had been given lists of questions for which they had to obtain answers. Not all of the questions were "legitimate" and the "bogus" ones really made us think creatively in order to come up with plausible answers the plebes could give to the upper-classmen.

On Saturday retired Fleet Admiral Ernest J. King visited the ship and full honors were presented to him. When his car arrived on the pier his Marine orderly got out, marched to the right, rear seat and opened the door. The Admiral got out, walked up the brow, saluted the colors and OOD and requested permission to come aboard. It was not until later that we realized that all this time his orderly was supporting him, for Admiral King was very ill. On Sunday the ship was open to general visiting and we had to act as tour guides.

We again returned to the PNSY on the 12th after conducting training exercises in Chesapcake Bay. On 14 November I was advanced to Radarman first Class (RD1).

Miami, Florida

Just before Thanksgiving we provided escort services for USS BANG, SS-385, while she was undergoing sea trials out of Norfolk. On Thanksgiving Day we had guests aboard for dinner consisting of the traditional holiday fare. However, I was not aboard for this dinner, I was fortunate enough to go home to New York for the weekend and to spend the holiday with family and friends.

In December, after conducting ASW exercises with USS CUSHING, DD-797, we stopped in Miami where we moored to the east end of the MacArthur Causeway. During this visit several of us decided to visit a serpentorium south of town. A young lady was demonstrating a black snake that she had around her neck. At one point she was explaining that snakes were not slimy and flipped a loop of the snake over my head. I froze. Unfortunately, I happened to have a pint in my waistband that went down through my pant leg and smashed on the ground. Everyone had a good laugh as the snake handler removed the snake from around my neck.

After leaving Miami, we headed home to Philadelphia. On the way back we had a serious casualty occur in the Forward Fire Room when a soot blower failed.[7] When this happened, it allowed live superheated steam to fill the fireroom and personnel had to evacuate before anyone got scalded. Fortunately no one was injured. But once again we had to go into Keystone for get repair.

The Christmas holidays of 1954 were spent in Philadelphia so I took leave and spent a few days in New Jersey with a yeoman shipmate and his family. Christmas Eve was a special time for this family, and as part of their tradition, all his female relatives bought different typical Italian dishes to a dinner party. His grandfather, who spoke no English, showed me his wine cellar, locked us inside, and insisted that I had to sample each of the nine barrels. The ladies had to pound on the door before he would unlock it. The next morning I went home to Richmond Hill. The ship was still in PNSY over the

New Year's holidays. However, the OOD did not follow naval tradition and the New Year's Eve deck log was not written in verse.

After leaving Keystone on the 11[th,] we returned to the PNSY and on the 29[th,] we left for Miami. That Sunday, in Miami, several of us decided to rent a convertible. We had a great time until the driver decided to watch the sights and not the car in front. It stopped for a red light and he did not, at least not in time to avoid hitting him. The front end of our car got a little banged up, but his was undamaged. We took the car back to the rental place, which, lucky for us, happened to be closed. We left a note explaining that we were leaving the following morning. I never did find out the outcome of this incident, but undoubtedly we were not the first sailors to enjoy liberty at the rental agency's expense!

We left Miami on the 31[st,] and returned to the PNSY.

Miscellaneous Incidents out of Time Sequence

One night my shipmate, Mike, took me over to New Jersey to visit some of the local night clubs. At some point in the evening, he came over to me, handed me his car keys, and told me that he and a lady that he met were going to another club. He asked me to follow in his car. This was all right except that his car had some sort of hybrid fluid drive transmission that I did not know how to operate— besides, I did not have a license! With many starts and stalls, I finally made it safely to the other club, which was about a mile away.

Another shipmate, Glenn lived in New Jersey and owned a souped-up 1949 Mercury sedan. He would race anyone over a quarter mile without even discussing what the other car had under its hood. He also would not let anyone look under his hood. On many occasions he would take me to his home for the evening. While there, we would frequent various nightclubs and stock car events.

One of my collateral duties was Master At Arms. One evening, shortly after 11 P.M., I was summoned to the quarterdeck and as MAA, directed to attend to some sort of rowdyism in the wardroom. This created quite a dilemma—I was not sure that my responsibility included the wardroom. I decided that it did and entered the wardroom. What I found were several young reserve officers with a young lady. The wardroom table on a destroyer does double duty as an operating table when needed and is equipped with operating room lights. These officers were performing "surgery,"—they had the young lady on the table with the operating lights on, and they were shaving her legs. When I asked what was going on, they realized that they were out of order and broke up the party without any further action on my part. I remained on the quarterdeck until all the participants left the ship.

All the electronic equipment we had in CIC was WW II vintage and we did not have any trained electronics technicians (ET) aboard. We did have a sailor who had taken a TV course and had taken and passed the exam for 3rd Class ET. One afternoon, several of us were sitting around in CIC when our ET came in and walked around a corner into an alcove. After awhile our CIC officer, a reserve officer who had finished last in his class at Notre Dame, came in and asked what the ET was doing sleeping in the corner. He had been working on a scope and unknown to us, electrocuted himself and lost consciousness. Base medical was quickly summoned and in a matter of minutes our ET was revived—much to everyone's relief.

One of my most memorable shipmates was the BT1 in charge of the forward fire room. He was inordinately insistent on cleanliness and safety, so much so that he insisted that the fire room personnel change out of their oily shoes and dungarees before leaving the fire room. Down in the fire room he had installed large metal boxes containing such items as a coffeepot and a 45-rpm record player. These boxes would normally be unlocked. Each morning he would go down into the fire room and walk around. If the state of cleanliness was not up to his standards, he would not say a word. He would just snap locks on the boxes and leave the fire room. Later he would return and find the fire room looking as clean as an operating room. If it did he would unlock the boxes.

Two other characters were seamen from the coal mining area of West Virginia. They would go ashore and go to a local bar. After a few drinks, one would turn to the other and say "Ready? Whose turn is it?" with that decided, one would hurl off and punch the other. They would take turns doing this until they got tired (I guess, as I never stayed around long enough to witness the outcome).

On November 15 1954, I had been advanced to first class petty officer. One day I was cleaning under a plotting table in CIC when I felt someone kick my foot. When I crawled out, I saw that it was Captain King. He asked me what I thought I was doing and when I told him, he informed me that he had advanced me to first class and that if he wanted me to be doing seaman's work he would make me a seaman. I thanked him and left the bucket of water and cleaning gear right where they were. They were still there when I left the ship in February 1955.

On 17 January 1955, CDR Eugene P. Wilkinson, first commanding officer of USS NAUTILUS, SSN-571, sent his historic report, "Underway on nuclear power." This was the beginning of the modern nuclear Navy.

Earlier in the year, I had submitted a request to winter over[8] at Antarctica, but that was denied. When I submitted my request I knew that I did not have a snowball's choice in hell of having it approved; however, the Antarctica assignment did sound exciting. Shortly after being turned down for Antarctica, I submitted an application to change my rating from Radarman (RD) to Firecontrolman (FT).[9] My desire was still to learn the technical aspects of RADAR not just the operational uses. In February 1955, I received orders to report to Firecontrol School at Anacostia, Virginia, just south of Washington, D.C.

On 22 February 1955, the State Department announced that a small force of military advisors would be sent to South Vietnam. This was the start of the United States' involvement in South East Asia.

My leaving WILLIAM T. POWELL was not as emotional as leaving SOUTHERLAND had been. It also had not been a challenging tour and I knew that I was going on to a new phase in my Navy career.

Note

WILLIAM T. POWELL was again redesignated as DE-213 on 1 December 1954, and continued reserve training duties until September 1957. She was placed out of commission, in reserve, on 17 January 1958, and was struck from the Navy list on 1 November 1965.

CHAPTER 8: Firecontrol Conversion School, Anacostia, Virginia, 1955

At Anacostia, I attended the Firecontrol School (FT-A) where the curriculum addressed basic principles of electronics and fundamentals of firecontrol. This was followed by a series of C-school classes on specific firecontrol systems[1] and then advanced Firecontrol School (FT-B). Classes for FT-A & C schools were held during the afternoon—evening shift (3 P.M. - 10 P.M.). Classes for FT-B were held during the day. Including the A, C and B courses, I was at Anacostia from March 1955 until April 1956.

One of our collateral duties was participating in the honor guard that would line Pennsylvania Avenue whenever a foreign head of state visited Washington. We had to line-up along the curbs, double arm lengths apart, and stand out there for hours in the hot sun. Seldom did we know who was visiting; all that we would see is a limousine passing by with flags flying. Fortunately, I never caught this duty on a cold day.

On 14 May 1955, the Warsaw Treaty was signed establishing a mutual-defense organization in Eastern Europe.[2] It provided a unified military command and allowed the USSR to station its troops in the territory of participating countries. It was dissolved on 1 July 1991, 1 when the USSR was dissolved.

The FT School was adjacent to the Navy Musicians School. In the summer while on our supper break we would sit out on the grass and listen to them play (sometimes it was good, but mostly it was practice). After we got out of class at 10 P.M. several of us would go the VFW Club in SE Washington where prices for drinks were reasonable. This club was just up the street from "8th & I" where the Marine Barracks are located. On Friday nights, if someone had a car, we would go to the EM Club at Arlington. They had a dance on Friday nights and there would be WAVES[3] there who dance with us.

At other times, we would go into Washington and visit the various sites during the day. On weekend evenings, when I did not go to New York, we would frequently go to the Mayflower Hotel cocktail lounge where a lady played the piano. As many times as we went there we never heard anyone request a song that she did not know. At other times, we would visit one of the many jazz clubs downtown. One or two weekends a month I would take the train up to New York to visit with family and friends. This was approximately a four-hour trip so the porters restricted people in the club car to two drinks each. I found that if I tipped them generously, I could spend the entire trip in the club car.

While at Anacostia we would get paid by check. On a particular payday in August, my check was made out for several thousand dollars! When I inquired at the disbursing office, I was told that personnel had changed my active duty base date (ADBD) and that I had back pay coming. Somehow my ADBD had been changed to my mother's birthday! Disbursing told me that I had two choices: either keep the check or return it, in which case I would not get paid until the problem was resolved. I kept the check and opened a bank account with it. Eventually the situation was straightened out and I was not paid for several months but was able to live on the banked money.

One particular Saturday morning several of us were sitting on the barracks steps swapping lies about the previous night's liberty and the young ladies that we met. There was an older petty officer sitting

98

on the rail, sucking on a piece of grass, and taking this all in. Finally he interrupted and said, "You can have those young ladies who are looking for experience; give me the older ladies who are looking for enjoyment."

At an air show held at Tushino, outside of Moscow, on 3 July 1955,[4] the Soviets flew both Bear and Bison long-range bombers multiple times over American visitors. This caused an exaggerated assessment of Soviet inventories of such bombers and led to the so-called "Bomber Gap." As a result, North America's continental air defense systems were strengthened, including the so-called DEW Line (Distant Early Warning) and the setting up of the so-called "Barrier Patrols" (to be discussed in Chapter 10). Eventually the bomber gap was disproved by U-2 over flights of the USSR.

One of the more humorous events that occurred at Anacostia concerned the 3"/50 gun mounts with the firecontrol radar antenna that were situated on a hill overlooking the Navy Exchange area, about 500 yards away. For amusement, while on class breaks, we would aim the antenna at one of the exchange shops and when someone would approach the door we would modulate the radar beam by shouting into the antenna. We would say something like "Don't touch that door knob!" Our voices would carry down and the unsuspecting customer would stop suddenly and look around to see who was talking. Of course they could not see us up on the hill. We also discovered that if we aimed the antenna down the boulevard, we could light up the neon signs on the shops. We did not do this very often, but the knowledge gained would come in handy in later years.

One afternoon I was walking back to the barracks after lunch when another student, a Chief Petty Officer (CPO), approached me. He proceeded to take me to task for something he thought I did the previous evening. Apparently his irritation with me concerned a lady in one of the clubs in town. Eventually I convinced him that I was in the barracks all night and, therefore, it could not have been me that offended him. That evening, during a class break, he again approached me and escorted me to another classroom where he told me

99

to wait outside the classroom door. A few minutes later the door opened and I thought I was looking in a mirror! There stood my first cousin whom I had not seen in over fifteen years! He was also a student changing his rate to Firecontrolman. Eventually he was commissioned and served as a communications officer in Vietnam.

On 17 August, Admiral Arleigh A. ("31-knot") Burke was appointed CNO (Chief of Naval Operations). Burke was to serve three terms as CNO.

One weekend that winter I took the train up to New York for a weekend at home. The weatherman was forecasting snow Sunday afternoon and evening so I decided to take an early Sunday afternoon train for the normally four-hour trip back to Washington. When the train was south of Wilmington, Delaware, it became snow bound and could not move which caused me some distress. I was due in class at 8 A.M, but due to the weather conditions, I did not make it back to the base until about 9 A.M. Monday morning. Fortunately I got off with just a warning from the Training Officer.

In February 1956, a destroyer patrol was established in the Red Sea in response to growing tension in the Middle East. This action focused centered around the Suez Canal.

After completion of Firecontrol B-School in April 1956, I was ordered to USS CASCADE, AD 16,5 a destroyer tender (a repair ship) stationed in Newport, Rhode Island for OJT (On-the-Job Training) as a FT.

CHAPTER 9: USS CASCADE AD-16: Newport, Rhode Island, 1956

History of the US Navy in the Mediterranean Sea

The US Navy's involvement in the Mediterranean Sea goes back to the early days of our country. In 1801, President Thomas Jefferson "sent a small squadron of frigates into the Mediterranean, with assurances to that power [Tripoli and the Barbary States] of our sincere desire to remain in peace, but with orders to protect our commerce against the threatened attack." In 1803 the frigate USS PHILADELPHIA, William Bainbridge commanding, ran aground and her crew and captain were captured. Later that year, naval actions and a naval blockade by Commodore Edward Preble in his flagship, the frigate USS CONSTITUTION, followed by further actions led by Commodore John Rogers in 1805, led to the United States achieving freedom of movement in the Mediterranean and highlighted the fact that the new nation would not tolerate interference with American shipping. The US Navy has had an ongoing presence in the Mediterranean Sea ever since. From the end of WW II until the collapse of the Soviet Union, the Sixth Fleet's task[1] was to provide air power support to the North Atlantic Treaty Organization (NATO) forces in the southern part of Europe. Destroyers have always played a major role in that "presence." For instance, between 5 and 9 April 1946, USS POWER, DD-839, accompanied USS MISSOURI, BB-63, to the Bosphorus, in Turkey. MISSOURI's mission was to return the body of the Turkish Ambassador to the United States, but a secondary mission was to influence Soviet Middle East policy by showing the flag and our determination to exercise our right of "freedom of the seas."

CASCADE'S History

Motto: "We Serve"

USS CASCADE, AD 16, was built by Western Pipe and Steel Co., San Francisco, California and was commissioned on 12 March 1943. She served in the Pacific Theater of Operations from June 1943 until March 1946. In 1947, she was decommissioned and placed in a reserve status. On 5 April 1951, she was again placed in commission and assigned as a tender for destroyers based in Newport, Rhode Island. Operating out of Newport, CASCADE made routine cruises to the Caribbean and the Mediterranean where she serviced the destroyers of the U.S. Sixth Fleet. The primary mission of CASCADE was service to the fleet: destroyer-type ships that were assigned availability dates during which time repair and maintenance beyond the capacity of the ship's company were performed by the tender. Supplies of every description were available on CASCADE as well as medical, dental, and religious services.[2]

Life Aboard CASCADE

When I reported aboard CASCADE in Melville, Rhode Island. on 27 April 1956, the CO was Capt. Edward L. Robertson, Jr., USN. The XO was CDR John F. Bauer, USN. CDR. Henry Frye, USN, was the repair department officer and LT Harry D. Christenson was the ordnance repair officer. On 11 June, CASCADE deployed to the Mediterranean Sea (the "Med") where she operated in support of the U.S. Sixth Fleet. On the 16th, while enroute, one of the seamen fell through an open hatch and fell four decks receiving three compound fractures of the skull (including the base; a broken rib, and a dislocated shoulder). CASCADE changed course and headed toward the Azores Islands. The next day, the 17th, we received an air drop of medical supplies delivered by an aircraft from Lajes Air Force Base. The seaman then received additional medical attention until an USAF crash boat arrived and he was transferred to Lajes Air Force Base. We later received word that he would recover from his injuries.

Shortly after we left Newport, I went to visit CIC. When I went in I received an emotional shock: I was no longer a "radarman" and was no longer "one of them." CIC is a "need to know" workplace and I no longer had a need to know what was going on. I was not asked to leave, but the watch standers made it obvious that I was not welcome by their body language and their turning documents upside down. This became a non-issue once we arrived in the Med and took up our repair tasks.

Cannes, France: First Visit

After dropping off our injured shipmate, CASCADE arrived in San Raphael Harbor, Cannes, France on 23 June, where she relieved

USS TIDEWATER, AD-31, and assumed the duties of the Sixth Fleet Service Force flagship. TIDEWATED departed for home on the 26th and CASCADE got underway on the 27th for operations with the fleet. While we were anchored off Cannes, we had an opportunity to visit the Kingdom of Monaco with its world-famous casino. We also ogled the sunbathers on the sands of the Riviera.

Up until this time, it was the Navy's policy to keep several tenders stationed in the Med. These normally included a seaplane tender, a submarine tender, and a "heavy" ship (cruisers, aircraft carriers, etcetera) tender. CASCADE'S mission in the Med was to do all possible to assist the Sixth Fleet to maintain a high state of readiness. In 1956, it was decided that one tender could handle the entire Med workload. It was now CASCADE'S turn. However, the Navy did not count on all the events of 1956 including the Suez Crisis and the Beirut, Lebanon crisis. In addition, the Hungarian Revolt of 23 October put a temporary stop to President Eisenhower's process of détente. As a result, CASCADE spent much of the time in the Eastern Mediterranean and, therefore, missed two port calls in Spain.

As part of the "repair department" aboard CASCADE,[3] we were not considered as "Ships Company." My only responsibility vis-a vis the ship's daily routine was maintenance of the four WW II era 40-mm antiaircraft gun mounts. Our working space was a large room that opened onto the main deck. Except for work benches along the sides and a few tables and chairs, it was barren. There was a loft over the space where we stored large replacement items. One afternoon a shipmate and myself were rearranging some of these items when he gave a crate a shove in order to reposition it. Unfortunately, the first joint of the small finger on my right hand was in the way: in a split second the finger was broken, and to this day it is crooked.

When we were at sea we had plenty of free time and during this period I learned to play pinochle. This skill stood me in good stead for the rest of my naval career as it was the game-of-choice in most messes.

While CASCADE was in port, we had to respond to work orders submitted by all types of ships and for all types of equipment and systems, many of which we had little familiarity with and lacked documentation. Fortunately, in most cases, the requesting ship's company appreciated the situation and could solve their own problems with little assistance. In many cases, all they required were replacement parts.

One of my more memorable shipmates was the Ship's Serviceman (barber) who owned a bass fiddle that he took ashore in just about every port that we visited. He would go into a local club and jam with the resident band. Unfortunately, I never had an opportunity to hear him except when he practiced aboard the ship. However, shipmates who did hear him related that he was excellent.

Between port calls, CASCADE operated at sea with the Sixth Fleet, replenishing the Fleet with whatever logistic support they required to sustain operations. This included refueling, rearming, reprovisioning, and providing medical services. During these at-sea periods, the repair department personnel would study the work orders for the upcoming tender availability period. If we were lucky, we would have the technical manuals that could assist us in analyzing the submitted problems. Several times while at sea servicing the fleet, we would anchor for the weekend in the Gulfo de Palmas, Sardinia. However, these were not liberty periods. In addition to CASCADE, there were other support ships present in the Med including USS AUCILLA, A0-56; USS ALTAIR, AKS-32; USS DENEBOLA, AF-56; USS ELKOMIS, AO-55; USS MISSISSINOWA, AO-144; and USS MAZAMA, AE-9.

Livorno (Leghorn), Italy

On 26 July 1956, while CASCADE was Med-moored[4] at Anadana Degli Anelli, in Livorno (Leghorn), Italy, the Italian passenger ship S/S Andria Doria and the Swedish vessel N/V Stockholm collided in the North Atlantic. USS EDWARD H. ALLEN, DE-531, rescued the Andria Doria's captain and 76 crewmembers. As a result of America's efforts to assist in this tragedy, we were exceptionally well received by the grateful Italians, although we had no role in the rescue.

Once, while in port in Leghorn, I was assigned shore patrol duty and wound up patrolling with the Italian State Police (the *Carabinieri*). Some of the places we visited included "upscale" houses of prostitution. These looked like something from a Hollywood movie set with wide, curving marble staircases and statuary all around. Of course, the young "ladies" lounging around did add a special touch. On another occasion, I was on SP with a young sailor off another ship who was from the mid-West. We were called into a bar to try to calm down some potential trouble. I told the other SP to stay slightly behind my left shoulder and do exactly what I told him to do. I then went to the back of the bar where some sailors and B-girls in a booth were arguing with sailors and B-girls in a booth across from them. The girls were encouraging the sailors to either ignore my orders or to instigate a brawl between me and the sailors. When I looked behind me I my SP partner talking to some friends in the front of the bar. In my most diplomatic manner I extracted myself from that situation.

Also while in Leghorn, each division had an opportunity to have a beach party at a private beach (Bagno Rosa). To get there, we had to ride a LCM (M-Boat) for about a half-hour. In addition to the sailors riding the M-Boat, there was plenty of Italian beer, *Birra Peroni*. At some point during our party, a shipmate cut himself and had to be ferried back to CASCADE for treatment. After several hours, when the M-Boat had not returned, and the beer was running out, a few of us went looking to see if we could find any replacement. After walking up the beach about a half-mile, we came across a farmhouse and met the farmer. Of course there was a language barrier: he did not speak English and we did not speak Italian. However, he did understand "vino." I think that we bought out his entire cellar! Some time later the M-Boat did return, but by that time we didn't much care.

On 6 August, CASCADE departed Leghorn for fleet exercises.

Cannes, France: Second Visit

On 13 August, we were moored out off La Napoule, Cannes, and I was assigned a work order to repair some equipment on a Landing Ship Dock (LSD).[5] The ship was complete with a Marine combat team, and when I boarded the ship I saw the well deck was full of tanks and trucks with Marines sitting on them cleaning their battle gear. As the ship's company FT led me with all my test equipment, tools, and manuals through the passageways, we encountered four Marines sitting in the passageway playing cards. I asked them to excuse us so that we could get by, but without looking up they told us to "Go another way Swabbie, we're playing cards." I then identified the highest ranking one there and ordered him, "Corporal, clear this passageway now." At that he looked up and saw I out-ranked him by several pay grades and immediately cleared our way. The ship's company FT told me, "You shouldn't have done that, now they [the Marines] will make life miserable for us." He would not tell me what the Marines meant, but I informed him that sailors had to stand up for their rights.

Our time anchored in Gulf Juan off of Cannes, off the French Riviera, was not all work. Monte Carlo was only a short bus ride away. Unfortunately sailors in uniform were not allowed inside the casino—all that we could do was look. However, we did get to enjoy the beach. Whenever possible when in port, another FT and myself would get on a local bus and take it to some outlying area. Then we would get off and walk the local neighborhood. One day while in Cannes, we took a bus to the last stop and got off. We stopped in a local bar where the owner greeted us with open arms and an open champagne cellar. After a short conversation we learned we were the first American servicemen to visit the town since WW II. On that day in 1945, when the allies landed in the south of France, his family's execution had been scheduled at the hands of the Germans. The bar owner's appreciation was immeasurable.

Other times when I had time off I would wander into a local wine shop and spend hours with the owner and any customers. Of course, I did not speak any Italian or French, but the language of wine is universal.

We again visited Cannes in October.

Palermo, Italy

On 28 August, CASCADE was moored at *Piave Pier*, Palermo, Sicily. When we got up the next morning, we found that several U.S. submarines had moored alongside. This was unscheduled and about two days later they left as surreptitiously as they had arrived. This provided my first and only experience in repairing or servicing equipment aboard a submarine. Unfortunately, no one in our shop had any experience with submarine firecontrol equipment; fortunately, the submarine crews understood the situation and were only too glad to receive any assistance. Our assistance was mostly limited to providing generic parts and loaning test equipment.

Taranto, Italy

When we were scheduled to make a port-call in Taranto, Italy in early September, the Captain asked the Public Information Officer (PIO) to prepare an informational handout for the crew. The PIO consulted an old encyclopedia and then wrote some disparaging items about the Italian Navy, our hosts, and their actions during WW II. These concerned events that took place at the beginning of WW II. Fortunately the Captain read a copy shortly before we anchored and we managed to scour the ship and collect all the copies. While there, the Italian Navy arranged for a bus to take some of us up to Bari for an International Fair that was in progress. We had lunch in Bari and then went to the fairgrounds. We were on our way back to the ship when the bus broke down. Of course, the driver did not speak English and none of us spoke Italian. When the driver went off to seek help and did not return for awhile, I walked into a town about a quarter of a mile up the road. In town I found what would be referred to as a delicatessen in New York. The aroma of salamis and cheeses hanging from the ceiling was so inviting, I felt pangs of homesickness.

After negotiating for a piece of salami, a piece of cheese, and a bottle of wine I returned to the bus and sat down with my back against a rear wheel to eat my lunch. Some of the other sailors smelled what I had and questioned my rationality in eating what I considered a New York feast. After they saw I was serious about devouring my food find, and did not get sick, they asked for directions to the shop. I am sure the shopkeeper never had such a prosperous day. Eventually the driver returned, fixed the bus, and we were on our way with full stomachs.

On 19 September, CDR Paul W. Dodson relieved CDR Bauer as XO. Then on the 25th CASCADE departed Taranto for exercises with the fleet.

On 10 October, Don Larson of the Yankees pitched a perfect game during the Yankees-Dodgers World Series.

Piraeus (Athens), Greece

When we were in Phalenon Harbor, Salamis, Piraeus, Greece, in October we had a division of destroyers alongside. One of the ships, USS LIND, DD-703, was having a problem with her Mk 1-A Analog Firecontrol Computer.[6] After troubleshooting the problem, I determined that a gear located at the bottom of a four-foot shaft had broken loose. On top of the computer there was a crank attached to the shaft that the operator would turn in order to match other computed data. In order to gain access to the gear, it was necessary to completely dismantle the computer. This was a process that had never been done before[7] and there were no procedures for doing so. I informed the destroyer's firecontrolmen, gunnery officer, and captain that I wanted to take each module out, place it on an individual sheet of paper on the plotting room deck, and then remove the shaft. They were also informed this could only be done if there was a guard posted on the plotting room door 24-hours a day in order to avoid any parts accidentally getting mixed up.

This procedure was agreed to; however, the task had to be completed in less than a week—the ship was scheduled to leave for the Red Sea. My boss essentially told me to get to it and not to return until the work order had been signed off. Eventually the shaft was removed and taken to our machine shop where the gear was re-pinned. All parts and modules were reinstalled and the computer was put back together; appropriate tests were run and the work order signed off minutes before the last mooring line was cast off.

I literally had to jump from the destroyer to CASCADE in order to avoid going to the Red Sea with them. I did manage to get six hours off during this inport period to go into Athens and see some of the sights. These included the Plaka, the Acropolis, and the Parthenon, dedicated to the goddess Athena. CASCADE departed Piraeus on the 23rd enroute to Barcelona, Spain, to be relieved.

Barcelona, Spain

Our last stop in the Med was for two days in Barcelona, Spain in late October where we moored to Muele de Poniente Pier. While there, CASCADE was relieved by USS SHENANDOAH, AD-26. Here I had the opportunity to see bullfighting, Spanish-style. In contrast to the bullfights in Tijuana, where a large percentage of the spectators are usually tourists, the majority of the spectators were Spaniards who were there for a day's outing at their national pastime. Another main difference was the presence of pairs of machine gun carrying army guards stationed at each entrance to the bullring. While in

Barcelona I also took a tour to Montserrat with its monastery in the clouds.

On 29 October, Israel attacked Egypt. The next day the United Kingdom and France sided with Israel. The United States opposed the invasion and the 6th Fleet amphibious forces evacuated over 2000 endangered Western nationals from the region.

Upon CASCADE's departure from the Med on our way home on the 29th, we received a message from Commander, Service Force, Sixth Fleet as follows:

> *Your cheerful assistance under a two-tender load was outstanding performance by a fine ship and crew. Good luck.*
> *P.S. While we've heard a better poem glad for you heading home.*

Prior to reporting to CASCADE, I had put in for NSEP (the Naval Scientific Education Program). Early in our Med cruise I was informed the requisites had been changed and that I should resubmit in accordance with the new requirements, including a physical. I fulfilled these new requirements and while we were in Barcelona on our way home I received word the requisites had been changed again and that I was now too old for the program.

In November 1956, Premier Khrushchev of the USSR told the United States "Whether you like it or not, history is on our side. We will bury you" (Now, in 2002, Khrushchev's son is an American citizen!).

When CASCADE returned to Newport (actually to the State Pier in Fall River, MA) on 9 November, there was a delay in the crew leaving the ship, or dependents boarding. We did not know if we would be staying or if we would be fitting out for a quick return to the Med. The CNO had ordered all naval forces to maintain readiness to execute emergency war plans as a result of Soviet plans to send six ships from the Black Sea into the Mediterranean. While we waited to find out what was happening, we were entertained by DesLant's band playing on the pier. After several tense hours, the situation was resolved, things settled down to normal, and the alert status was canceled on 13 December. Upon our arrival in Fall River we received the following message from ComDesLant:

> *Welcome back from an arduous Med tour. Reports all indicate you have maintained the outstanding reputation of DesLant tenders.*

This completed my period of OJT as a FT and I was transferred to USS CHAMBERS, DER-391, also home ported in Newport.

Note

CASCADE was stricken from the Navy Register on 23 November 1974. For service at Okinawa during WW II, CASCADE earned one battle star.

CHAPTER 10: USS CHAMBERS DER-391: Newport, Rhode Island, 1956-'59

While aboard CASCADE, I had received orders to report to USS CHAMBERS, DER 391, a radar picket ship also stationed in Newport, Rhode Island. CHAMBERS was assigned to the North Atlantic Barrier Patrol, the seaward extension of the Distant Early Warning Line (DEW line) and was one of the first ships to "set the watch" on the Barrier.[1] CHAMBERS and her sister ships were normally berthed at East Dock, Goat Island[2] in Narragansett Bay, a five-minute free ferry ride from downtown Newport. At any given time, a number of DERs of Escort Squadrons (CortRon) 16 and18 could be found nested at East Dock including USS CALCATERRA, DER-390; USS CAMP, DER-251; USS FESSENDEN, DER-142; USS HAVESON, DER-316; USS HISSEM, DER-400; USS JOYCE, DER-317; USS KETCHNER, DER-329; USS KIRKPATRICK, DER-318; USS MILLS, DER-383; USS OTTERSETTER, DER-244; USS PILLSBURY, DER-133; USS PRICE, DER-332; USS RHODES, DER-384; USS ROY O. HALE, DER- 336; USS SELSTROM, DER-255; USS STRIKLAND, DER-333; USS VANDIVER, DER-540; and USS WAGNER, DER-539.

CHAMBERS' History

USS CHAMBERS (DE-391), an Edsall-class destroyer-escort, was launched 17 August 1943 by Brown Shipbuilding Co., Houston, Texas. She was reclassified DER-391 on 28 October 1954, and began conversion to a radar picket escort vessel. She was recommissioned 1 June 1955. CHAMBERS was named after Russell Franklyn Chambers, a naval aviator who was killed in the Philippines in 1942. I was not related to Ensign Chambers, but my shipmates did have a lot of fun with new arrivals when they first reported on board. Whenever they asked a question, the stock answer was, "Ask Petty Officer Chambers, it's his ship." Enlisted sailors had to wear a ship's name patch on the right shoulder of their dress uniforms. Having "USS CHAMBERS" on my shoulder and telling people that my name was Chambers frequently raised questions as to my truthfulness.

North Atlantic Barrier Patrol

DER sailors [performed] tough and difficult work; they [accepted] as normal circumstances the combination of bad weather, confinement, solitude, and extended time at sea; a combination which [at that time was] common to no other type of naval duty.

> LCDR Everett A. Parke, USN
> Former Commanding Officer
> USS SELLSTROM DER-255

As part of the DEW line, there were four twenty-mile radius circles equally spaced between Argentia, Newfoundland,[3] and the Azores Islands. Four radar picket ships would each assume one of these stations and stay there for three or four weeks, depending on the particular station. As the years went by, this practice was changed to a ship spending only about a week on a station and then rotating to another station. It was not unheard of for CHAMBERS to be relieved late due to weather or other unforeseen conditions. Also, on occasion, CHAMBERS would relieve late for the same reasons.

Our assigned task was to watch for Soviet aircraft or missiles coming over the eastern horizon or any aircraft violating the North American Air Defense Identification Zone (ADIZ) and alert the North American Air Defense Command (NORAD) of any intrusions. NORAD would then scramble jet fighters to investigate. The ships would cruise to the windward edge of their assigned circles and then cut engines and drift to the lee edge of the circle. Then we would steam back to the windward edge and repeat the process. This went on day after day, regardless of weather conditions, until our patrol time was up and we were relieved. Fortunately we never saw any Soviet aircraft. Except for the watch in CIC, about the only excitement we had was when we arrived at either the windward or lee sides of the circle and the word was passed, "Stand-by to come about."

Life Aboard CHAMBERS

When I reported aboard CHAMBERS, she was moored at Pier I at the Newport Naval Station. LCDR George K. Dress, USN, was the commanding officer and LT Howard Hurst was the XO. Reporting aboard CHAMBERS provided me with my first real experience in taking over a leadership position where I was new to the established order. I knew that if I just tried to exercise my rank I would be doomed to failure. I also realized I had to get to know the firecontrol crew, their strengths and weaknesses, and what problems existed, if any, before making any changes. As in CASCADE, I attempted to visit CIC, but normally met with the same type of reception. However, when they were short of RDs, I would be called upon to fill in as a voice radio operator reporting contact information to NORAD. This situation did not occur very often.

This was my first visit to Newport. When a sailor left the station by the Main Gate, he would find there was a road that turned sharply left and the road to town went straight ahead. Diagonally across from the gate was a bar. As the sailor left the Gate, he would see a sign on that bar that identified it as "Leo's First Stop." When he returned to the base, he would see a sign that identified it as "Leo's Last Stop." When we were moored at Goat Island, we were at a disadvantage for liberty—there was no ready access to service clubs. We also had problems with other sailors who resented us being at Goat Island. They thought that we had it easy mooring there. This sometimes led to bar fights.

Living conditions aboard CHAMBERS were about the same as those aboard SOUTHERLAND or WILLIAM T. POWELL. One main difference was that diesel turbines instead of steam turbines drove CHAMBERS and her CIC and radar equipment was the latest in technology. Another main difference was that just about every Wednesday afternoon was Rope Yarn Sunday and every Sunday was holiday routine. I was MAA and many Sundays I would assist the duty cook prepare and serve brunch. Another difference was a particular rack in the Gunnery Department berthing compartment. This rack had an eight-inch fire water main running directly over it with about six inches of clearance. On one patrol we had our full compliment of sailors aboard so an FT2 volunteered to take the restricted rack. To get into it he had to reach up, grab onto a cable hanger, pull himself up and the put his legs out horizontally. Then he would slide under the water main.

On 28 November, CHAMBERS left Newport to relieve JOYCE on picket station 14, located east of Atlantic City, New Jersey. On 18 December, we were relieved by RHODES and proceeded to the Boston Naval Shipyard, Charleston, Massachusetts. CHAMBERS then spent the Christmas and New Year's holidays in the shipyard.

While we were in dry dock, one of the gunner's mate seaman was chipping paint in a forward magazine when he chipped right through the hull. He reported this to me and I reported it to the Officer of the Deck on the quarterdeck. The OOD panicked and wanted to call out the damage control party before I had a chance to remind him that the ship was in dry dock!

This shipyard period gave me my first opportunity to visit "Old Ironsides," the oldest commissioned ship afloat in the U.S. Navy, in fact, in the world. This frigate had "set the course" for Navymen and women to follow. It is stilled manned by active duty Navy men and women who continue the heritage of this ship. It was quite a moving experience to compare a ship built at the beginning of the 19th Century to our current day ships.

New Year's Eve, 1957

On New Years Eve I went to a party, but by midnight it was getting out-of-hand so I returned to the ship. Ensign C.W. Gerhard had the midwatch and, according to naval tradition, wrote this deck log entry in prose:

I'm now on watch and all is well
There are no high winds or even a swell
The decks are covered with inches of snow
The ship is at the disposal of the C.D.O.
We are in Boston Shipyard at Pier Number Five
The yard on this eve is not very alive.
Receiving services from the dock
The harbor is calm; not even a rock.
Moored portside to DE-246
We know our neighbor, we're not in a fix;
We have standard lines out and nothing to fear
We are as secure as crypto in this very New Year.
To check the lines the deck I roamed
My mind was really on a party at home.
It is now Midnight, I can tell
I feel like sounding the G.Q. Bell.
We have on board a skeleton crew
Half, at least, I bet are feeling blue.
We're surrounded by ships all snowy and white
It looks like a ghost fleet on an erie night.
There are DD's, DE's, and even an LST
Ships all around as you can see
A fighting fleet, that's what we are-
No other nation is up to our par;
With God's help we'll remain the same.
Happy New Year to all—whatever your name!

LCDR Robert J. Loomis, USN, relieved Captain Dress on 5 February as commanding officer. On 15 March, as MAA, I had to escort a prisoner to the RecSta, Boston. This sailor had been convicted of assault and rape and was being transferred to the Retraining Command at Portsmouth, New Hampshire. We went in a Navy car, with a civilian driver, and I was required to wear a sidearm.

During the last two weeks in March we went to sea several times to conduct sea trials. On 4 April, we left the shipyard having received the first operational unit of the AN/SPS-28 air search radar in the U.S. Atlantic Fleet. We loaded ammunition from a barge in Nantasket Roads, and returned home to Newport. After conducting training exercises in the local OpArea, we departed Newport on 1 May for Argentia and picket station duty and evaluation of the AN/SPS-28 radar. Then on the 11th we were relieved by HISSEN and returned to Argentia to refuel before returning home to Newport. We visited Argentia many times over the following years, but seldom stayed longer than a few hours, just long enough to refuel.

The Isolation of the Sea

While at sea sailors frequently receive news of tragedies at home. Whenever possible, they are transferred to transport home. If a ship is fortunate enough to be operating with an aircraft carrier, the sailor can be transferred to the carrier and ferried back to land in an aircraft known as COD, or Carrier On board Delivery. On 13 May, while returning to Newport from Argentia Harbor, CHAMBERS stopped all engines and lowered the National Ensign to half-mast. Then Captain Loomis made the following announcement over the 1 MC:

> I deeply regret to announce that one of our shipmates, Chief _____, has lost his son. Chief _____ received word that his boy was critically ill while we were up North and managed to carry on in a stronger manner than most of us could have, including myself. Now with this latest blow there is, unfortunately, little that we can do. There is one thing each of us can do in his own small way, however. Will all hands now rise, un-cover, and observe a moment of silence and offer a prayer to God for the boy, and for his mother and father that they might have the courage to carry on. [At this time a moment of silence was observed.] May the Grace of our Lord Jesus Christ be with them for ever more"[4]

This was the first, and only instance that I heard a commanding officer make a public announcement of a crewmember's hardship.

While on our way from Argentia to Newport something, either a length of line or wire became tangled between the hull of the starboard screw and the shaft strut bearing. CHAMBERS had to lie to while the XO went over the side to investigate the situation. When he returned aboard the decision was made to continue on to Newport. When we arrived in Newport on the 14th, we moored at Destroyer Pier One where drivers inspected the starboard screw. It was found that the tip of one blade was rolled (15" x 5 ½") on the tip of the blade, a condition that would not impair the ship's operational readiness.

CHAMBERS had a single 3"/50-caliber gun mount on the forecastle that was our main battery, which was mostly underwater when we were out on station. This gun mount had a receiver-regulator box (a control box) mounted on its side that had a tendency to leak despite its rubber gasket. Frequently I would spend a great deal of in-port time overhauling this box. One Saturday morning Captain Loomis came onboard and saw me working on the gun mount. He suggested that I just replace the entire receiver-regulator. I determined there was one available at the Naval Supply Depot in Pennsylvania and ordered it. That Monday we received a message from the Fleet Commander wanting to know why we had not reported our main battery inoperative. Certainly, this was not in our maintenance budget! Eventually this mount was replaced with a closed-in mount.

Our 40-mm guns were controlled by a manually operated, lead-computing optical gunsight (a Mk 29) that would transmit electrical control signals to the guns. One of our FTs had an uncanny ability using the gunsight. He was able to adjust his aiming point by watching the tracer shells. When we went through Readiness Evaluations, the Check Sight Observer would criticize the fact that he did not keep his reticle on the towed targets. However, he did hit the targets.

Caribbean Operations, 1957

CHAMBERS departed Newport on 22 May, underway for refresher training out of Gitmo. During the week, we were in and out of port as we conducted various training exercises. Over the weekend of 15 June, we visited Kingston, Jamaica where we moored at the Hanover Street Wharf. After completing training, we departed Gitmo enroute to Norfolk, Virginia where we ran antenna calibrations in Lynnhaven Roads. We returned to Newport on 25 June before moving up to Fall River, MA for the Fourth of July and a tender availability period alongside USS GRAND CANYON, AD-28.

Return to Picket Duty

After this upkeep period, we resumed picket duty on Station 4 where we relieved PRICE on 16 July. After relieving PRICE, we conducted ASW exercises with USS SAILFISH, SSR-572. We also conducted ASW exercises with USS THREADFIN, SS-410, on the 27th. One night during this picket, the engineering Oil King[5] was taking readings on a tank under the deck department living compartment when he noticed a stalking figure. All the lights were out except for a single red night light on the opposite side of the compartment. When he shined his flashlight on the figure, he saw a sailor with a dogging wrench[6] in his hand getting ready to strike a sleeping first class Boatswain's mate. The next day Captain's Mast was held and it was decided that this Seaman Apprentice should be reduced to Seaman Recruit and confined for his own safety until he could be brought before a court martial. We had a 40-mm clip shack unloaded and modified with a porthole and a bunk and confined him there. At his court martial he was convicted of willful disobedience of a senior officer, insubordinate conduct toward a non-commissioned officer, and failure to obey an order or regulation. We kept him in his makeshift cell until 28 July.

On 2 August, we were relieved by PILLSBURY and returned to Goat Island. Then the Seaman recruit who had been confined went

AWOL. He eventually was picked up in Philadelphia by the Shore Patrol.

On 7 August, LT Alexander D. Thompson, USN, reported on board as relief for the XO. On our next picket we relieved KETCHNER on Station 3 on 21 August.

On 21 August, the Soviets launched the first ICBM (Intercontinental Ballistic Missile), using their R-7 8K71 rocket system. This system was also used to launch Sputnik on 4 October 1957.

On 8 September, CHAMBERS was relieved by PILLSBURY and returned to Newport where on the 16th divers from CASCADE inspected the sonar dome and found no problems. CHAMBERS next relieved PRICE on 9 October. During the afternoon of the 20th, I was directed to hold small arms training for a couple of new officers. I drew some weapons from the armory and met my students on the forecastle. One of the weapons, a BAR (Browning Automatic Rifle) had a habit of misfiring. I instructed a LTJG that if it did misfire he was to keep it pointed toward the water and alert me of the problem. I was instructing the other officer when the first called me and said, "This gun won't fire." When I turned toward him, he had it pointed at my stomach and was pulling the trigger! I reached out and jerked the weapon out of his hands and it went sliding over the deck until it got caught in the rat lines. At that he started screaming, threatening me with court-martial proceeding for assaulting an officer. Fortunately the CO saw the entire incident from the bridge and paged the officer to report to the bridge immediately. Nothing further came of this incident as far as I was concerned, but for the officer, the incident undoubtedly taught him a new respect for firearms.

We were relieved by HISSEM on 28 October and returned to Goat Island.

In November, we underwent a tender availability alongside USS ARCADIA, AD-23, in Melville.

As with my assignment aboard SOUTHERLAND, one of my collateral duties was ship's MAA. On Thanksgiving we were having dependents and guests aboard for the holiday dinner—only the commissary man neglected to stock enough turkey and ham to feed everyone who showed up. The duty cook called me and asked if there was anything that I could do about the situation. I approached the deck division duty section and asked for their assistance is solving the problem. They advised me to take a walk and come back in about ten minutes. When I did, due to some miracle, they had two large canned hams. As frequently happened while loading stores, some items get "misplaced." These saved the day.

On 9 December, we were enroute to station 1, but on the 13th we were diverted to a special SAR station Alpha as part of "Operation Friendship," President Eisenhower's flight to Paris to attend a NATO Conference, scheduled for 13 thru 20 December. This entailed being on station for an overfly of Air Force One. On 15 December, we relieved OTTERSTETTER on Station 1.

New Year's Eve 1958

Christmas 1957 and New Year's Eve 1958 were spent on Picket Station #1 off Newfoundland. LTJG J. H. Mc Elroy had the mid-watch and wrote this deck log entry:

Have you ever been on the briney deep,
So far from a bar you'd like to weep,
And waited cold-sober for the New Year to start,
While you wished for a drink with all of your heart?
It makes you wonder it really does,
If the Navy's worth it, or ever was.
Oh, but we're having such liquorless fun,
Patrolling Barrier Atlantic Picket Station One!
It's more than just ordinary fun, to ride the swells,
And realize, main engine number 2 will answer bells.

A View from the Deckplates
Two Decades Aboard Destroyers during the Cold War (1950-1970)

> *While 15 minutes is all you need,*
> > *To have number 4 up to speed;*
> *Not to mention the entertainment of knowing,*
> > *That in 30 minutes 1 and 3 could be going?*
> *Sure we have fun!*
> > *Lying to on Picket Station One.*
> *A civilian would say, "it's only a myth,*
> > *To be underway 'in accordance with'",*
> *But nothing happens in this old Navy,*
> > *Without an order from higher authority.*
> *Now we can illustrate this, and make it clear,*
> > *By telling who it was that sent us here.*
> *COMDESLANT is one that we could name,*
> > *Whose quarterly Employment Sked's to blame;*
> *COMBARLANT also helped arrange our fix,*
> > *With something called 0p-Order one dash fifty six.*
> *(We hope wherever they are, they're having a few,*
> > *For the thirsty sailors of the CHAMBERS crew.)*
> *Now, don't you believe it's fun,*
> > *To be aboard TE 81.2.1.1?*
> *To have the mid watch on a New Year's eve,*
> > *Is a privilege far greater than being a CTE.*
> *For while our Captain sleeps, I have the deck,*
> > *And hence enjoy Modified Condition III's effect.*
> *It feels so good to be awake,*
> > *And welcome nineteen fifty eight!*
> *On this day which has just begun*
> > *USS CHAMBERS is TE 81.2.1.1,*
> *And we want you to fully understand,*
> > *That our Captain's in complete command—*
> *Although about all we ever do,*
> > *Is steam during chow, and then lie to,*
> *It must be piles of fun,*
> > *To be CTE 81.2.1.1.*
> *Yet, despite all the happiness being here brings,*
> > *As the watch slowly passes, and the Sonar pings,*

We can't help thinking how extremely far,
    It really is to the nearest bar.
Baker is set, so we couldn't sink,
    But wouldn't it he nicer to have a drink?
Yeah, Station One,
    Lot-sa fun.
In case you're interested in what generator's in use,
    Number one's supplying the ship's electrical juice.
At zero one ten a white light hove into view,
    19 thousand yards away, bearing zero two two.
So we lit off the radar for surface detection,
    And discovered him heading in a westerly direction.
He plodded along at a slow 12 knots,
    According to the best of Combat's plots.
Eight miles was the closest he ever came,
    As a contact he was exceedingly tame.
Now the horizon's clear, not a ship in sight
    As the mid watch ends on a New Year's night—
But some how it just wasn't right,
    Not to have been a little tight.

Station Storms

On 3 January we were relieved by GARY and put into Argentia to refuel before returning to Goat Island. During this inport period we went from Storm Condition I[7] to Storm Condition III on several occasions.

We relieved RHODES on Station 2 on 21 January. Then on the 30th, we were hit by a severe North-Atlantic storm. The winds averaged 55 knots and the seas were in excess of 20 feet high. During the storm we frequently took rolls in excess of 55-degrees! At 1332, the winds were 60 knots, the seas were running 50 feet high and we were experiencing 55-degree rolls when our primary air search radar (AN/SPS-28) antenna was carried away. For several days all that we could do was keep the bow into the wind (heading due north) and maintain steerageway. When the duty radioman took the message board to the bridge with a message that said we could expect clear weather, the Captain threw the board over the side! Between the wind and the high seas, we lost all radar antenna, boats, ready service lockers, and other topside gear. The shield around the forward 3-inch gun mount was caved in and the mount was partially torn from the deck. There was a 5-inch crack in the main deck at the gun shield seam. The port anemometer and its bracket were carried away. Many rivets were loosened or parted and there was leakage at the junction of the aluminum deck house and steel hull, at multiple sites on main deck. There was also one inch splits in the deck house at several sites. After the storm finally abated, we returned to Argentia with about 11% of our fuel left on board. At that time, Navy Regulations prohibited a CO from letting fuel levels get below 16%; unfortunately there were no diesel stations out on the North Atlantic. For doing so, the CO received a mild letter of reprimand. This was followed by a glowing commendation for saving the ship and crew.

When GARY relieved us in February, instead of being moored at Goat Island, CHAMBERS moored at Destroyer Pier 1 at the Newport Naval Station. On several occasions during this inport period, we went to Storm Condition III. On 1 March, CHAMBERS was once again underway to picket station, and the next day we were hit by a severe storm. Winds were in excess of 26 knots and waves were over seven feet high. The splinter shield around the forward gun mount was bent back along the seam with the main deck for two feet. The weld at the junction of the splinter shield and main deck was broken, allowing water to flood the amplidyne room and adjacent passageway, shorting out the power panel. This resulted in the loss of power to Mount 31 and the hedgehog mount. After repairs were made in Argentia, we proceeded to Station 3.

During this picket we were plagued with a series of equipment casualties. First the AN/SPS-8A air search radar failed; next the Number 4 engine overheated. This was followed by failure of the navigation lights. The emergency generator failed, ending our series of equipment malfunctions. On the 11th we transferred mail to

126

PILLSBURY using the "Barrel Method" of transfer.[8] On the 21st we destroyed another floating barrel by gunfire. This was also considered a menace to navigation.

On 9 March, Congress approved the so-called Eisenhower Doctrine, stating "the United States regards as vital to the national interest and world peace the preservation of the independence and integrity of the nations of the Middle East." Then in April, after anti-government rioting broke out in Jordan, the 6th fleet was rushed to the eastern Mediterranean and lands a battalion of Marines in Lebanon to "prepare for possible future intervention in Jordan."

Lisbon, Portugal and Gibraltar

This spring we had several rotations on and off picket station. Just prior to Easter, CHAMBERS was assigned to Station 3. Before departing Newport, the Captain took a poll amongst the crew to determine how many wanted to go to Lisbon, Portugal for a port visit after the patrol instead of returning directly to Newport—Lisbon won. On 22 March, after attempting to transfer mail, supplies, and personnel for seven and a half-hours SELLSTROM relieved us off station. Due to heavy seas, attempts at high-line transfer were abandoned and eventually transfer was made by a rubber life raft. CHAMBERS then proceeded to Lisbon. While enroute we continued to experience equipment casualties, including a fuel leak to Number 2 main engine; failure of the gyro followup system; and loss of all electrical power. When CHAMBERS arrived in Lisbon on 26 March, we were scheduled to moor at the *Poço do Bispo Wharf* in the *Rio Tejo* (Tagus River). However, due to adverse weather conditions, we anchored in the *Man-of-War* anchorage. The current in the harbor was very swift with winds up to 31 knots. The Captain warned the crew to be very careful—if any crew member fell over board, they probably could not be rescued. The following day the Harbor Pilot came aboard, and CHAMBERS then moored port side to the *Poço do Bispo Wharf.* This is just above the *Praça do Comércio*, the so-called *Black Horse Square* with the equestrian statue of Don Jose I.

On Saturday a small Portuguese tanker vessel moored abaft of us and was emitting a strong licorice odor. A shipmate, "Ray," who was French-Canadian and thought we should pay them a visit and find out what their task was. Between Ray's French, and their limited French and Portuguese, we were able to find out that they transported an anise liquor to a distillery. They "insisted" that we have a drink with them. When they handed me my glass, they asked if I wanted it cut with water, but I declined—after one taste I changed my mind and they all had a good laugh at my expense.

On Easter Sunday, 6 April, I had an opportunity to attend a Protestant Easter sunrise service on the beach at Estoril. The sun coming up over the mountains to the East was quite beautiful and the services were very moving.

While we were in Lisbon, one young sailor went ashore and had his first experience with drinking. He also had his first experience with B-girls. In an attempt to keep him from getting in trouble, he tied a line around his waist and the bitter end around a shipmate. However, some of the other sailors paid a B-girl to "fall in love" with him. We never did find out how he got loose from the line around his waist.

Liberty in Portugal afforded me the opportunity to once again watch the bullfights. Only in Portugal, as contrasted with the Spanish bullfights, it was not the practice to kill the bulls. Two of my shipmates and I met three American ladies who were tourists and we were all enjoying the fights with promises of further adventures after the fights were over. We were enjoying each others company until a sailor in the next row who had a little too much to drink while in the hot sun, vomited, soiling himself and those within proximity of him. Our lady companions said they were going to the ladies room to wipe themselves off and would be right back. We never saw them again.

CHAMBERS left Lisbon on 7 April and moored in Gibraltar on the 8th. On the way out of Lisbon with a local Harbor Pilot at the conn,[9] CHAMBERS struck a mooring buoy, port side amidships. After our visit to Lisbon, we went to Gibraltar to refuel, to reprovision, and to have the port screw inspected. Subsequent inspection in Gibraltar revealed that one blade on the port propeller was bent back six inches. It was decided that this was the result of a prior incident and not as a result of striking the buoy while departing Lisbon. While we were in Gibraltar, various merchants came aboard and set up their wares on the mess decks. I bought several cashmere sweaters. Other shipmates bought items for delivery in the U.S.

Return to Picket Duty

On 11 April, we departed Gibraltar and returned to picket station 4 for another three-week tour. We were relieved on 29 April by KRETCHMER. When we returned to Newport on 4 May, we found out some of the crew's spouses and mothers had lodged a complaint with the Navy regarding our Lisbon port of call and our two consecutive tours on station. As far as I know this was never done again. Apparently they did not want their men to "Join the Navy and See the World." Later we discovered that a senior petty officer would stand by the quarterdeck in the evening and take notes as sailors returned off liberty. He would then write this gossip to his wife who would spread it around.

During the last week of May, we conducted training exercises in the Narragansett OpArea. Then, from 31 May until 20 June, CHAMBERS patrolled picket station #2, having relieved GARY. On the 26th we were relieved by CALCATERRA and went to Argentia to refuel. While there, General Partridge, USAF, COMNORAD, and his staff paid us an official visit. When CHAMBERS returned to Newport LCDR C. T. McGrath, USN, relieved CDR R.J. Loomis, USN, as commanding officer in ceremonies held in Newport on 26 June 1958. LCDR McGrath had reported aboard while CHAMBERS was in Argentia on the way home from picket.

On 15 July 1958, President Eisenhower sent 70 naval vessels and 5,000 Marines to Lebanon.

After the Fourth of July holiday, we spent about two weeks conducting training exercises. Then on 21 July, CHAMBERS was dry-docked in Davisville, Rhode Island, to have her port screw repaired. It had a section 15" long by 4" wide that was bent aft at a 45° angle. In addition, 15% of our body paint was missing, there was moderate sea growth about the hull, and the hull zinc anodes were 75% corroded. While in the dock the bad spots in body paint were scraped and repainted, the sea chests were freed of marine growth, the sonar dome was cleaned, water was removed from the rudders, the port propeller was replaced, and all the zinc anodes were replaced. We left the dry-dock on the 22nd.

On 28 July, CHAMBERS was again at sea and relieved ROY O. HALE on station 2 on 1 August. On the 17thth the Northern Lights were sighted and then on the 20th we reported "off station" due to the weather. The winds were in excess of 30 knots and the waves were over 25 feet! On 20 August we had to leave station due to 31-knot winds and 25-foot waves. On the 23rd, we were relieved by PILLSBURY. On our way back to Newport the

> [S]hip passed through a definite line of demarcation at Lat 41-17 N, Long 64-23W extending in the direction of 045 - 225° T[rue]. Characterized by 5' waves of short period and heavy whitecaps from about 200° T, winds from 220° T, 22 kts on the easterly side of the line and long 3' swells from 245° T with no whitecaps, winds from 220, 22 kts on westerly side. Pronounced line on radar. Believed to be meeting of Gulf Stream and Labrador current traveling in opposite directions.[10]

The south-flowing Labrador Current interacts with the north-east flowing Gulf Stream south of the Grand Banks. There can be as much as a 20° temperature difference between the green-colored Labrador Current and the blue-colored Gulf Stream. When these two currents collide they can create heavy fog and violent weather conditions.

The next day while we were enroute to Pier One, Newport Naval Station, I was doing some work that required the use of a knife held in my left hand. During the process the knife slipped and made a 1 ½" incision in my right forearm. When I reported to sickbay, our chief corpsman told me there was a new method for closing such wounds, known as a "butterfly clip." He installed two of them and the wound healed leaving a ½" scar on my arm.

On the 28th, Hurricane Condition II was set in the Narragansett Bay area so we moved from the pier to a buoy. The next day we returned to the pier.

In early September we were undergoing an In-Service-Inspection (INSERVE) when a crusty Chief Warrant Gunner (CWO4) asked me when the 3" gun mount was last lubricated. I told him the procedure had been performed in accordance with the prescribed lubrication schedule. He then told me something that I have never forgotten: "Manuals are for the direction of ignorant people and for the guidance of intelligent people, which are you?" I then asked him to ask me about the mount lubrication in the morning, at which time I replied, "Last night, Sir."

This gun mount was controlled by a radar system (Mk. 34) that had its antenna mounted on the mount. At random the radar would just shut itself off. We knew there must be an open circuit somewhere, but after hours of troubleshooting we could not find anything wrong. Finally, on a Sunday afternoon, I swallowed my professional pride and sought assistance from our 1st Class ET who knew nothing at all about this particular radar set. As I was walking him through a descriptive explanation, I mentioned that "this is the main power connector" and grabbed the connector. At that, the radar shut down! During our troubleshooting efforts, we had the connector off several times to check it, but had never touched it with the power on.

Close inspection revealed a broken wire that would open with the ship's motion.

On 12 September, we were again underway to Argentia and then to Station 4 where we relieved RHODES. On 7 October, CAMP relieved us and we returned to Goat Island. On the 20th we held a dependents cruise where the wives, children and other guests went to sea to observe what their sailor's did aboard ship. However, being single, and without family in Newport, I took a brief leave over this period.

The Lost Screw

When CHAMBERS left Pier 1 at the Newport Naval Base on 6 November and attempted to twist ship, there was no effective response to backing bells on the starboard shaft. We then anchored before returning to the pier. On the way back, the captain became very upset with the OOD because the helmsman could not keep on course. Finally he announced, "The Captain has the conn." This relieved the OOD of maneuvering responsibility. The Captain then proceeded to give the engine room various orders, "forward," then "back," in an attempt to bring the ship alongside another DER. Despite the Captain's efforts he could not understand why the ship was not responding. We had an anchor "at the dip" when we finally went alongside another DER, ripping out the stanchions on her main deck.[11] Divers were sent down to inspect and found the starboard propeller was missing! A few days later the following ad appeared in the local newspaper.[12] It is believed that this ad was placed by the commanding officer of CALCATERRA, the ship CHAMBERS had been scheduled to relieve On the 10th we were towed to dry dock in Davisville to have a new propeller installed. CALCATERRA on picket station but was unable to do so.

ATTENTION LOBSTERMEN!

LOST

One Bronze Three Bladed Ship Propeller
Vicinity Brenton Reef Lightship

Finder return to Commanding Officer USS CHAMBERS

Liberal Reward

We finally relieved RHODES on the 24th on Station 4. About that time the release mechanism for number 1 and 3 life rafts failed, dropping them in the water. They were later retrieved by the deck force. Later during this picket we destroyed another floating barrel by gunfire. This was considered to be a hazard to navigation. We were relieved by SELSTROM on 30 November and returned to Melville. On 26 December we left Newport and relieved HISSEM on station 3.

During the 0000-0400 watch on 1 January 1959, the OOD, LTJG M.P. Bassock, USNR, penned this deck log entry:

Underway all alone,
Steering a course far from home.
On 195 we sail the blue;
Our speed 7 knots that's 172
And why are we here on Atlantic Barrier Picket Station three?
Cause COMSUFBARARGENTIA wills it to be.
O3120 their Notice so tame,
Places us here all the same.
They're not alone in this presumptuous act,
COMDESLANT quarterly Op-sked verifies that fact.
And how do we glide so swift o'er the water?
Why main engine four is answering our order.
If it comes to pass; and, if need be

133

We can depend on main engines one, two and three.
Like farmers in spring awaiting the locust,
The engines standby on 30 minutes notice
And, if you ask what feeds the mighty engines, I'll rant,
Generators 1 & 3 operating in split plant.
Modified condition of Readiness III,
Allows all hands to sleep peacefully.
And now the Chambers goes for broke
For set is Material Condition Yoke.
The thing that's distracting about this whole verse,
Many of the lines couldn't be worse.
The next line you'll see is so hard for me;
CHAMBERS composes TE 82.2.1.3.
Commanding Officer Chambers is CTE;
His number of course is 82.2.1.3.
To all who read this log by the fire bright
We wish a Happy New Year on this New Year's night.

We were relived on 12 January and returned to Goat Island where, on 26 January, LT R.H. Loyd relieved LT A.D. Thompson as XO. On the 28th we once again got underway for Argentia and then to Station 1. On 21 February, we departed station for Newport, but our orders were changed, directing us to head for Argentia. The next day we were ordered back to Station 1 and once again ordered to proceed to Argentia. Enroute we encountered ice packs, the temperature was in the low 20s, and the winds were in excess of 10-knots.

Pursuit of a Russian Trawler

One of the Navy's "Super Constellations,"[13] the airborne barrier patrol, spotted a Russian trawler suspected of attempting to interfere with the five American-owned trans-Atlantic communications cables.[14] On the 26th Commander Barrier Force Atlantic (ComBarLant) ordered CHAMBERS to put to sea, with orders to pursue and board the trawler, and to seize any evidence of tampering. CHAMBERS cleared the harbor and we were lying to by the breakwater with the sea and anchor detail still set and not knowing what was going on, when we spotted a helicopter heading towards us. One of the sailors pantomimed arm signals directing the helo to land on our fantail. Was he ever surprised when the helo did hover over the fantail and deposited an investigative team consisting of Commander Escort Squadron (ComCortRon) 18, a lieutenant, junior grade (LTJG), and a Russian-speaking AD3 (Aviation Machinist Mate).

While heading for the last-known location of the trawlers, we encountered thick ice. Captain McGrath ordered me to form an armed boarding party and to be ready to board the trawler and to protect the "brass" and the interpreter. When I requested specific orders or instructions as to what actions I should take under specific conditions, I was told was "Chambers, you're the petty officer in charge, use your discretion." My main concern was that the Captain insisted on part of the team being a hotheaded Gunner's Mate from the backwoods of Maine. He was to carry a machine gun. CHAMBERS chased the suspected trawler north into the rapidly thickening ice pack. Before we could catch the trawler, ComCortRon 18 decided the ice was too much of a threat to our 3/8-inch steel sides so we were forced to break off the pursuit. I was relieved that we did not have to board the trawler, as fear of starting an international incident was uppermost in my mind. While we were enroute back to Argentia, we encountered heavy concentrations of pancake ice and, at one time, our rudder was blocked by the ice. We had to make some erratic maneuvers to get free.

While CHAMBERS' part in this operation was underway, ROY O. HALE, one of CHAMBERS' sister ships, did intercept, stop, and board a Russian trawler also suspected of interfering with the trans-Atlantic cables. However, they found no evidence of any tampering. This "visit and search" operation was carried out under provisions of an 1884 Convention concerning protection of undersea cables. After this operation was canceled, and as we headed back to Argentia, we encountered heavy concentrations of pancake ice. When we got close enough to Argentia, our passengers departed by helo. On 1 March, on our way home to Newport, we encountered grease ice, pancake ice and occasional growler ice. [15] Once we cleared the ice fields, we dropped depth charges for pre-overhaul structural tests. We moored at Goat Island on 3 March. After 31 days at sea ComCortRon 16 came aboard and held a surprise administrative inspection! The next day we went to State Pier, Fall River, where we had a tender availability period alongside GRAND CANYON, AD-28.

Reenlistment

On 12 March 1959, I again re-enlisted for another 6-year cruise. This would be the penultimate reenlistment in my career. I was getting ready to go on leave to see my mother in New York for St. Patrick's Day when a shipmate asked if he could go with me. I told him he was welcome to join me, but cautioned him there was no place at my mother's for him to stay. In New York we visited several places and finally took a cab to the local YMCA where I left him, telling him I would meet him in the morning. The next day went I went to the YMCA, but he was not there. I walked around the local area checking some places where he might have gone for breakfast without any luck. Then I realized that I was tired of walking and decided to buy a car. I went to a local Ford dealer and bought a black and yellow 1955 Mercury Monterey, my first car.[16] When I called my mother to see if my shipmate had called. He was there so I drove home. We went out, he was in uniform and I was in civilian clothes, to check out a few local places. At the first place we went into, he experienced the esteem that Long Islanders had for sailors. After a few free beers I suggested that we go get him some civilian clothes, but instead he insisted that I go put on my uniform. I did and we proceeded to have a great day of drinking and meeting people.

Memorial Day Parade, Watertown, Massachusetts

On 16 March, CHAMBERS left Newport and went to the Naval Weapons Station, Earle, New Jersey, to off-load ammunition prior to entering Boston Naval Shipyard, Charlestown, Massachusetts. On

136

Memorial Day we were in Boston for an extended shipyard period (March to June) when the Captain received a request for CHAMBERS to participate in a parade in Watertown, Massachusetts. We had nothing that even resembled a ceremonial detail and nothing to equip one with if we could put one together. In any event, the Captain assigned me the task of putting together and training a ceremonial detail to represent CHAMBERS in the parade. I agreed to do so provided that I had complete control of the off-duty time of those whom I could get to volunteer to be a part of the detail. With this agreement, I was able to recruit the needed 27 "volunteers" to participate.

Fortunately, at the time there was a WW II "Jeep" carrier in the shipyard that was being prepared for scrapping. The shipyard commander had invited inport ships to salvage whatever they wanted from the carrier. When we went aboard, we found little of value until one of my team stumbled on a hatch to a GSK storeroom. When we opened it up we discovered the compartment was filled with some kind of gas (most likely ammonia). We had seen some oxygen breathing apparatus (OBA) around, so I tried one of the canisters and found it to be sweet and breathable. Using lifelines and OBA, we entered the storeroom and found wardroom dishes, tools and landing team accouterments that our parade detail could use. These included leggings, web belts, and helmet liners. While we were in the compartment, a junior officer off CHAMBERS showed up and questioned what we were doing. I explained the circumstances and even brought out some of wardroom china to show him. At this, he said "Very well, carry on." We salvaged some china as well as what we needed for our ceremonial detail. These landing team accouterments were olive drab so later we painted them with white enamel so that they would look sharp in the parade.

Now all that we needed were weapons and training. I went to the Marine Barracks in the shipyard and asked the leading Marine if he could provide us with assistance. This marine had just been promoted tp Sergeant Major during the first promotions to the newly formed E-9 pay grade. He was a poster Marine, about 6' 3" tall and looked like Burt Lancaster was made to look in his movies. Anyway, he agreed to train us to march only under his conditions. His three conditions were (1) he would first drill me one-on-one for several days, (2) his Marines would drill our company for a week, treating them like Marine recruits, and (3) I would then drill the company under his supervision. I agreed to these terms and drilling began. We also arranged for the loan of 27 M-1 rifles. On Memorial Day we were bused to Watertown, participated in the parade and captured "best in parade," beating out a Marine reserve outfit! Our detail consisted of the Officer-in-Charge, LTJG Michael P. Bassock, in ceremonial dress whites complete with sword, myself with a .45-caliber automatic pistol, and our 27 "recruits." After the parade we were all invited to a party in the local VFW hall. This was the typical party where guys related stories over a can of beer. We all enjoyed ourselves except we received no recognition for our achievement once back aboard the ship.

Gloucester, Massachusetts

After a period of sea trials when we were in and out of Boston, CHAMBERS returned to Goat Island on 19 June after loading ammunition in Nantasket Roads. Then on the 26th we completed our ammunition load at NAD, Prudence Island. Over the July 4th weekend, CHAMBERS paid a visit to Gloucester where we moored at the State Fish Pier. The people there treated us extremely well. In fact, it was not unknown for a sailor to have a lobster dinner in a restaurant and not receive a bill. Many bars had bowls of clams out like other places put out peanuts! On the day we were due to depart, the Harbor Master delayed our departure until later in the day. We had to wait for the next high tide.

When we tried to leave the pier on 6 July, we had problems with the severe currents. At one point, we only had one 3-inch nylon line out through the after portside leading to the pier. I was in charge of the fantail detail and was ordered to hold the line as the Harbor Pilot was attempting to pivot the bow on the stern line. This line was extended about 150 feet and was under so much tension that it was taut as a piano wire and was smoking. At some point I determined it was too dangerous to have the sailors near the line and ordered them to clear away. A few seconds later the line snapped and recoiled back through the chock with a whip-like motion. If the sailors had not cleared out surely limbs would have been lost.

Once we got underway, we went to the Caribbean and Gitmo.

Caribbean Operations, 1959

While undergoing shakedown training out of Gitmo, we visited Cap Haitien, Haiti where CHAMBERS relieved USS ROSS, DD-563. This was unusual for a DER to relieve a destroyer. After we arrived, the Captain found out the U.S. Government was anticipating an uprising in Haiti and we were in Cap Haitien, not for R&R, but to evacuate U.S. citizens if necessary. The Captain told the crew we might have an uncertain departure time and if the ship's whistle blew three times, we should immediately return to the ship.[17] We were in Cap Hatien from 19 to21 July. On the day we departed I was the duty MAA when the CO, XO, and the city mayor were coming down the pier. The OOD paged me to the quarterdeck and told me to remove an intoxicated sailor from the quarterdeck before they got to the gangway. It turned out that instead of leaving, the sailor wanted to fight me—a proposition that just didn't work.

After Cap Haitien, we visited Port-au-Prince, Haiti, arriving there on 1 August.

When we arrived in Port-au-Prince, we moored alongside USS DAVIS, DD-937. As we were coming alongside DAVIS, a local Harbor Pilot had the conn.[18] At this time there also was a bum boat alongside the DAVIS. We got the bow line over when the Pilot gave the commands to bring our stern alongside the DAVIS before the man in the bum boat decided to move. He waited until the last minute and then started to row frantically to get out of our way. He succeeded, but our stern missed him by inches. After all lines were over, the

OOD asked the Pilot if he saw the man in the bum boat. The OOD knew the Pilot had seen him as the lookouts and our fantail detail had all reported him. The OOD had also reported him to the Captain and the Pilot. When the OOD asked the Pilot what he would have done if the boat had not moved out of the way, he acknowledged, yes he saw the boat, but just brushed it off and that doing so was common practice.

We departed Port-au-Prince on 3 August, bound for Gitmo.

While in the Caribbean we had a problem with sailors coming back to the ship drunk and being rowdy and causing disturbances after lights out. As MAA, I went to the XO to seek his approval for a plan that I wanted to implement. Before liberty the next day I put out the word that drastic measures would be taken if there were any more incidents. That night, when a sailor was acting up, I shackled him, spread-eagled, wrist and foot, in the middle of the passageway between the heads and showers. A foul weather jacket was placed under his head and the cuff keys given to the quarterdeck watch with orders not to release him except in an emergency. When the crew got up in the morning they had to walk over the sleeping sailor. We had no further problems.

During this shakedown we were conducting ASW exercises when the CO ordered the hedgehog mount[19] to fire. It failed to do so, and at that the CO personally passed the word on the 1MC for me to report to the hedgehog mount immediately. The hedgehog mount is located immediately below and forward of the pilothouse. Because we were at GQ, it took me a few minutes to get there, but as soon as I arrived, the CO was banging on the pilothouse window and beckoning me up to the bridge. When I reported to the bridge the CO proceeded to chew me out wanting to know why the mount did not fire and demanding an estimated time for when I would have it repaired (up until that point the mount was not my responsibility). As I had not had a chance to talk to anyone at the mount, I had no idea what the problem was, but took a SWAG and replied, "Two minutes after you let me off this bridge." Fortunately my guess as to what was wrong was correct and I was able to replace a blown fuse with a paper clip and enabled us to continue the exercise.

Just before we left the Caribbean for Newport on 13 August, our chief cook became ill. As the only chief aboard at the time, he also functioned as Chief MAA. One day he called me to the Chief's Quarters and told me that he was due to reenlist for the final time when we returned to Newport and did not want any formal recognition of being ill. He asked if I could cover for all his MAA duties. I agreed and he had me move into the Chief's Quarters. When we returned to Newport on 17 August, he had his problem taken care of and then invited me to his home for a barbecue where I was served the biggest steaks I have ever seen.

During September, CHAMBERS again performed picket duty, rotating between stations. On 29 September, while returning to Newport, we had to go south to avoid a hurricane and then put into the US Naval Station, Bermuda, BWI, on 2 October. We left on the 5th bound for Newport

Miscellaneous Incidents Out of Time Sequence

While out on one extended patrol someone thought the thing to do would be to hold a beard-growing contest. By unofficial polling, mine was the hands-down winner. However, on the evening of the judging the bulkheads in our living compartment were sweating so much that we had to continually wipe up the water—and I missed the judging.

In the summer, if we were out on the most southern station, we would frequently have swim call. Of course there were sharks in the water so we'd have sharp-shooters stationed on the bridge wings and on the main deck. In the motor whale boat another sharp-shooter was armed with carbines in case any of the threatening predators showed up. There were also sailors stationed with life rings and other life saving equipment. However I do not remember ever having trouble with any sharks.

During a gunnery exercise we had a misfire in the after gun mount and I was ordered to investigate the cause of the problem. The mount was on the main deck and trained out over the port side for safety. As I was descending the ladder from the 01 deck to the main deck, the gunner's mate inside the mount decided to try the "stinger" one more time. This time it worked and the concussion knocked me off the ladder onto my rear end. Fortunately I was holding on and did not get hurt, but my ears rang for a long time thereafter.

One of my firecontrolmen strikers was a young sailor from south Boston. He was what we referred to as a "sea lawyer," one who though that he knew all the rules and regulations. He also had a reputation as a "screw-up" and always seemed to do things incorrectly. When he was taken to task, he would start quoting his "rights." One Saturday, after I had occasion to order him to complete his assigned tasks before going on liberty, he read me off in front of other crew members, and told me that I did not have the authority to tell him what to do since I was in civilian clothes (at the time I had received permission from the OOD to be aboard out of uniform—not that it mattered). On Monday I told him to clean up one of the equipment rooms and then went to the ship's office and picked up Navy Regulations, the Manual for Courts Martial, the Constitution, as well as several other publications. I took these to the equipment room and dogged down the door. Then I told him "Here are your rights, are we going to have any more problems?" After that there were none. Shortly thereafter I sent him to school in Dam Neck, Virginia. When he returned I asked him how he did and he told me, "I finished second in my class." When the official report was received it showed that there were three students in the class—and two of them tied for second place!

Our normal procedures when returning off station were to assign all the lower rated personnel in the deck and weapons divisions to all required at-sea watches. Then all senior petty officers, including the 1st class petty officers, would man the watch in the after steering station.[20] This sometimes resulted in a six or seven man watch rotation. After Steering was also the space where a poker game was usually held. One evening when I had the watch there was a blanket spread on the deck surrounded by several players and covered with several hundred dollars, when the XO entered the compartment. He asked me if I knew anything about the money and I told him, "No, Sir." Then he asked each of the players, in turn, if the money was theirs to which they all replied, "No, Sir." At that he announced if the money did not belong to anyone, it must belong to the ship's Welfare and Recreation Fund. He then scooped it up and left after admonishing me to, "Keep a taut watch."

Later in the year I was sent to Boston to attend a shipyard briefing. After hearing of my impending trip, and a sonarman asked if he could ride along with me. He had to take a BT (bathythermograph)[21] to the shipyard for some testing. I agreed, welcoming the company. When we stopped for lunch, I observed he had a couple of stiff drinks but I was not too concerned about it since I was doing the driving That evening we went to Fenway Park to watch a concert by Dakota Staton where I observed he was never without a beer. The next evening when we arrived back at the Goat Island ferry I dropped him and the BT off at the landing. The next morning the ASW Officer asked me what the sonarman had done with the BT. After some investigation, we discovered he did not get on the ferry, but instead hid the BT in some bushes and went to a bar where he got drunk, and as a consequence forgot what he did with it. That is when we started comparing notes and uncovered the fact the man was an alcoholic. While at sea he had been "borrowing" after-shave lotion and never returning it. After a few days he was transferred to the Newport Rec-Sta for further transfer to a Naval Hospital for evaluation and disposition.

At one point during my tour of duty, we received a new division officer onboard. This officer came from an Army NROTC Program and was an Army "brat." Consequently, he knew the routines for performing facing drills as the Army performed them and not how the Navy performed them.[22] As division leading PO, I tried to explain the difference to him, but he insisted we do things his way. Shortly thereafter, at a change-of-command ceremony, he confused the division in front of the new skipper. That evening, at a party in the club, I was sitting in the back of the room when he approached me with two pitchers of beer and asked if I minded if he joined me. I invited him to join me and he sat down and started baring his soul. Eventually he was crying and asked me to help him become a good naval officer. I did all that I could to assist him from that time on.

I had submitted a request to attend TALOS Missile School, which was denied due to the phasing out of the TALOS System. In late summer a new personnelman (PN), who had been stationed in Washington, reported on board. In conversation on the messdeck he asked how long I had been on board and why I did not get shore duty. I told him that shore billets for FTs were primarily limited to instructor duty. He then asked where I would like to be stationed if I could get shore duty and I jokingly responded, "New York." Shortly thereafter I received a set of orders to Recruiter School and then to recruiting duty in New York! I served aboard CHAMBERS until October 1959, when I was detached to report to Bainbridge, Maryland to attend Recruiter School. I was detached early thanks to some of our crewmembers who got into trouble in town one night. The CO had warned the entire crew that if it happened again he would volunteer us for early patrol. They did and he did.

Decommissioning

A new radar became operational in 1960, which resulted in the decommissioning of the CHAMBERS and many other DERs. LTJG John Conroy wrote the following words to the tune of Ghost Riders in the Sky.[23]

Our DER went sailing out one blowy blusty day,
And on a wave she rested, as her radars searched away.
When all at once a message came right from the CNO,

Turn off your radars boys those bombers, they don't show.
Fare thee well, fare thee well,
Good-bye to the picket line blow.

The skipper said clean up the ship, and boy it really shines,
The paint's all white, the bright work's bright,
Short haircuts suit us fine.
We even use our men, just like the XO said,
But now our shop is closing up, the Barrier is dead.
Fare thee well, fare thee well, the Barrier is dead.

Oh Mr. L no more shall tread on E divisions toes,
And Frinizi, Smith and Koch are free of lookout woes.
The radarmen shall wax their decks and watch their scopes in peace,
And Mr. L sure hopes like hell on ships no more he'll feast.
Fare thee well, fare thee well, no more will we sail east.

A few more months we'll all be gone the CHAMBERS will be dead,
391 will sail no more to scare off Russian Reds.
The moths will come and eat her up and that's the sad sad end,
Of picket lines, of heavy seas and Schopenhauer's bread.
This is the end, this is the end, the Barrier is dead.

Note

On 20 June 1960, CHAMBERS was placed out of commission, in reserve, at Philadelphia. She was sold for scrap 24 September 1975.

CHAPTER 11: Recruiting School, Bainbridge, Maryland, 1959

When I was detached from CHAMBERS, I took 30-days leave and went home and worked with a friend for a few weeks as a metal-lather, installing re-bar for a new water treatment plant in Yonkers, New York.

Due to my early detachment from CHAMBERS when I reported into Bainbridge I was told that I had no duties until classes started and that I should just check in periodically. One day, while waiting for the course to start, I visited the FT A-School to see if I knew any of the instructors. As I passed one classroom the instructor saw me, came out, and dragged me into the classroom. He introduced me to the class as someone "fresh from the fleet." With that and without any warning he turned the class over to me and left the room. I had to give an impromptu lecture on the power distribution system of the AN/SPG-34 firecontrol radar. In that era the entire schematic of the radar was posted around the room over the chalkboards so I had no problems explaining how it functioned.

While at Bainbridge we would go into the clubs in Havre de Grace, Maryland for liberty. Havre de Grace is across the Susquehanna River and in Harford County, another county from Bainbridge. In Harford County the bars would close one hour earlier on the Bainbridge side so at the closing hour there would be a mad dash back across the river for "last call." On weekends we would drive to Lancaster, Pennsylvania to watch Franklin and Marshall College football games—engage in other social activities. Of course, it did not hurt that Lancaster was where the Wave recruits would be bussed for their liberty.

On 8 November John F. Kennedy defeated Richard M. Nixon for the presidency.

The most difficult part of recruiting school was learning to type since recruiting papers had to be typed—letter-perfect. Also, I had to learn to drive a manual transmission truck. Fortunately one of my classmates took the time to teach me.

Periodically we had to stand a duty officer watch and part of the task was inspecting the Waves[1] barracks prior to lights-out. We made it a point NEVER to inspect the barracks unless we had their duty MAA with us.

One evening I had been into town and when I returned some classmates convinced me to go to bingo. On my first card I made an "X" and won a portable TV, a portable radio, and an electric shaver. So much for beginner's luck!

At the completion of this schooling I carried out my orders to report to the Recruiting Station, New York, NY.

CHAPTER 12: Recruiting Duty, New York, 1960-'61

When I reported to the main Navy Recruiting Station at 346 Broadway, New York City, I found that I was one of only two FTs on recruiting duty in the entire Navy, the other being on humanitarian shore duty. Our office was in a suite on the first floor of a Federal building; the Marine's had their office in a suite on the opposite end of the floor. The female Navy recruiters had their office on the second floor. The Army and Air force recruiters were on higher floors.

On 1 January 1959, Fidel Castro and his guerrilla forces overthrew Fulgencio Batista's extreme right-wing dictatorship in Cuba. Then, on the 7th the U.S. Government recognized Castro's government. However, he eventually entered into agreements with Moscow and set up a Communist regime. This was a precursor to the "Guns of October" 1962.

My assignments varied from the main recruiting office, to the Washington Heights office at the northern end of Manhattan Island, to the recruiting booth in Times Square. The Times Square station had four desks and was shared with recruiters from the other services: Marines, Army, and Air Force. Our main task here was to interview candidates and send those that showed promise to the main station for further testing and processing. This booth, built in 1950, was finally closed in July 1995, and was replaced in June 1996. Duty here was without much excitement, although we did get to spend a lot of time watching the sight-seeing tourists. Mostly young men of draft-age would stop in looking for information to assist them in making up their minds about their future. Occasionally we would get some ex-sailors who would drop in to say hello and to reminisce with us about their Navy days. One day a "young lady" came into the office and wanted to enlist. She had obviously been living on the streets for several days as her white blouse was filthy and had many sweat bands under the arms. When I turned her down she approached the Marine, the Air Force, and then the Army recruiters with the same result.

At the main station, our daily routine consisted of interviewing walk-in candidates, both male and female. Those females who appeared to be likely candidates we sent to see the female recruiters on the second deck. For males, we administered a screening test, took their fingerprints, typed background checks and other recruitment papers. A good number of young men would come in and deliberately flunk the test in the belief that this would excuse them from the draft. This scheme did not work well because, as prescribed, we would turn their names over to the draft board. I remember one applicant who managed to score zero on two different versions of the screening test. This was quite an accomplishment as when things were quiet we would take score cards and arbitrarily mark them and never "score" below 23-25%. We retested this applicant using another test and again he scored a zero! This approach to avoiding the draft did not work either. That is when we found out that he wanted to tell his draft board that he had been turned down for the Navy so that he would be classified 4F.

On enlistment days we would take the new recruits to the Hoboken ferry that would take them to the train to Great Lakes. A shipmate from my WILLIAM T. POWELL days who lived in New Jersey generally carried out this task. Then he would ride the train to his stop and get off, leaving the "boots" on their own.

We were also required to give talks in high schools. However, in the City the only school that we visited regularly was in Washington Heights in Upper Manhattan. Even then, we went as a team with one member from each service. First one member would give a generic overview of military service, pay benefits, and more. The others would then give a brief overview of their particular service. The main problem that we would encounter was in the halls when the female students would crowd around us. We had to be extremely careful to keep each other in sight and to keep our hands at our sides.

On 5 May 1960, Francis Gary Power's U-2 spy plane was shot down over the USSR. On 19 August he was sentenced to ten years in prison. Then, in 1961, he was exchanged for a Soviet spy.

As the new man in the recruiting office, I was assigned collateral duty as the publicity man for the station. One of my tasks each month was to change the recruiting posters (A-boards) located around Manhattan. This involved driving a pick-up truck to the various locations, picking up the old sign and replacing it with a new one. Once I was driving a motor pool pickup truck west across 42nd Street and was just crossing Broadway when the truck died. Then I heard sirens. Looked up I saw the John F. Kennedy presidential motorcade coming down Broadway. I managed to coach the truck to the far side of Broadway where I left it parked at the curb. After the truck had been towed back to the motor pool and checked for possible problems it turned out the transmission had been serviced in the motor pool and they neglected to put oil in the transmission gearbox before checking it out to me.

On 30 December, USS GEORGE WASHINGTON, SSBN-598, the first ballistic missile carrying submarine, was commissioned.

During December 1960, USS CONSTELLATION, CVA-64 caught fire in the Brooklyn Navy Yard, across the river from the Recruiting Station; 32 civilians lost their lives. There was a fire station around the corner from the recruiting station and I was detailed to go there, explain shipboard fire fighting, and comment upon why their comrades died.

On 20 January 1961, John F. Kennedy was inaugurated president. Then on 11 May President Kennedy ordered a contingent of 400 Special Forces soldiers to Vietnam. This signaled the start of the escalation of U.S. involvement in Vietnam.

Another publicity task was to arrange for recruiting commercials to be shown on the local TV stations during their public service segments. In this I was a dismal failure; I could not even get an appointment with the appropriate directors. However, all was not lost. In the summer of 1961, a naval aviator, a member of the famed Blue Angels, was assigned to the Main Station for humanitarian duty. He would visit a station, show his Blue Angels card, and doors would open for him.

I was also responsible for providing audio-visual support for various Navy-related functions held in the City. One such event was a meeting of the Naval Academy Alumni Club held in the Waldorf Astoria Hotel in the fall of 1961. Admiral Arleigh Burke, ex-three times Chief of Naval Operations, was the guest speaker. President John F. Kennedy had recently chastised him for making remarks that the President considered "out of order" so Admiral Burke declined a fourth term. After Admiral Burke was introduced, the first thing he bellowed was, "Are we all Navy-men here?" The response was a resounding, "Yes!" Next the Admiral bellowed, "Are all the doors locked?" again the reply was a resounding, "Yes!" Then Admiral Burke proceeded to defend his comments and views to standing ovations. Mostly he spoke about the Navy's lack of preparedness and retention problems, particularly in the so-called "skill" ratings. Subsequent events have proven him to be correct on all counts.

Nineteen hundred sixty-one turned out to be one of our busiest years. After the Hungarian Revolution in 1956, refugees with minor children were allowed to immigrate to the United States. In 1961, many of these young men became of age and eligible to enlist. Completing their enlist papers was quite a chore as many did not know where they had been in the intervening years. Each individual was processed on a case-by-case basis.

Several incidents that happened in the office stand out in my memory. The first was when the CO received a letter from an executive with one of the oil companies doing business in Saudi Arabia. He said that he would be coming to New York and wanted to have his son enlisted in the Navy. He further stated that he would have only a couple of days in the City. I was ordered to prepare the paper work to enlist his son provided that he passed the screening test and physical. I objected to this quick turn-around, noting that it did not allow time for proper background checks. When I met the young man, my suspicions became aroused so I located residences of his close relatives. I then sent finger print cards to law enforcement agencies in each of those locations, including Los Angeles where an aunt lived. A few days later we received a telegram from the LA Sheriff's Office informing us the young man was wanted for suspicion of burglary. We were asked to hold him and told that a deputy was being sent o pick him up. Unfortunately by this time he was on his way to the training center at Great Lakes. I never found out the end of that story.

Another time I was typing the papers for a recruit and his father was waiting to sign them. In those days we had to put a letter on the papers to indicate the applicant's race. I typed a "C" for Caucasian. The father saw this and asked: "What are you doing? My son is as white as you are." This practice was later discontinued.

One of the more rewarding applicants was the young man who came in and told me he wanted to enlist, but he had been on parole for statutory rape. Through questioning I encouraged him to explain his statement. It seems that there was a neighborhood girl who was consentually taking care of several of the local boys and this young man happened to get caught by her father. There was something about him that impressed me so I consulted the Officer in Charge of Recruiting who said if I wanted to do the extra work required and he proved to be a viable candidate, he would forward the papers to Washington for approval. In the end I must have sent out thirty character references and personally interviewed several of them. Some of the references he provided included my 7th grade science teacher and the priest who was going to officiate at my sister's wedding. I also met with some-

153

one from the court who informed me that the record was "sealed and [I could not] see it." However, the court representative let me know, in an off-handed way, the file was on his desk. He then left the room for a few minutes, and as a result I ascertained that his story was basically true. The Bureau of Naval Personnel in Washington finally approved enlisting this applicant providing he passed a lie detector test. This was set up with NIS (Naval Investigative Service) and he passed. He made it through boot camp and hopefully went on to a successful career.

Normal procedure was for the recruiters in the outlying stations to interview their female applicants, give them a basic screening test and send them into the Main Station for further processing, including their physicals. One female, after processing in the Main Station, returned to her local recruiting station in Connecticut. The Chief there asked her how she did on her testing. She replied that she passed the mental test. He then asked about her physical and she replied, "What physical? I told them that you already gave me one." It took him a few minutes to realize that he had been set up as the butt of a joke.

Perhaps the most memorable sailor at the Recruiting Station was the 1st class yeoman (a clerk/typist) on the support staff. He was studying psychology and had several quirks. Perhaps the main quirk was that when someone would pass him and say something like "Good morning" he would look after them, scratch his head and say, "What do you suppose that he meant by that." He was writing a book that was supposed to be an expose of communists in New York City government. Somehow this effort came to the attention of the NIS (Naval Investigative Service) who made an investigation, which resulted in the yeoman being transferred to less-sensitive duty.

At one time the Marine recruiting major, who's office was in our building, noticed some discrepancies in an upstate sub-station's telephone bill, including many long-distance calls to Brooklyn. The major and sergeant major visited the recruiting sergeant and asked for an explanation. The Marine thought fast and replied that he had been processing an applicant for the Woman Marines. When asked why all these calls had been placed to the Brooklyn phone number, the sergeant replied that the female was visiting an aunt nearby when he started the processing. This explanation was accepted with the proviso that the applicant be in the Main Station within a week. She was not and the Marine was no longer in his field assignment—in a matter of days he was back in the Main Station scrubbing the marble with a toothbrush after hours.

This reassignment apparently did not alter the Marine sergeant's behavior patterns. Each year at the Outdoors Show at the NY Coliseum, as part of our duty, we were required to man an exhibit. Each day a recruiter from the different services would lead a color guard in "mounting the colors" following the opening of the show. One day it was this Marine sergeant's turn, but he had obviously had a few snorts that morning. We tried to convince him to let one of us lead the color guard, but he refused claiming the he was "a Marine and Marines can do anything." Unfortunately for him, his major and sergeant major were in the audience that day. The next day he was relieved of recruiting duty and transferred to Camp Lajune, North Carolina.

One evening I was detailed to drive a semi-truck with Navy recruiting displays in the trailer and loud speakers mounted on the outside. I was given the location and did not think much about it until I got there and saw that it was directly outside the Democratic Party headquarters. The use of the truck was ostensibly for an American Mothers Committee rally. I told the organizers that as an active duty Navy man, in uniform, I could not be involved with any political campaigning. I told them they could use the loudspeaker system, but if I heard any campaigning that I would shut it off instantly. For the most part, they honored this request. However, some did manage to broadcast their message that they represented a particular district and that they were running for a particular office.

On another occasion we received a request from a Texas recruiter to have enlistment papers signed by an applicant's father who would be visiting the City. He was the Chief Engineer aboard a merchant ship that would be unloading in Brooklyn. On the day they were in port I took the papers to the ship and had them signed. However, the recruit's father and his shipmates would not let me leave the ship. Instead they insisted I stay for lunch and swap sea stories afterward. When they finally let me go, they gave me some tax-free cigarettes and Scotch to take with me.

One of the tenets that they preached to us in recruiting school was that you do not find recruits in bars. That might be true in most places, but not in the boroughs of New York City. In New York, bars are like clubs in other places; they are where young men "hang out." When I visited the several bars of my youth in Queens County, I would constantly be called aside by friends and friends of friends, and asked questions about their military obligation and the Navy in particular. In order to avoid any charges of "poaching," I would direct all those who were sincerely interested to go to the local sub-station.

As part of routine procedure, whenever a sailor was discharged, the recruiting station nearest to his home would be notified. We were then expected to contact him and try to get him to reenlist. Before his 90-day grace period was up, we were supposed to make eyeball-to-eyeball contact with him. In our station this was seldom done; in most neighborhoods in Manhattan there were no street addresses on tenement buildings and if the building could be identified, there was seldom any lighting in the halls or numbers on the apartments. In addition, most residents were suspicious of any strangers coming around and asking questions. When we received a new recruiting officer, he visited our office and inspected our files, in particular the tickler file that we maintained on discharged sailors. It was obvious to him we were not making the required calls and he wanted an explanation. When we explained the local conditions he replied, "Keep up the good work." However, when we had an applicant we really wanted, we would go to his neighborhood in teams and with advance notification of our visit.

Later in 1961, we received a new CO who did not like the idea that station personnel wore civilian clothing on their way to work and to home. He thought we should wear our uniforms for their public relations value. However, after several days of fighting his commute from New Jersey and after having a pair of shoes ruined by people stepping on them, he realized the downside of wearing a uniform in the subways and rescinded his order.

In the fall the CO received notification there were some Butler buildings[1] available at the Naval Air Station in Atlantic City. He thought we could use them as recruiting sub-stations so a Seabee Chief, two support sailors from the recruiting support department, and I went down to claim two of the buildings. When we arrived on Tuesday afternoon base personnel asked when we thought we would need a fork lift to load the components onto a truck. We told them that a truck was scheduled for Friday. They did not believe we could dismantle the buildings that fast. We started at first light on Wednesday and, except for a quick lunch, did not stop until after dark. By Thursday evening we were finished and they had an open-bar party for us at the club. Friday the truck came and we went home.

Before we left I told one of the other members of "The Gang" to see a civilian friend of mine (a "scalper") and get tickets to that Saturday's Army-Oklahoma football game in Yankee Stadium. When we met him the next morning he had eight tickets on the 50-yard line—only they were in the first row and all that we saw most of the game was the backs of the Oklahoma players!

While stationed in New York I met a lady who was to have a major influence on my life. One of our potential recruits, Kenneth Thornton, was under age and needed his parent's signature approval to enlist. Ken's mother was ill at the time and physically unable to come into the recruiting station so I took the papers to his home in Woodside, Queens to have them signed by her. On the morning of 16 April 1960, I knocked on the Thornton's door, which was opened by Ken's sister, Jacqueline (Jackie). From that instant I knew that my days as a bachelor were numbered. While working in Times Square I made friends with someone in the USO Office, and therefore, was able to get tickets to Broadway shows whenever I wanted them. Jackie and I went as often as her college and after-school work schedule permitted. She exposed me to "the better things in life" and made me realize there might be more to life than just the Navy and typical bachelor sailor activities.

Formal religion never played a big part in my life up until the time that I met Jackie. However, after she invited me to accompany her to Sunday Mass, I began to attend Mass with her on a regular basis. Then I started to question those religious principles that I thought I knew and realized these were mostly based on hearsay. I also started to question the life style that I had been living.

On 17 April 1961, the aborted "Bay of Pigs" invasion of Cuba by CIA-trained Cuban mercenaries took place.

Later that summer, I had a Friday afternoon appointment to have the brakes on my car replaced. However, before I left the station the XO called me and told me to standby to drive to the Teterboro, New Jersey airport to pick up the CO. They were afraid that Floyd Bennett Airfield in Brooklyn, his original destination, would be fogged in. Turned out that I did not have to go get him, but I missed my brake appointment. The next morning Jackie and I were driving to the beach when the brakes on my car failed and I crashed the car. I was all right, but Jackie spent several days in the hospital as a result of delayed shock.

In August 1961, the Soviets begin building a wall around Berlin in order to keep people from East Berlin from escaping to the West. This wall was finally taken down on 9 November 1989. The reunification of East and West Germany followed shortly thereafter.

Not all of our time was spent working—we did manage to find time for R&R. When ever we planned a station party, we would visit various suppliers in and around the City, and request donations (beer, hamburgers, hot dogs, pretzels, and any other party items) and we were generally successful. One summer day we had arranged an out-door party at a recreational site in upstate New York and I had ar-ranged with the motor pool to check out a stake body truck. I was then going to pick up all the party stuff and drive it to the party site. What I did not know was that the truck had a governor on it that re-stricted it to 45-mph; therefore, the drinks and food arrived about an hour late. The proprietors of the recreation site based their fee on the number of people attending, so we volunteered to have a sailor keep count using a hand counter. I believe the counter only clicked once for each two attendees.

On another occasion Jackie and her classmates wanted to put on a production of South Pacific in a citywide competition with all the other nursing schools. Five of us from the recruiting station loaned them our white uniforms and made certain the first few rows of the auditorium were filled with sailors on the night the girl's performance took first place. Four of these sailors shared a large, first floor apart-ment in Jackson Heights, Queens and several female flight attendants had the upstairs apartment. One winter night the five of us went to a party at the home of one of Jackie's classmates. This party was about ten blocks from the guys' apartment. At some point during the eve-ning it started to snow. By the time the party broke up, the roads were impassable. However, we guys knew the girl's would need a car the next day, so we shoveled the snow in the street then pushed, pulled, and carried a car all the way back to their apartment. Of course, a Boda bag of brandy helped in the process. Late the next morning, when the girls showed up at the apartment, the guys were still sacked out. We had many great weekend parties in the guys' apartment but because all the girls were attending a Catholic college, we ensured everything was proper and above board.

At that time it was routine for recruiters to receive an exten-sion on their tour of duty. However, when I requested an extension, my detailer in Washington said, "No way, as an FT you don't belong there in the first place." Shortly thereafter I received orders to FT B-School at Great Lakes.

CHAPTER 13: Advanced Electronics Schooling, Great Lakes, Illinois, 1962

In December 1961, I was detached from recruiting duty and was ordered to Great Lakes to attend FT B-School. I left New York after the holidays and drove straight through to Great Lakes with stopping only for gas, food, coffee, and brief naps.

While there, we spent many hours studying for our advancement exams. Then on 16 May 1962, I was advanced to Chief Firecontrolman (FTC). The CPO (Chief Petty Officer) initiation was a unique experience! One of my classmates was Jim Kilpatrick, a Senior Chief Firecontrolman (FTCS), who bought charges against me. These charges were: (1) "Impersonation of a Superior: In that Chambers resorted to several methods to pass himself off as a CPO. For example, Chambers and another first class petty officer were heard to refer to each other as 'Chief' and he had been heard on several occasions to refer to his living quarters as the 'CPO Quarters,' and (2) Immorality: In that while in the presence of younger sailors, Chambers used vulgar and profane language and made nasty and obscene innuendoes that would defame the reputation of CPOs." I had no defense against these trumped-up charges and pleaded guilty. After doing my just penance, I accepted the creed as a Chief Petty Officer (Appendix B). Career-wise, Jim and I would serve together for the next several years.

While attending school at Great Lakes I decided it was important to me that I take religious classes with the intent of converting to Catholicism as a prerequisite to marrying Jackie Thornton, the lady I'd met while stationed in New York. Up until the time I started dating her, I essentially had not attended any particular church, and certainly did not practice any religion, but while escorting Jackie to Mass every Sunday, I realized that something was missing in my life.

On 20 February 1962, USS NOA, DD-841, recovered Project Mercury astronaut Lt. Col. John H. Glenn, Jr., USMC, from the waters of the Atlantic Ocean after his historic three orbits of the earth in his Friendship Seven Capsule.

One of my classmates had difficulty understanding magnetism and transformer theory. When an instructor explained a particular power supply conversion process the student asked where the power came from to begin with. At that, the instructor took his chalk and drew a line from the schematic on the chalkboard and around the room's baseboard to an electrical outlet and explained, "That's where it came from."

On 1 April 1962, the Destroyer Force, Atlantic Fleet was combined with the Cruiser Force, Atlantic Fleet to form the Cruiser-Destroyer Force, US Atlantic Fleet (CRUDESLANT). CRUDESLANT was disestablished on 31 December 1974, when it was combined with other forces to form the Naval Service Force, Atlantic Fleet.

On 19 July 1960, while making the transit between Seal Beach and San Diego for decommissioning, USS Ammen, DD-527, was struck by USS Collett, DD-730. The collision killed 11 Ammen sailors and injured 20 others.

One Saturday we were playing pinochle in the barracks when somebody announced it had started to snow. By noon, when the snow had started to drift up to the windows, we decided we had better get dressed and go to the messhall for lunch. After bundling up and fighting our way to the messhall, we found the cooks had come up with a new innovation: pickle burgers! These were hamburgers with a pickle slice stuck inside before they were grilled. Considering the weather and the walk to the messhall, these tasted pretty good. The cooks at Great Lakes were always trying to be innovative!

At the completion of FT-B School, I had orders to TERRIER Guided Missile Radar School in Dam Neck, Virginia.

CHAPTER 14: Missile Guidance Radar School, Dam Neck, Virginia, 1962

When my technical schooling at Great Lakes was completed in August, I reported to Dam Neck, Virginia where I attended TERRIER Guided Missile Radar (AN-SPG-55A) School. [1] Again one of my classmates was Senior Chief Jim Kilpatrick who was doubling classes: taking radar classes during the day and Mk 119 Firecontrol Computer classes in the evenings. At this time the Navy had three surface ship missile systems: (1) TARTAR, a short-range anti-aircraft system, (2) TERRIER, a medium-range shore, anti-surface and anti-aircraft system, and (3) TALOS, a long-range anti-aircraft system.

Cuban Missile Crisis

On 14 October, photographs taken by high-flying U2 aircraft confirmed that the Cubans were building launching sites for offensive missiles. These sites were for Russian-built intermediate range ballistic missiles (IRBM) and medium range ballistic missiles (MRBM) being supplied by Soviet Premier Nikita S. Khrushchev. On 22 October, President John F. Kennedy demanded that Khrushchev remove all the missile bases and their deadly contents and declared that, "a strict quarantine on all offensive military equipment to Cuba is being initiated." This was intended to prevent Russian ships from bringing additional missiles and construction materials to the island. Many differ-

165

ent military units from all of the armed services took part in this quarantine including Navy aircraft carriers, aircraft squadrons, oilers, stores ships, transports and at least 102 destroyers and destroyer-types. These included 67 destroyers (DD), 13 radar picket destroyers (DDR), 5 guided missile destroyers (DDG), 2 destroyer-leaders (DL), 4 guided missile destroyer leaders (DLG), 5 destroyer escorts (DE) and 7 radar picket destroyer escorts (DER). The quarantine was successful in that on 28 October Khrushchev agreed to remove all missiles and other offensive weapons from Cuba. On 21 November the quarantine was terminated.

During the infamous "Thirteen Days of August"[2] all students were on alert for possible assignment to ships in the event the normal crews of those ships could not be recalled in time for possible deployment to Cuba. This deployment never took place and on 1 September 1962, Chaplain Ralph Handren performed the marriage ceremony for Jackie Thornton and me in the chapel at NAS Oceana, Virginia. Both our families and Jackie's best friend-maid-of-honor were there. It was an extremely hot day and I was in my dress whites, and at the appointed time, Father had not yet arrived. Apparently Father was having an exceptional round of golf and lost track of the time. He finally showed up—wearing his golf cleats!

Jackie had a year of college to complete so she continued to live with her mother in New York. At the end of my TERRIER Radar schooling I received orders to a TERRIER ship being built in Bath, Maine.

CHAPTER 15: USS HARRY E.YARNELL, DLG-17:
Norfolk, Virginia, 1962-'65

At the end of October 1962, I detached from Dam Neck with orders to the precommissioning detail for USS HARRY E.YARNELL, DLG-17,[1] a guided missile destroyer-leader being built in the Bath Shipyard, Bath, Maine. Captain Charles E. Nelson, who was regarded as a martinet, was the commanding officer. Captain Nelson was a 1937 graduate of the U.S. Naval Academy. During WW II he served in USS MORRIS, DD-417; USS MOALE, DD-693; and USS HYMAN, DD-732. He commanded USS TAYLOR, DDE-468, and he also served in an APD and a heavy cruiser, as well as several shore and staff billets. CDR Robert C. Pringle was the Executive Officer, LCDR R.K. Albright was the Weapons Officer, and LT. W.T. Swayne was the Firecontrol Officer.

HARRY E. YARNELL's History

Motto: "Quickdraw McDraw"

USS HARRY E. YARNELL was built by Bath Iron Works, Bath, Maine. She was named in honor of Admiral Harry E. Yarnell. Admiral Yarnell served in the Navy for 31 years, spanning three wars—the Spanish-American, WW I, and WW II. As a young officer, he served in several destroyers before assuming command of USS DALE, DD-4.

Precommissioning, Bath, Maine

When I reported to the precommissioning detail in November, my initial assignment was Leading Firecontrolman. However, in the spring of 1963, Senior Chief Kilpatrick reported aboard and assumed that role (he had been attending TERRIER Computer and System Schools at Dam Neck). I was then given the responsibility for the Weapons Control System and the gun firecontrol systems. I have a lot to be thankful for to Senior Chief Kilpatrick, who took an inordinate amount of time to explain the TERRIER System to me and ensuring that I learned my lesson well. Our main job while in the builder's yard in Bath was to learn as much about the new ship as possible, which included locating every fitting, identifying every

switch and circuit breaker was and what they controlled, and organiz-
ing all documentation.

Those of us who did not have their families in Bath were quartered in an old hotel across the street from the shipyard. Most weekends I would drive a car pool to New York, leaving on Friday afternoon and returning Sunday night. This was normally about a six-hour
drive; however, one weekend we hit a severe ice and snowstorm and
the return trip took over twelve hours! The windshield defrosters
hardly had any effect at all and every few miles we had to stop and
scrape the ice off the windshield. Fortunately we were aware of the
weather report so we wisely left early Sunday afternoon, arriving back
on time.

HARRY E. YARNELL was one of a "new breed" of destroyer-leader and TERRIER Missile ships. She was a so-called
"double-ender" in that she was capable of launching missiles from
either of two missile launchers, one forward and one aft. Targets
would be designated to the firecontrol system from the Naval Tactical
Data system (NTDS) in CIC. Digital target information would be sent
to the Weapons Control System (WCS), also in CIC, where it would
be converted to analog data and transmitted to the firecontrol computers. Once in flight, a missile would be guided by an ANSPG-55A
missile guidance radar.

An unfortunate thing happened while the ship was being constructed in the shipyard. We had four missile guidance radars and
four firecontrol computers. All the radars and computers were from
the same lots and with the same consecutive serial numbers, 42, 43,
44 and 45. Except radar number 43 was dropped while being hoisted
aboard the ship and it was replaced by a radar, number 46, from a different lot. This caused us many configuration control problems over
the next several years, as the external records never caught up with
the changed serial numbers. We kept receiving changes for radar
number 43 that we did not need and not getting changes for radar
number 46.

Commissioning, Boston, Massachusetts

HARRY E.YARNELL was commissioned in the Boston Naval Shipyard on 2 February 1963, a cold and rainy day. My assignment was "pier monitor," directing visitors to the seating area where my normally heavy bridge coat soaked up additional tons of rainwater. Jackie came up to Boston for the ceremony, which was followed by a great party in the CPO Club in South Boston.

Perhaps one of the most emotionally moving ceremonies in the Navy is the commissioning of a new ship. This normally takes place in a Navy yard with many dignitaries and Navy brass present in full dress uniforms. The first key event takes place when a high ranking Naval officer, on behalf of the Department of the Navy, accepts the ship for service from the builder and orders it to be placed in commission. At that point the national ensign and union jack are hoisted at the bow and stern respectively and a commission pennant is hoisted at the main mast. This all takes place during the playing of the National Anthem. Next the prospective commanding officer reads his orders, assumes command, and orders the executive officer to "Set the watch." At that time, the crew, who have been standing at attention in their dress uniforms on the pier, run up the gangway and man the ship. This brings the ship to life.

Even though the ship is now in commission and theoretically is a "Navy ship," it has been said that a ship does not truly become a "Navy ship" until the last member of the precommissioning crew is transferred. While the ship is in the building yard, members of the precommissioning crew take responsibility for decisions that normally would not be in their area of expertise. Once the ship is in commission and questions come up, it is typical for the answer to be "See _____, he was part of the precommissioning crew." When that last member departs, the crew is forced to consult the manuals, regulations, and other resources for answers. It is then the ship truly becomes a "Navy ship."

Following commissioning the new ship goes through several trials. First there is the Builder's Trials, followed by Preliminary Acceptance Trials (PAT), and ultimately Final Acceptance Trials (FAT). Builder's Trials are conducted after fitting out has been completed. These trials allow the builder to test the underway operating capabilities and limitations of all shipboard major systems. PAT is conducted under the auspices of the Board of Inspection and Survey (InSurv) and are designed to recommend acceptance of the ship by the Navy. After the ship has operated for a period of time, and all systems have been operated and tested by the crew, including live weapons firings, FAT is conducted, again under the auspices of InSurv.

Earlier it was mentioned that Captain Nelson was a "martinet": however, this might not be the most accurate evaluation of him as captain. In his own words he was the "Leading Petty Officer of the Ship." He was known to see a seaman painting a specific area and either correct him or reassign him to paint elsewhere. While in the shipyard, he once had the deck force painting by drop light in freezing weather. Normally the executive officer would set leave policy and liberty hours for the crew; not so under Captain Nelson—he set liberty hours. The XO could not even approve an early liberty. For instance, on one occasion I received word that Jackie, who was still living in New York, was ill. There was a late afternoon flight out of Norfolk so I went to see the XO to request permission to leave about two hours early enabling me to catch the flight. He commiserated with me, tears came to his eyes, and he told me that he could not approve my request. I had to take a bus to Washington where I was able to catch a red-eye flight. However, HARRY E. YARNELL did develop the reputation of being the best DLG in the Atlantic fleet.

My personal living situation aboard HARRY E. YARNELL was quite different than what I had been used to aboard my other ships. Prior to being assigned to HARRY E. YARNELL, I had been promoted to Chief Petty Office so I was now entitled to live in what was referred to as the "Goat Locker"[2] or Chief's Quarters. We also had our own mess where our own mess cooks served our meals family-style.

Search for USS THRESHER

On Wednesday, 10 April 1963, shipyard personnel had to take the ship to sea for a few hours to check for sea worthiness, loose equipment, and miscellaneous squeaks and noises. There was little food aboard and we only had the clothes on our backs. Little did we know that we would be at sea for several busy, stressful days. As it happened, later that day we received word that the nuclear submarine USS THRESHER, SSN-593, was missing at sea. We were ordered to proceed to her last known position and conduct a search. We were the first ship on the scene, but after finding nothing but an oil slick, we returned to Boston on Friday.

Transit to Norfolk, Virginia

After completion of fitting out at Boston, we steamed south to our homeport of Norfolk, Virginia. A major difference between the destroyer-leader class ships and WW II era destroyers was that CIC was located on the same deck and immediately abaft the bridge. As any tactical operations were expected to take place many miles from the ship, the commanding officer's GQ station was now in CIC, where the he would have the best and most complete view of the entire tactical situation. On our way south we passed several anchored Russian fishing ships, including a large replenishment freighter, VALADIVOSTOK, No. 788. Alongside her to starboard was SHEMCHUNG, PT-334. Also in the area was a Russian coastal freighter KORSAKOV, all homeported in Kalingrad. Captain Nelson ordered that we approach the ships in order to take pictures of them. Our XO did not think this was a good idea, advising Captain Nelson that the Russians would get more intelligence data than we would. However, the Captain prevailed and we took their pictures. When the Russian freighter dipped her colors, we replied. We attempted to communicate with them using international flag signals and flashing light, but received no reply so we proceeded to the U.S. Naval Weapons Depot (NAD), Yorktown, Virginia, and then to Pier 7, Naval Operating Base (NOB), Norfolk.

Shakedown Training

From 8 May until 14 July, we operated in and out of Norfolk conducting shakedown training. Then on 15 July, we entered the Norfolk Naval Shipyard (NNSY), Portsmouth, Virginia to have new turbines installed. We left the shipyard on 23 October and went to Yorktown to load ammo before commencing shakedown training.

From 28 October thru 26 November 1963, HARRY E.YARNELL was in the Caribbean operating out of Gitmo before returning to Norfolk. Most of the Weapons Department's time was spent engaging in Ship Qualification Testing (SQT) assisted by a Ship Qualification Assistance Team (SQAT) out of the U. S. Naval Ship Missile Systems Engineering Station (NSMSES), Port Hueneme, California. This team consisted of a Naval Officer in Charge and a contingent of civilian engineers. One of our most time consuming tasks was revising and proving what was known as DSOT, or Daily System Operability Tests. As the name applies, these tests were run each day, normally before breakfast, to check the proper functioning of all elements of the weapons system. There were four different tests, each one testing parameters in a different quadrant, and they required personnel with sound-powered telephones to be stationed at different locations throughout the weapons systems. At first, Senior Chief Kilpatrick acted as test conductor, running the tests from the Weapons control Area in CIC. During this time I functioned as an observer-trainee. When our confidence in the operation of the system, and my knowledge increased, we would alternate as test conductor.

On Friday, 22 November we were in the Bahama Islands conducting sonar tests in the so-called "Tongue of the Ocean," a partially enclosed basin that is greater than 6500 feet deep,[3] when word was received that President John F. Kennedy had been shot and killed in Dallas, Texas. Later that day Vice President Lydon B. Johnson was sworn in as president. These events had a very profound impact on the crew. Once again we realized how cut off we were from timely news.

We completed trials on 25 November and headed back to Norfolk. At that time LT. T. Klish made the following entry in the deck log:

> *This Man-of-War successfully accomplished her first task and cruise away from U.S. Coastal waters since being commissioned this year. This is the day President John F. Kennedy, her past Commander-in-Chief, is to be buried in our national cemetery.*

> *Shortly after assuming the presidency, President Johnson introduced his "Great Society" program and the 1960s became the era of the "New Generation."*

When we returned to Norfolk I went shopping for an apartment in anticipation of moving Jackie to Norfolk. I found one that I thought fit our budget and put a temporary hold on it. When Jackie came down she was not impressed so we found another in a complex where one of her college classmates already lived. A few days before Christmas we moved into our first home. After we got settled in Jackie insisted on having a Christmas tree. Wanting to provide my bride with the traditions of Christmas, even at such a late hour, I went looking for an acceptable tree. Around 9:30 P.M I finally saw a single tree outside of a market in the ghetto area beyond East Main Street. As I reached for it, a black hand reached out from the side and also grabbed it. The shopkeeper finally solved this impasse by splitting the tree down the middle and selling us each a half. When I got it home we put it in the corner, making it a very memorable first Christmas tree.

On 1 January LCDR R. L. Bauchspes, Jr., wrote the traditional New Year's deck log in this verse:

Our six lines are out and all sure doubled,
But we are ready to the call of trouble,
D & S Piers is the place we be,
Norfolk, Virginia the city by the sea,
We're starboard side to at pier number twenty,
with our missiles and guns ready for plenty,
The winds are high and the seas are rought,
but our number two boiler will call its bluff,
Our number two generator has a crosslite at our [__],
for those to see who are not at Mass,
Two little boys at our port side too,
the SAPSON and CONNYNGHAM will do their job true.
VADM GRENFELL is SOPA who wishes the boys a
"HAPPY NEW YEAR TODAY".

Now New Year is here, we bow our heads,
to Him who gives us Daily Bread,
We remember all the joy and sadness of last year,
with an amen that we all are here
We lost a great leader last year
Twas a sailor he was who had no fear,
He taught us though seaman or flag, which ever we be,
T'is our job to keep our country free,
Our stars and our stripes do fly at our mast,
For all nations to see that they will always last
For sailors we are and good ones we be,
For to keep the Peace and all nations free,
A star did shine so long ago,
and we are here so it may always glow,
He watches on us from on high
who has our names in His sky,
We shall go to wherever called
so that free men shall never fall,
The old will go and the new will come,

> *to do the Job which must be done,*
> *T'is not our Job to cause alarm*
> *but to keep all free nations from what harm,*
> *Sail on O'Sailor's of the sea,*
> *for this is a job that will always be,*
> *So a happy New Year to all who hear*
> *For we are sailors who must be here,*
> *To welcome this New Year*
> *And Proud to say*
> *"WE ARE HERE"*
> *For you to know*
> *and never fear.*

On 13 January 1964, USS MANLEY, DD-940, evacuated 54 U.S. citizens and 36 nationals of other countries from revolution-torn Zanzibar, Africa. MANLEY returned on the 20th, ready to conduct additional evacuations, if needed. This is a typical example of humanitarian operations conducted by destroyers.

We spent a good part of the late winter and early spring operating in the Jacksonville, Florida OpArea and on the Roosevelt Roads, Puerto Rico missile range qualifying our missile systems. On 13 February ADM Eli Rich, head of the Navy's surface missiles program, visited us. The Admiral, Senior Chief Kilpatrick, and I were taking a stroll on deck and discussing the problems with the missile systems. We told him the major problem was the inaccuracy or unreliability of target designations from the AN/SPS-39 three-dimensional height finding radar. He asked if we had any recommended solutions and I, jokingly, said, "Give the maintenance responsibility to the FTs." ADM Rich asked if we thought we could handle the task and Jim and I exchanged nods whereby Jim replied, "Yes, Sir." A short time later responsibility for the height finding/target designation radar was transferred from the Operations Department to the Weapons Department. This led to the usual problems encountered when one group loses responsibility and another group assumes the role. Until the day the transfer became effective, we were not allowed into the radar spaces or permitted to review the technical manuals.

In February, HARRY E.YARNELL was again in Gitmo. On the morning of the 16th, a Friday, several Chiefs had to make an early "inspection" of the Chief's Club. As we were returning about 1:30 P.M., our Chief Hospital Corpsman saw an admiral standing on a pier waiting to meet a transport ship. All of a sudden "Doc" ran over, grabbed the admiral in a bear hug, and swung him about. Needless to say the rest of us were mortified and feared a court martial for Doc. When the dust settled we found out that the admiral was Rear Admiral (RADM) John D. Bulkeley of WW II PT Boat fame,[4] the Commander of the Naval Base, and that Doc had served with him. We invited the admiral to coffee in the Chief's Mess the following morning and he accepted.

On the next morning, the 17th, the quarterdeck received a call that the admiral would be arriving shortly. Somehow we had neglected to inform Captain Nelson of the admiral's visit. When RADM Bulkeley arrived, Captain Nelson wanted to escort him to the Wardroom, but the Admiral informed Captain Nelson that he was only aboard to have coffee with the Chiefs. Buckeley also told his aide that he did not want to be disturbed under any circumstances. However, his aide did interrupt to relay to the admiral some information that apparently could not wait. At that the admiral excused himself, left, and ordered that the water pipelines coming into the base be cut and a section removed to disprove the accusation made by the Cuban government that the United States was stealing water from Cuba. A 38-inch, 300-pound section of the 14-inch pipe and a 20-inch section of the 10-inch pipe were cut and lifted from the ground. The openings were permanently sealed with RADM Bulkeley personally using the welding torch.

Ocho Rios, Jamaica

On 14 March, we visited Ocho Rios, on the north coast of Jamaica and moored to the Reynolds Inning Pier. The owners of a resort hotel invited us to use their pool and locker facilities. While doing so we were playing a water game when I left the area for a few moments. When I returned, I saw someone standing poolside with his back to me. Thinking that I was just continuing the game, I shoved him into the pool. That is when I found out the he was the XO who had just arrived! Fortunately he was a good sport about it.

The problem we had in Ocho Rios had to do with the red bauxite dust that was everywhere. If a sailor sat in it or rubbed his white uniform against a wall, the uniform had to be scrapped.

Virginia Capes Operations

We returned to the Destroyer/Submarine (D/S) Piers at NOB. On 1 May, CDR L.J. Fay, USN relieved CDR Pringle as our XO. Then on 6 June, Captain Guy C. Leavitt, USN, relieved Captain Nelson at the D/S Piers, Norfolk. Captain Leavitt had destroyer experience in USS NIELDS, DD-616; USS BROWNSON, DD-868; and as commanding officer USS FORREST SHERMAN, DD-931.

On 19 June, we conducted a Saturday dependents' cruise. This is a Navy-sponsored event that gives the crew's family members an opportunity to spend the day observing regular ship operations and to get a feel for what it is like to be at sea on a missile cruiser. This was Jackie's first opportunity to see the ship in action at sea. At one point HARRY E. YARNELL had to cut across the wake of USS FORRESTAL, leaving several guests unprepared for the sudden rolling motion. One elderly lady in particular, who was sitting on a folding chair, fell over, injuring her shoulder. She was taken to sick bay to be treated by both our doctor and chief hospital corpsmen who were seasoned combat veterans. Neither had the slightest idea of how to treat a woman but knew my wife Jackie, who was a nurse, was on board. I was escorting Jackie around the ship when she was paged and asked to attend to the problem.

As part of the shipboard tour, I took Jackie into the Weapons Control Area of CIC and showed her how the Missile Control System operated. Following some minor instruction I let her order training missiles (T-SAMs) loaded from the below-deck magazine to the launcher rails. This experience led to a humorous incident during a latter dependent's cruise aboard USS FOX, DLG-33.

Career Information and Counseling School

From 24 June until 24 July I was sent to Career Information and Counseling School, a Class-C School at Schools Command, Naval Training Center in Norfolk. Without consulting me, I was nominated for this assignment as the ship was going to be visiting New York and since I was from N.Y they rationalized that I wouldn't miss going there. This was a great disappointment as it was the only potential opportunity that I had during my entire career to show off my ship to family and friends. Never again did a ship that I served in visit New York.

Like every other Navy course I attended, I approached my studies with determination to do well. After I took up my shipboard duties as Career Counselor, I convinced Captain Leavitt that to improve morale it would be a good idea to pick one division as "outstanding division" at the Saturday personnel inspections. The Fire-control Division (F-Div.) was selected three weeks in a row and just barely missed in the fourth week, mainly due to one individual who did not get his hair cut since earlier in the week. By the time that I was going to discuss this with the individual, others in the division told me not to worry about it as they had already squared the offender away. When I asked how they did this, I was told, "Chief, you don't want to know."

Norfolk Naval Shipyard

Later in July a problem developed in one of the ship's main engine turbines (which we learned was the result of a design deficiency) and we had to put into NNSY, Portsmouth for it to be replaced. While there, we learned details of our schedule for our forth-coming Mediterranean cruise. This schedule called for us to be at Cannes, France over the Christmas/New Year's holidays. I promptly called Jackie and informed her of this schedule. When I returned home that afternoon she had already made travel arrangements for herself that would enable us to spend the holidays together.

On 2 August 1964, in another part of the world, in the Tonkin Gulf, off the east coast of Vietnam, USS MADDOX, DD-731 was at-tacked by North Vietnamese PT boats. Then on 4 August two United States Navy destroyers, USS MADDOX and USS TURNER JOY, DD-951, reported they had also been attacked in the Tonkin Gulf by North Vietnamese PT boats. This incident led to the congress passing the so-called "Gulf of Tonkin Resolution" that gave President Johnson approval to use "all necessary resources" to resist "Communist ag-gression" in Vietnam and allowed Johnson to expand the increasingly unpopular war.

Sixth Fleet Operations, 1964

On 14 September 1964, HARRY E.YARNELL deployed to the Med to operate with the U.S. Sixth Fleet. During this cruise we made goodwill visits to eight foreign ports before returning to Norfolk in February 1965. These ports were Amsterdam; Suda Bay, Create; Athens (Piraeus), Greece; the Island of Rhodes; Tripoli, Libya; Genoa and Naples, Italy; Cannes, France and Barcelona and Valencia, Spain.

Before reporting to the Sixth Fleet, we were conducting NATO anti-submarine warfare (ASW) training operations between Scotland and Norway when a Russian destroyer, DD-096, appeared. We also encountered a Russian ELINT trawler KRENOMETR, out of Shehermentro. We received orders to trail the destroyer to find out where she was being re-supplied or re-fueled. As we proceeded fur-ther into the North Sea and crossed the Arctic Circle on 21 Septem-ber,[5] a failure developed in the anti-freeze system of the antenna of missile guidance radar #2 located up over the pilothouse. In order to repair the antenna, FTs had to climb up the backside of the antenna and remove waterproof access covers. The wind was severe and the temperature was extremely cold, so to work with any attempt at comfort we would turn the antenna so that the front pointed into the wind and we could work on the lee side. The cold was so intense that one individual could only stay exposed for about a minute. When the Russians observed our plight, they altered their course in such a way, that by following them the wind would blow across the back of the antenna. Again, we would turn the antenna. This "cat and mouse" game went on until the repair task was successfully completed. We tracked the Russian destroyer without success for several days before we were relieved.

On 18 September, USS MORTON, DD-948, and USS PARSONS, DD-949, opened fire on suspected PT boats off the coast of Vietnam.

After breaking off tracking the Russian destroyer, we had been scheduled for a port call at Portsmouth, England, but the incident with the Russian cruiser pre-empted this visit. Instead, on 29 September, HARRY E.YARNELL transited from the Zuiderzee, entered the Ijmuiden Canal for the ten-mile passage through thirteen locks, for a port visit to Amsterdam, Netherlands. As we made our way to Amsterdam, many of us were somewhat uneasy being confined in the locks. After we moored I had the first watch on the quarterdeck when I noticed several youngsters crawling on the ship's mooring lines. This was an extremely dangerous practice because the ship could surge, and any limbs dangling between the lines could be cut off. Attempts by the security watch to keep the children off the lines were unsuccessful so I looked in a phone book and saw something that looked like "Marines" and I called the listed number. I identified myself to the person who answered in English and I told him of my concerns. He informed me that he would take care of the situation. A few minutes later a company of Royal Dutch Marines, in full dress uniform, came marching down the pier. They assumed a position in front of the gangway and the sergeant in charge told me that he would station a Marine there, assuring me that I would not have anymore problems. True to his word, a Marine guard was on duty the entire time we were in Amsterdam, thereby alleviating any potential problems.

One night Senior Chief Kilpatrick and I found a local neighborhood bar where we were welcomed and were treated like visiting family. The next evening, several other Chiefs wanted to join us. We were sitting in a back room drinking large Heinekens when someone asked what should we do with the empties? It was decided that we would place them on a ledge that ran around the room. I do not know how far around the room the bottles extended, but it was impressive. During the course of the evening, we got into an arm wrestling contest. I was able to take all comers. Later someone came and told me they had someone who I could not beat, but it would be awhile before we could have the contest. At the appointed time, they instructed me to sit with my back to the door, then presented my opponent—a woman! This lady beat me handily and honestly, two out of three. When I turned around I discovered the reason why my back was to the door: the CO and XO were both standing there watching my humiliating defeat!

After we departed Amsterdam on 2 October, and had transited twelve of the thirteen locks leading to the sea, we saw hundreds of people waiting on the final lock to wish us bon voyage. Once clear of the Ijmuiden Canal, we sighted a surfaced submarine flying the Soviet Naval ensign. We attempted to communicate with them by flashing light, but they did not reply. Shortly thereafter we sighted a second Soviet submarine. They eventually joined up and went on their way, a course set in the opposite direction of HARRY E. YARNELL.

In October 1964, Leonid Brezhnev ousted Khrushchev as General Secretary of the Soviet Communist Party.

From October 1964 until January 1965, HARRY E. YARNELL operated in the Mediterranean participating in scheduled Sixth Fleet exercises and various training operations, including missile firings off the island of Crete.

The mission of the Sixth Fleet was still the same as it was when President Jefferson sent a squadron of frigates to the Mediterranean Sea in 1801 and when I was last in the Med aboard CASCADE in 1956. The main difference between HARRY E. YARNELL's mission and CASCADE's was that we were a front-line warship responsible for protecting the fleet's aircraft carriers and their strike aircraft. Our station was normally to the east of the carriers where our long-range radar could provide early warning of any Russian aircraft or missiles. At the National Command Center, our ship had a life expectancy of six minutes from the time attacking Russian aircraft or missiles were detected crossing over the Balkans. We were expected to fire all of our missiles and from that point on we were out of the war planning process. Anything else that we could contribute after that was considered gravy.

Visits to Piraeus, Greece and Rhodes

After a missile firing exercise off Create in early October, we paid a visit to Piraeus, Greece, that allowed many of our sailors to make their first visit to Athens. While in Piraeus, Senior Chief Kilpatrick and I took an all-day tour to Corinth and Mycenae. This was unusual since it was our practice that both of us not be away from the ship at the same time. The Corinth Canal particularly impressed us, noting that St. Paul lived and preached there for over two years. In Mycenae we visited the citadel of Agamemnon, the King of Mycenae, and commander-in-chief of the Greek coalition that attacked Troy. Agamemnon was slain by his wife Clytaemestra who then ran away with her lover.[6]

Starting in August, during a period of growing tension on Cyprus that centered on proposed changes to the electoral system, a Carrier Battle Group (CVBG) and an amphibious force operated off the island.

When we departed Piraeus on the 15th, we spent a few days on the destroyer evacuation station near the trouble-ridden island of Cyprus. Our task was to standby and to be ready to evacuate American citizens if the political situation demanded that they leave. While on station we stopped the ship's engines and held swim call. After we were relieved we visited Rhodes and passed through the twin breakwaters where according to legend, the famous bronze statue, the *Colossus of Rhodes*, stood. With us were USS LIND, DD-703 and USS ZELLERS, DD-777. While in port we held open-ship and also hosted a party for orphan children on 18 October. While we were in Rhodes I got the chance to walk the same beach where St. Paul landed in about 60 A.D on his way to Jerusalem.

Our Official Visit to Tripoli

At the end of October, ComDesRon 26, CAPT. E. Higgins, Jr., who was embarked in HARRY E. YARNELL, was named as President Johnson's personal envoy to the Prince of Libya. The lease we had for Wheelus Air Base at Tripoli was due to expire at the end of 1970, and the United States was attempting to extend it. As a result, we had the highest priority on replacement parts and other needs before we made a port call at Tripoli. When we arrived at Tripoli, we fired a 21-gun salute. While in port HARRY E. YARNELL was visited by U.S. Ambassador Edwin A. Lightner, Jr., the governor of Tripoli, the German ambassador to Libya, and the Crown Prince of Libya. We were warned that due to the political situation we should not leave the short main street and also to travel in teams.

Local U.S. citizens who worked for the oil companies had extended invitations to various crewmembers to visit their homes. Senior Chief Kilpatrick and I accepted one such invitation to dinner. A lady, Mrs. Anne Kleckner, picked us up at the ship and told us that her husband was called away to the oil fields, but if we wanted to join her and her children for dinner we would be welcome. We did accept. When we arrived at their home we were being introduced to her three children when a messenger arrived requesting Anne's immediate presence at a medical emergency, as she was the "duty" nurse. Apparently one of the oil company workers had splashed acid in his eyes. Jim and I made ourselves at home and entertained the children until Anne returned. After that we had a lovely dinner and Anne drove us back to the ship. Jackie exchanged letters with Anne for several years thereafter until we lost track of each other as a result of our many relocations.

Return to Sixth Fleet Operations

After our port call and as we were leaving the harbor, I was informed there was a problem with the #3 missile guidance radar. The problem turned out to be an oil leak in a train (rotational) drive motor. Replacing one of these huge electrical motors is normally not a ship's crew's responsibility so we were not trained to do so. However, we had to find out what was wrong and whether or not we could repair it. We managed to jury-rig a block and tackle and then lower the motor. It turned out that an oil seal had actually scored the motor's stainless steel shaft, allowing oil to leak onto the coils, causing them to burn out. A replacement motor had to be air-expressed from the Sperry plant in Lake Success, N.Y. Fortunately we still had the presidential envoy priority for replacement parts and it arrived within a day; it was delivered by helicopter after arriving aboard a carrier via COD (Carrier On-Board Delivery).

For the next week we operated in the Levantini Basin, in the southeastern Med, before making a port visit at Genoa, Italy.

On 3 November, Lydon B. Johnson was elected president in his own right, having completed the term of assassinated President John F. Kennedy.

Visit to Genoa, Italy

When we visited Genoa with USS GEARING, DD-710, from 7 thru 12 November, I managed to get the Sunday off so I went into town with the Chief who had the bunk next to mine. This Chief had a habit of eating whole raw onions! The metal partition between our bunks helped, but not completely.

After we left Genoa we again returned to fleet operations.

Visit to Barcelona, Spain

When we left Genoa we went to the Ceres missile range off Crete and had a successful missile firing exercise. As usual, after a successful missile firing exercise, all hands participated in the joy of our combined efforts. After operating in the Tyrrhenian Sea with the 6th Fleet, including USS FORRESTAL, CVA-59; USS SPRINGFIELD, CLG-7; and others, we proceeded to Puerto de Barcelona, Spain. In Barcelona, we moored at the Darsena National Pier. During this period the Navy had been losing pilot-less helicopters at an alarming rate for no known cause. After I went into town I met a Navy aviator in a bar and we started discussing the problem. Eventually we decided that maybe the helo's blades were hitting small birds. At that we cleared the table and started trying to figure how fast the tips of the blades would be traveling if they hit something in flight. As the night wore on, others joined our discussion, but or brandy-influenced calculations were never completed.

We left Barcelona on 2 December enroute to Naples, Italy.

Visit to Naples, Italy

From 5 thru12 December, we were in Naples, Med-moored to pier Molo Angiono, where the congressman from the 2nd Congressional District of New York paid us a visit. While there, myself and about a dozen other FTs went to a local bar to celebrate our prior successful missile firings. After we got settled in a side room we were inundated by B-Girls. We asked them to leave, but they were persistent in their attempts to have us buy them drinks, leaving me no choice but to speak to the manager. I told him that we were just in to celebrate and did not want to be bothered by the "ladies." I warned him that if the intrusion continued I was leaving with my team. He asked me, "Who the *&%# did I think I was?" I told him, then showed him,…then I told the gang, "We're out of here." We then went to another place where we celebrated in our own style. We left Naples on 8 December, and rejoined the Fleet at sea. We also conducted another missile firing exercise before heading to Cannes.

Visit to Cannes, France

We spent the Christmas and New Year's holiday anchored off Cannes, France. By this time I had reenlisted for another six-year hitch, so I requested and received approval for two-weeks leave. Jackie closed our apartment in Norfolk, went to New York and took a nursing job where she earned enough money to fly to Paris. I took a "Red Eye" train from Nice to meet her there for a delayed honeymoon. I was not familiar with the various classes of service on the French trains so I bought a Third Class ticket. This is the class of service French the peasants used. However it was a very enjoyable night as other passengers kept giving me wine, bread, and cheese. Jackie and I had planned to visit both Paris and Switzerland, but at the last moment before I left the ship I was informed that foreign military personnel were not allowed to wear their uniforms in Switzerland, a neutral country. Because I did not have civilian clothes aboard, I faced quite a dilemma. Finally I asked LCDR Albright if he had anything that I could borrow. He loaned me an old, summer-weight Glen plaid suit that barely fit. However, it served the purpose in Switzerland and Jackie and I had an enjoyable belated honeymoon.

One quiet afternoon there were only four chiefs in the Chief's Mess. The other three, including Senior Chief Kilpatrick, wanted to play bridge but needed a fourth. They asked me to play but I told them I never had and didn't know how. They promised to teach me and not to get mad if I made mistakes. I agreed and sat in as Jim's partner. The first hand I messed up and that was excused. When I messed up the second hand, which I later learned was a potential "Grand Slam," Jim lost his temper and leaped over the table at me. Nothing came of this other than it ended my bridge playing career.

<u>New Year's Eve, 1965</u>

On New Year's Eve we were anchored in the harbor at Cannes, France when Ensign A. R. Taylor wrote the following deck log entry:

Eight bells and all is well
Here on the HARRY E.
Old '64 has gone ashore
'65 is the new arrivee.

There is 105 out the center spout
Down to the ocean floor
We're anchored in sand off the beach of Cannes,
Ten minutes from the shore.

There's one on the line for five minutes time
In case a storm's abrewing,
But we're riding still with a slight evening chill
So we don't expect to be moving.

COMCARDIV FOUR is SOPA once more
With FORRESTAL flying his flag;
He's probably on the beach making a howl and a scream,
As are all but this midwatch stag.

So only 30 days more and we'll see the shore
Norfolk our homeport we agree;
It might not be the best, but we're ready for rest
Every man on the HARRY E.

Valencia, Spain

We left Cannes on 6 January, and again conducted missile firing exercises. From 8 to 16 January we were on ASW Barrier patrol in connection with Operation MEDCANDEX, a joint exercise with Canadian forces. We were on station around Golfo Di Teulada, south of Capo Spartivento, off Sardinia. Our last port of call before returning to Norfolk was the weekend of 16 to 18 January in Valencia, Spain, where we moored to Pier Espigon No. 1 del Turia. While there, another Chief and I were assigned to shore patrol duty. We had orders to report at 1400 hours to the shore patrol officer—a lieutenant off one of the carriers—at Fleet Landing. When we reported he told us that he would not require us until 1800 hours and that we were free to go into town until then. At 1800 we returned to Fleet Landing and assigned our posts. We were assigned the duty of maintaining order and checking sailors attempting to take liquor out to their ships. About 1900 hours the shore patrol officer was relieved by a Marine warrant officer who asked how long we had been on duty. When we told him since 1400, he said that he did not need us and that we were relieved. Now that we were off duty we could enjoy a few hours in town.

While in Valencia, HARRY E. YARNELL was relieved by USS DAHLGREN, DLG-12 and departed the Med.

In 1965, USS TURNER JOY, DD-951, while operating in the Gulf of Thailand, conducted the first-ever naval gunfire support mission on South Vietnam's west coast.

On 20 January, we transited the Straits of Gibraltar in company with USS ZELLERS, DD-777; USS CECIL, DDR-835; USS

189

GEARING, DD-710; USS NORRIS, DD-859; USS BEATY, DD-756; and USS SABINE, AO-25.

Norfolk, Virginia

HARRY E.YARNELL arrived home in Norfolk on 1 February, and LCDR Albright was relieved as Weapons Officer by LCDR Jackson. In early February, I was detailed to RCS Service Corp., Alexandria, Virginia, ostensibly to attend a training class for a new TV system that was being installed in CIC. However, this turned out to be a briefing session for highly classified operations in which HARRY E.YARNELL would be participating. A good part of the next several months was spent preparing for and participating in those classified operations with various units of the Atlantic Fleet.

On 5 February, CAPT Kruchfield relieved CAPT Higgins as COMDESRON 26.

These exercises were designed to test the interoperability of the different types of missile ships, with different types of missiles and different missile guidance radars. In order to effectively carryout the needed research, the majority of the missile ships in the Atlantic Fleet had to operate in close proximity to each other for extended periods of time. Needless to say, this caused COMLANTFLT (Commander, Atlantic Fleet) many days of anxiety as he envisioned another Pearl Harbor; therefore, security was extremely tight. As usual, when conducting missile firings, we had to contend with Russian trawlers in the OpAreas. This testing required us to keep our systems at a high state of readiness while we had civilian engineers making various modifications to different operating parameters. One day, while conducting DSOT, one of the engineers asked me how I knew that a FT at a remote location in the ship was giving me the correct answer for a test measurement. Because we only used four different tests, he thought the FT could memorize the correct answer and not really make the required measurement. I informed him that if I could not trust the FT to give me a correct reading, I could not trust him to adjust the radar in the first place. He never asked me again.

On 15 April, Students for a Democratic Society sponsored the first major anti-Vietnam War rally in Washington, DC.

In Norfolk, on 15 May, a Sunday afternoon, while we were moored outboard of a French destroyer, *Bouvier*; D-624, they extended an invitation to our officers to attend a party with spouses. For some unknown reason, there was no officer available so the Command Duty Officer (CDO) asked me to attend. I informed him that I had the mid-watch on the quarterdeck that evening—but he told me to go anyway. I called Jackie at home and she met me on the pier. We had a great time and Jackie was the hit of the evening. She was crowned with a French sailor hat and awarded the ship's ribbon, which she was instructed to wear like a beauty queen. Eventually we had to leave the party so that I could stand my watch.

Roosevelt Roads and San Juan, Puerto Rico and Miami. Florida

During June, we sailed to Annapolis and embarked some midshipmen on our way to Roosevelt Roads to fire missiles. After the missile shoot we visited San Juan from 18 to 22 June, where we moored at the Fernando Juncos Pier. Following that we spent several days in Miami moored at the Dodge Island Causeway before returning to Norfolk on 2 July.

Miscellaneous Incidents Out of Time Sequence

On another afternoon we were nested outboard of a tender when a new ensign on our ship decided on his own, to test our security detail's response time so he tried to loosen the dogs (latches) on a forward magazine. Unfortunately for him, the armed roving patrol was in a berthing compartment right above the magazine. At that time I just happened to be passing the armory where a gunner's mate was working on a small arm. He handed me a pistol and told me the location of the alarm. When I got there, the roving security patrol was detaining the ensign at gunpoint. He tried to tell me, "good work, the situation is over," but I told him the situation was just beginning and that he was under arrest. I then called the CDO, whose emergency post was on the quarterdeck, and reported the situation. I escorted the ensign to the quarterdeck where the CDO took charge. Meanwhile, when our alarms went off, the tender who had the radio guard for the nest, following protocol radioed Washington that we had a potential nuclear incident. I do not know how this problem was resolved, but undoubtedly due to the seriousness of the incident, the young ensign had quite a bit of explaining to do.

One day we had a visit by an Italian navy captain, the prospective commanding officer of the cruiser GARIBALDI which was being outfitted with Terrier Missile Systems. Using Dynotape, the FTs in the forward missile radar room had named their radar sets "The Pig" and "FUBAR." After I had explained the functions of the various equipment, the captain had one question: "What does FUBAR mean?" I did not know how to explain that it was an acronym for "Fouled Up Beyond all Repair," so I told him that he should know how young sailors are—they make up words.

On 5 July 1965, after standing the 0400-0800 in port Officer of the Deck (OOD) watch in Norfolk, I detached from HARRY E.YARNELL with orders to TERRIER System School at Mare Island, California. My ultimate destination being USS JOUETT, DLG-29, which was under construction in the Puget Sound Naval Shipyard, Bremerton, Washington.

Note

HARRY E. YARNELL continued to operate with the Atlantic Fleet until she was decommissioned in October 1993.

CHAPTER 16: Terrier System School, Mare Island, California, 1965

On 14 December 1964, while HARRY E. YARNELL was in the Med, I had re-enlisted for another 6-year cruise and requested assignment to any new guided missile ship being constructed on the West Coast. As a result, I received orders to USS JOUETT, DLG-29 being built in the Puget Sound Naval Shipyard. Enroute I was to attend seven weeks Terrier Weapons System School at Mare Island, Vallejo, California. Jackie and I decided this would be a good opportunity to see the country, so I took leave and we took our time driving to Mare Island. When we arrived at Vallejo, we found a nice, small apartment in a ten-unit apartment building.

Just before I completed Terrier System School, the Training Officer, LT Walter Carter called me into his office and inquired about my future plans. I immediately noticed my service record was sitting open on his desk and I became a bit suspicious. I told LT Carter that I had orders to JOUETT, whereby he informed me that she was delayed in construction and he asked what I would like to do instead. I told him that I did not care which ship I went to as long as it was new construction scheduled to be home ported on the West Coast. He then informed me that DLG-33 was being built in San Pedro, California and would be the next ship to be commissioned—I readily agreed to a change of orders to FOX.

Two days later LT. Carter again called me into his office and informed me that my change of orders had been approved and that he would be the Firecontrol Officer in FOX. He also informed me that I had my pick of any students currently attending FT School at Mare Island. He encouraged me to select a cadre for my firecontrol division team. Then he let me know that I would be attending a Naval Tactical Data System/Weapons Designation System (NTDS/WDS) Operation course following completion of the Terrier Weapons System course—for another seven weeks of training.

This change of orders put Jackie and me into a financial bind. I had borrowed money for our cross-country trip, thinking that I would receive my travel allowance to pay it back without incurring any interest charges. Now I would not be getting the extra money until FOX was commissioned the following May. In addition, I still had quite a few bachelor debts and Jackie had some student loans to pay off. As a result, our entertainment was limited to an occasional movie, watching high school football games, and attending "demolition derbies." We ate more than our share of hamburgers, hot dogs, and tuna fish during this time. On weekends we would visit the wineries and sample their free wine and snacks. We did go into San Francisco on occasion. One time in particular stands out. That was the Friday evening when I put a quarter into a side pocket to ensure that we would have the necessary toll to get back across the Golden Gate Bridge.

On 15 and 16, October anti-war protests were held in about 40 American cities.

On 3 December 1965, I detached from Mare Island with orders to report to the FOX precommissioning detail in San Pedro. When Jackie and I arrived in Long Beach, we spent several days in an efficiency motel before we moved into a new apartment in North Long Beach.

CHAPTER 17: USS FOX DLG-33: San Diego, California, 1966-'68

FOX'S History

Motto: Faire Sans Dire
("To do without saying" or "Action without words")

USS FOX, DLG-33, was built by Todd Shipyard, San Pedro, California. She was the fifth US Navy ship named FOX and the third to honor Gustavus Vasa Fox, Assistant Secretary of the Navy from 1861 to 1865. The first ship to honor Secretary Fox was Torpedo Boat 13, commissioned in July 1899, and decommissioned in 1916. The second was DD-234, commissioned 17 May 1920. In September 1944, this ship was reclassified as AG-85 and decommissioned 29 November 1945. The third ship to honor Secretary Fox was DLG-33 commissioned on 28 May 1966.

Precommissioning, San Pedro, California

My first view of FOX was quite a nerve-racking experience. When I drove up to the main gate at Todd Shipyard, San Pedro, I asked the security guard where I could park. Instead of directing me to a parking place he ordered me to move my car anywhere where it would not block the gate. At that moment I heard sirens behind me and saw fire engines racing for the gate. I took the hint and moved my car off to the side. I waited in the car—with great apprehension, not knowing what was happening. It turned out that there was a fire in the bos'n locker area of the FOX and apparently no harm was done (at least nothing that was evident at that time).

There were several main differences between FOX and HARRY E. YARNELL. FOX was a "single-ender" in that it only had one missile launcher that was forward of the bridge superstructure. This launcher was loaded from a triple-ring, rotating magazine that held both TERRIER Missiles and ASROCS. Also, instead of having four missile guidance radars, FOX had two. Whereas target detection and target assignment were separate functions in HARRY E. YARNELL, in FOX, the NTDS and WDS were integrated. FOX had a helicopter hanger and helo landing area abaft the after stack. When helos were embarked, they were used primarily for SAR missions. FOX also had a different three-dimensional air search radar, the AN-SPS-48. This radar had beams that were scanned in elevation electronically. It also had a mode called "burn-through" where all the energy could be concentrated in a few beams rather then being scanned. One day we inadvertently had it in this mode and had it set to low elevation. Normally the antenna would be pointed out to sea when

196

operating in this configuration. However, this time it was pointing inland. I do not remember how we found out, but we did erase the computer systems at the Union 76 refinery a few miles from the shipyard. This experience, along with the experience we had with the radar at FT-A Schoo, would be useful when we went to Vietnam in 1967.

Commissioning, Long Beach, California

USS FOX entered naval service as a Guided Missile Destroyer-Leader (DLG)[1] on 28 May 1966. When she was commissioned at the Long Beach Naval Shipyard (LBNSY), our commanding officer was CAPT Robert O. Welander, USN. Captain Welander, from Jamaica, New York, was a graduate of the U.S. Naval Academy, class of 1946 and was a highly qualified destroyerman. During WW II he served in USS HUGH PURVIS, DD-709, and USS CHARLES P. CECIL, DDR-835. Prior to FOX, he commanded USS SEMMES, DDG-18, a TARTAR ship. Our executive officer was LCDR Earl H. Graffam, USN, our Weapons Officer was LCDR Donald G. Todaro, USN and our Firecontrol Officer was LT Walter Carter, USN. At 1409-hours, Captain Welander ordered the XO to "set the watch." Except for the location, the personnel, and the Southern California weather, this ceremony was essentially the same as that of USS HARRY E. YARNELL in 1963. On 30 May, FOX fired a 21-gun salute in honor of Memorial Day. The next day, RADM Zumwalt, COMCRUDESFLOT 7, made an unofficial visit to the ship.[2] FOX was placed in dry dock on 3 June and remained there until the 28th while work was performed on the sonar dome. Then on 4 July, FOX was rigged "dress ship" in commemoration of the signing of the Declaration of Independence.

During July and August we continued out-fitting in the LBNSY and going to sea for various trials and certification of systems. After completing out-fitting on 26 September, FOX got underway for the first time as an active, fully commissioned ship of the U.S. Navy. After going to the NWS, Seal Beach, where we loaded missiles and ammunition, we proceeded to the SoCalOpAreas to test fire missiles and guns. That afternoon we returned to Seal Beach, reloaded ammunition, and the next day headed for our homeport, San Diego.

My return to San Diego for the first time since 1953 was quite a shock. I could hardly believe how much the city had grown in 13 years. Perhaps most surprising of all was that we did not have to moor to a buoy out in the bay—we went directly to the base at 32nd Street. During my previous duty in San Diego aboard SOUTHERLAND, the *El Cortez Hotel* dominated the skyline. Now it could not even be seen. Also, the locker clubs, uniform shops, and most of the bars were gone from Broadway.

The cadre of a firecontrol division that we had picked at Mare Island was supplemented with additional fine sailors and excellent firecontrolmen. Only two shipmates presented us with obstacles to a smooth running firecontrol division. Neither man had ever served aboard a sea-going man-of-war. Both these individuals had spent their entire careers aboard an experimental ship, USS NORTON SOUND, AVM-1. Aboard this ship civilian engineers did all the work. One was a 1st Class Petty Officer who was assigned to several different jobs, but could not do any of them effectively. He eventually solved the problem by having an automobile accident that necessitated a transfer to the hospital. The other was a Chief who later was selected for warrant officer and was transferred shortly after we arrived in WestPac. Another individual who I particularly remember was the junior officer who reported aboard with only a pair of brown shoes—he would paint them with white shoe polish to wear with his white uniforms.

Shakedown Training

During the fall we conducted shakedown exercises, ASW training, and missile firing exercises off the Southern California coast. On 6 October, we had our "official" welcome by

COMCRUDESFLOT 11 as the first ship in the Pacific Fleet capable of launching both anti-submarine rockets (ASROC) and surface-to-air guided missiles from the same launching system.

Puget Sound Operations

In mid-October, we were scheduled to put on a demonstration of our integrated TERRIER/ASROC missile launching system for the Canadian Navy in Puget Sound. On our way there we stopped at NWS, Seal Beach and stayed overnight. Jackie came down from Long Beach that evening, picked me up at the Main Gate, and we went to dinner. After dinner, she dropped me off at the Main Gate and instead of waiting for base transportation, I started to walk down to the ship. The next thing that I knew I was surrounded by Marines and base security personnel. After they "briefed" me on not walking in unauthorized areas, they drove me to the FOX.

On 17 October, FOX moored at the Marginal Pier, NAD, Banger, Washington, and for the next several days we conducted various drills and tests in Dabob Bay, in the Hood Canal area of Puget Sound, near Keyport. On the 19th we were scheduled to make a full power trial run. Our Chief Machinist Mate (MMC) had a gut (intuitive) feeling that there was something wrong with one of the shafts (port side, I think). He recommended to the EO (Engineering Officer) that we abort the full power run; however he could not convince the EO there was anything wrong. Apparently the EO didn't tell the Captain of the Chief's suspicions so we did the run and the Chief was correct, we experienced severe vibrations in the #2 engine. Subsequent inspection revealed the reduction gears were damaged (I believe that the Chief logged his objection to making the run in the Engineering Log).

After leaving Bremerton, FOX conducted various trials in the U.S. Naval Test Range, Carr Inlet, Puget Sound. On 1 November, we moored to Centennial Pier 20 D, Vancouver, British Columbia. On the 3rd, we were on the Nanoose Underwater Weapons Range in British Columbia, for acoustic trials, self-noise tests, and torpedo firing tests. When these were completed, FOX returned to Vancouver in the evening. Then on 4 November, we tried to demonstrate our ASROC firing capability, but had a malfunction in the firing circuit from the Sonar Switchboard to the Weapons Control switchboard. Having two different divisions responsible for checking the same system (the combined missile and ASROC launcher) was a new experience for all of us, and the Weapons Officer had an administrative problem keeping both the Firecontrol Officer and the ASW Officer happy.

A heavy vibration was felt in the fantail as we were leaving the missile range. It was believed we must have struck some underwater object since Puget sound is infamous for partially submerged logs. On the 5th, we set course for San Diego, and after arriving in San Diego divers went down and found the starboard propeller had been damaged.

Early in November, a heavy oil-filled cooling unit failed in one of the missile guidance radars and a new unit was ordered. Shortly after the unit was delivered aboard ship, I noticed the radar crew standing around, not doing much about installing the replacement unit. When I asked why the unit was not being replaced the crew told me they were waiting for a block and tackle. Jokingly, I told them they should be able to lift it into place. The wisecrack was incentive enough for them to challenge *me* to position the unit in its proper place. I had lifted the unit about three inches off the deck when I actually heard and felt something snap in my lower abdomen. As a result, later in the month I wound up in the Balboa Naval Hospital with a severe left-side hernia and undoubtedly learned a valuable lesson.

Two days after my operation I was assigned duty as a parking lot monitor for the maternity ward. It was raining and as a result I contracted pneumonia and wound up back in bed. While I was on this duty I had the occasion to meet Mrs. Lewis B. Puller, wife of LT GEN "Chesty" Puller, the commander of the 1st Marine Division during the Korean War. General Puller was in the hospital and she was visiting. One evening I was in bed with an IV running into my left arm when Jackie showed up for a visit. She took one look at my arm and realized that the IV had infiltrated. She reported this to the charge nurse and had them re-do the IV. Meanwhile, she attended to other patients on the ward. Jackie would work a full nursing shift at a hospital in Long Beach and than drive down to Balboa. Attending to other patients, giving them back rubs, and attending to other care needs, became routine whenever she visited.

One day the Chief of Staff and the Head of Surgery had all the surgery patients line up for inspection. Of course, we were all naked as jay birds. When they stopped in front of me, the Chief of Staff exclaimed, "Who did THAT?" The Head of Surgery then replied something to the effect that, "You don't have to worry, he's been transferred." The hospital wanted to keep me until after the New Year, but I requested Captain Welander contact them and demand my release.

Missile Firing Qualifications

When Captain Welander reported to the precommissioning detail at Todd Shipyard, we made a bet on our Ship Qualification Test (SQT) missile firings. He promised to buy F-Division a case of beer for each successful firing. These missile firings took place in mid-December and FOX had 15 out of 16 successes, the last being a proven missile failure. However, I was in the hospital at the time so I did not get to see any of the firings. In spite of our noteworthy accomplishments, we never had a chance to collect any of the beer we won—our pace of operations never slowed enough for us to have a beer party.

That spring, the earlier fire in the bow came back to cause us many problems. In order to align (collimate) the radar's tracking and guidance beams, we had to radiate energy from the radar into a feed horn mounted on the bow. From there it would be transmitted via coax cable under the deck to test equipment in the Missile House.

One day the test setup was not working and after running some tests, we concluded that the connection from the feed horn to the coax must be defective. I had to crawl through the small openings in about fifteen "frames" (the ship's "ribs") in order to reach the connection. This entailed lying flat on my stomach with my arms stretched out in front of me, pushing tools and test equipment ahead and then pulling myself forward. When I got to the connection I found it to be corroded apparently from the water that was used to put out the fire back in the shipyard. After I replaced the connector I reversed my method for reaching the connection—backing out feet first through the ship's ribs.

One day I went down to the radar room where the crew was having a friendly, non-technical argument. When I showed, up one of the crew said, "There's the Chief, ask him." I do not remember the details, but I settled the argument, against the leading petty officer's point of view. He was a little miffed and told me, "Chief, the only difference between you and us is time." I have always remembered this admonishment when my head tended to get a little large.

On 23 December 1966, USS O'BRIEN, DD-725, was hit by shells from a North Vietnamese shore battery located to the north of Dong Hoi. This was the first direct hit inflicted on a US naval vessel during the Vietnam conflict.

New Year's Eve, 1967

On New Year's Eve, 1967, LT D. A. Brown wrote the traditional Deck Log entry in prose as follows:

Ahoy! You landlubbers, all based ashore
Take a look along Pier four
Feast your eyes of Baby Blue
Upon FOX, moored port side to.
See her missiles, all shiny and bright
And the big Thirty-Three, under the light.

Count the lines from one to six
Holding her snug at Berth Forty-six.
She's steaming on a boiler called Number Four
With smoke free macks, to protect the shore.
And down below—away out of sight
Number Three and Four Generators, provide the lights.
She is receiving supplies from the pier,
In the form of fresh water—not frosty cold beer.
For they with the watch—duty did call
While all of their shipmates are having a ball.
But thanks to a company that's called A.T. & T.,
Phone calls are made to their families.
The FOX is but one in three in a nest,
The KING and the WORDEN are nestled abreast.
The Senior Officer Present Afloat
Who looks over all of these ships and their boats,
Is located in the cruiser SAINT PAUL,
COMFIRSTFLT by name, that's known to all.
So now that you landlubbers all know the score,
Wander on back to your billets ashore.
Rest easy in bed and calm all your rears,
The mighty Grey FOX stands vigil here.
The man in charge is the O.O.D.,
"Mays" by name—an ETC
He's assisted by "SPIELMAN"—a DS2
Whose lonely job is protecting you.
There's one more man, who is running the show,
LT. E.P. JONES—the C.D.O.
Now that I've told you all of our might,
HAPPY NEW YEAR to All, and to all a good night.

Operational Training

FOX spent the period from 3 January until 18 March in the LBNSY, conducting various tests off the California coast. After this shipyard period, FOX returned to San Diego and entered a period of extensive training, both inport and underway. This training included gunnery firings, engineering casualty drills, ASW exercises, and missile firings. All this training culminated in a simulated "Battle Problem" where observers scored FOX and her crew in all areas of operations.

On 15 April, massive demonstrations against the Vietnam War were held throughout the US. Protesters in New York's Central Park burned about 200 draft cards.

A military coup occurred in Greece on 21 April. In response, the America CVBG was immediately dispatched to the Ionian Sea. Two amphibious groups were included in the contingency task force.

On 13 May, we held a Family Cruise out of San Diego. During this cruise I was showing Jackie our new version missile control system and explaining how it was upgraded from what she saw in HARRY E. YARNELL. About the time Captain Welander joined us, I was paged over the general announcing system, requesting I attend to some minor problem. Captain Welander told me to attend to the page, and that he would continue to escort Jackie. As he was explaining how the missiles were ordered loaded, she said something to the effect of, "Is this how it's done? Without hesitation she pushed the appropriate buttons to load the missile. Fortunately all that were loaded were T-SAMs (dummy training rounds). Needless to say, Captain Welander was greatly surprised. Jackie then asked Captain Welander where she could use a restroom. He told her to use the one in his sea cabin. While there, she picked up the voice tube and called out, "Guess who's in the Captain's head," not knowing this would be broadcast throughout the ship.

WestPac Cruise, 1967

On 5 June, Israel unleashed the Six-Day War against Egypt, Syria, and Jordan.

On 7 June, two days after the start of the so-called "Six-Day Arab-Israeli War," FOX deployed from San Diego for the Far East. On our way to WestPac we stopped in Pearl Harbor where we conducted gunnery and ASW exercises.

On 8 June, an American ship, USS LIBERTY, AGTR-5, was off the coast of the Sanai Peninsular in international waters of the Mediterranean Sea, collecting electronic intelligence and monitoring the course of the Arab-Israeli war. In an unprovoked attack by the Israelis, 34 U.S. Navymen lost their lives and 172 were wounded. Israel later apologized for the "mistaken identity" attack.

When FOX stopped in Hawaii, another FT Chief, Jim Culpepper and I, rented a car and decided to drive across the top of the island. After driving several miles down a single lane trail we encountered four ladies who were trying the same stunt. Only they could not go any further—there was a deep ditch across the lane in front of them, and there was no room to turn either car around. I backed ours up for about a half mile while Chief Culpepper backed out the ladies' car. After a few minutes of conversation I learned that one of the ladies knew my younger sister from when she worked in an insurance company in New York—small world.

After leaving Pearl Harbor on the 17th, FOX steamed west to Yokosuka. Before we left, we had contacted Hanna Barbera, of animated comic's fame, requesting permission to use their copyrighted character, Quickdraw McDraw as our mascot since the voice radio code name for FOX was "Quickdraw—and the music, "Tally Ho, the Fox." Hanna Barbera granted their permission so we had a large pennant made with the Quickdraw character on it and had a tape with the music. Thereafter, every time we went alongside a replenishment ship, an oiler, stores ship, or ammunition ship, when we broke away we would unfurl the banner from the foretop, play "Tally Ho, the FOX" over the topside speakers, and break away rapidly and smartly.

We arrived in Yokosuka on the 26th, and after a brief one day visit we got underway enroute to the Subic Bay Naval Repair Facility, in the Philippines, where we stayed for two days before heading to Vietnam and the Tonkin Gulf.

Olongapo City and Bagio

Just outside the Naval Base at Subic Bay in the Philippines is Olongapo City, the place where sailors and marines with the 7th Fleet went for liberty when their ships needed maintenance. The Navy made attempts to keep ship movements secret, but somehow every bar and club would know when a ship was due to arrive. Several times while in Subic Bay I pulled Shore Patrol on the Naval Base side of a small bridge over the Olongapo River. This river ran just outside of the main gate and the local inhabitants used it for bathing, cooking, drinking, and raw sewage. The river (or was it a drainage channel?) must have been one of the filthiest rivers in the world with all sorts of excrement, garbage, dead animals, and trash floating in it. CDR Nichols referred to Olongapo as a "pest-ridden mud hole [where] everything…was cheap: booze, floozies, and room and board."[3] The sailors called it the "armpit of the earth." Once a sailor crossed the bridge going on liberty, he would be subjected to street begging urchins, pickpockets, hookers, and every variety of con artist imaginable. Young children would dive from small boats into the river to retrieve coins that sailors would throw from the bridge. Standing Shore Patrol at the bridge during the evening was quite a demanding task when drunken sailors would come back and fight for the limited number of base cabs to take them to their ships.

Other than making visits to the Navy Exchange, for the most part I avoided going on liberty while in Subic. Most of my free time was spent in the CPO club on the base drinking and playing slot machines. However, in August I did manage to get up to Bagio for several days of R&R. We went there by way of bus during a Monsoon-like rain storm. The route followed the same route as the infamous "Bataan Death March" of WW II. As the bus climbed up past Clark Air Force Base, we could watch rocks as big as human heads floating down the roadside! Bagio was a typical golf resort with a huge, low-slung hotel where we each had our own room. However, due to the weather, there was not much to do but read or hang out in the bar. One afternoon, "Curly," one of the chiefs, left to visit the head. We thought nothing of this until we heard him scream when we went running to his aid. It turned out the commode had one of those old-fashioned flushing tanks mounted high on the wall. Curly had been trying to flush when a back pressure shot all the contents out of the bowl and all over him. We all had a good laugh before getting him hosed off.

Tonkin Gulf Duty

While deployed to WESPAC, in addition to conducting various training exercises, FOX supported the Vietnam conflict. Our primary station was off the coast of North Vietnam (NVN) as the northern Tonkin Gulf search and rescue ship. Our secondary mission was to control carrier-launched combat aircraft at PIRAZ (Positive Identification Radar Advisory Zone). PIRAZ was a picket station about 100 miles north of the carrier task force on "Yankee Station"[4] and about 20 miles south of Hanoi. As such, we were part of the so-called "Tonkin Gulf Yacht Club." The ship that was on PIRAZ duty was known as RED CROWN and had to stay in the vicinity of a buoy marking the station.

FOX took over PIRAZ duties from USS WAINWRIGHT, DLG-28, on 7 July. While the transfer was being made, USS POTERFIELD, DD-682 stood by as a gun ship. In her capacity as RED CROWN, FOX maintained constant radar and visual surveillance of the Tonkin Gulf and adjoining coasts for the purpose of identifying all aircraft in the zone and vectoring defensive forces to the interception of any possible airborne enemy intruders. Because of the relative immobility necessary to those duties, FOX also served as a reference point to guide American strike aircraft to their targets ashore. Since her duties afforded her a continual picture of the events occurring in the air over the zone, she also served as a base for SAR helicopters. The lessons the Navy learned during PIRAZ operations were put to good use in the design and development of the next generation of destroyers and cruisers, the so-called Aegis ships

The night of 11 July, our first night in the Tonkin Gulf was quite unnerving. Our surface search radar detected what we thought could be NVN motor torpedo boats. FOX went to GQ and tried to identify these "contacts," but was unable to do so. We tried to confirm them using other radars, again without success. After an hour or more of trying to evaluate these "contacts," everyone's nerves were getting extremely tense. About that time the junior FTC declared, "Those aren't real targets." Captain Welander demanded to know what he based this unsolicited opinion on. Never having been in a similar situation, the FTC had to retract his opinion. Eventually Captain Welander decided they were false contacts and we stood down from GQ. The next two nights we also tracked unidentified radar contacts, but these returned to land.

On the 18th, we sighted an unidentified object in the water and put a swimmer over the side to retrieve it. It turned out to be a piece of hard foam rubber. Putting a swimmer in the water was an unusual occurrence, but when necessary it was either a member of the deck force or a damage controlman, depending on the circumstances. On the 20th our helo picked up a downed pilot and bought him aboard. On the 21st, we sighted a Russian trawler, GIDROFON, a VODA—class ship. On 29 July, fire broke out aboard the USS FORRESTAL CVA-59 on "Yankee Station." FOX transferred some damage control personnel to FORRESTAL to assist with this emergency.[5]

While FOX was on station, all the Firecontrol Chiefs and Gunner's Mate Chiefs stood their watches in the Weapons Control Area of CIC. When things were quiet, I had time to converse with the various officers, both on watch and just visiting in CIC. These conversations were sometimes technical and many times philosophical; I owe a great deal to these gentlemen and their conversation for making me realize what I was lacking in my education. Although I was an avid reader, most of the materials were not very uplifting or educational. Although I had extensive technical training, I was sadly lacking in the liberal arts.

There were several times we had North Vietnamese MiGs[6] come out to test FOX. They would stay at what they thought was missile range and circle around. We would designate the firecontrol radar to try to lock on to them, but as soon as they saw the C-band transmitters on their threat receivers, they would dive for the deck and we would lose the on search radar and firecontrol radar. It is probably a good thing they did not know that at the time. However, they did appear to be well versed in the "Rules of Engagement" that specified we could not fire unless under direct attack. At other times the North Vietnamese would illuminate us with their firecontrol radar. When they did this, we would depress the height finding radar, train it on them, and put it in "burn through" mode. This concentrated high energy would burn out the crystals in their radar's receiver front ends and they would shut down. This is where the knowledge from FT-A School and experience with our height finding radar in Todd Shipyard proved useful.

Subic Bay and Manila

On 12 August, FOX was relieved on PIRAZ station by WAINWRIGHT and returned to Subic Bay. Enroute we conducted dual-ship attack drills with USS CUSK, AGSS-348. We arrived in Subic on the 14th, where a marker buoy was caught under the stern with no apparent damage. When conditions permitted, I would visit the CPO club and play the slot machines and have a few cold beers. On the 26th, we were visited by RADM Combs, COMCRUDESGRU 7th Fleet. Then on the 30th, a sailor who was absent without authorization, attempted to swim to the ship undetected. However, he was spotted and picked up by USS MISPELLION, AO-105. Before returning to the Tonkin Gulf, we spent several days in Manila where we moored to South Harbor Pier 13.

On 7 September, FOX again relieved WAINWRIGHT and assumed PIRAZ duties. On the 10th, our helo recovered another pilot who had ejected from his A-4 after a flame out. FOX was relived off PIRAZ Station on 14 October, by USS BELKNAP, DLG-26, and returned to Subic Bay where on the 21st, CDR William A. Lamm, USN, relieved CDR Graffam as executive officer. CDR Graffam detached to report as Prospective Commanding Officer of USS SCHOFIELD DDG-3. When we arrived in Subic Bay, the Chiefs were entertaining Captain Welander in the Chief's Club when our Chief Boilertender (BTC) arrived and informed the Captain that "The part for the boiler just arrived." The CO asked "What part?" Apparently he had not been informed that one boiler was out of commission and not available. That boiler provided the last 15% of the ship's speed.

Between 21 and 23 October, 50,000 people demonstrate in Washington, DC against the war.

We departed Subic on 22 October, for Da Nang, Vietnam. USS BUCK, DD-761 accompanied us. On a normal day FOX monitored the activity of up to 200 Navy and Air Force missions over Vietnam. On the 23rd, a FOX air controller directed two F-4 fighters from USS CONSTELLATION, CVA-64, to intercept and subsequently kill a North Vietnamese MIG-21 aircraft over Hanoi. It was the first time during the Vietnam War a shipboard controller had directed an intercept that resulted in a shootdown of enemy aircraft. I will let the words of the Tactical Action Officer in CIC tell the story:

> There were actually two separate shoot-downs as I recall, spaced about two days apart. Scenario went something like this:
>
> MIGs from Phuc Ycn airfield (we couldn't hit Phuc Yen because it was "off limits") outside Hanoi were specializing in jumping our Air Force attack aircraft returning to Thailand after strikes on downtown Hanoi. The MIGs would scramble about the time the raid was over, and intercept our guys while we were low on fuel

& headed home. Capt Welander proposed to OTC [Officer in Tactical Command] a scheme to beat the [NVN] at their own game, and received permission to execute the plan.

On strike days which were thought to be likely Phuc Yen MIG activity days, we orbited a flight of two F-4s in an area away from the return route of our aircraft and away from the notice of the gooks. We kept the F-4s topped up with fuel by using tankers. We manned CIC and controlled the "bar-cap" from FOX. One day (date not certain in my mind, though I was the CDO in CIC during the action) the MIGs took the bait. They scrambled to position themselves between our returning attack aircraft and the Thailand airfield, planning once again to pick off some of our guys. They didn't notice that our controller was vectoring our F-4s into a cutoff position on them, and by the time the MIGs wised up we had lock-on and the F-4s launched sidewinders at the MIGs. FOX's CIC speakers had the F-4's frequency piped in, and we all heard the report "splash one MIG". The place went crazy. Capt Welander & our Exec were both in CIC along with the rest of the team during the action.

I believe it was about two days later that the game played out again, with almost identical results, splashing one more MIG. [As] I recall, one missile ran hot under the wing of one of our F-4s and caused the flight crew to pop out. We recovered them but lost the F-4. In any event, that engagement ended the gooks little strategy of trying to pick off our returning Thailand-based strike aircraft as we continued to mount our bar-cap waiting for our next shot.

I'm about 90% certain that the first engagement was the first time since at least the Korean War that Navy

211

ship-based air controllers had vectored friendly fighters into an engagement that resulted in the shooting
down of enemy aircraft. I also believe we were
awarded the PUC for the action. Couldn't buy a drink
at the Cubi Point O Club after that as the airdales kept
FOX guys in booze for the rest of our tour.[7]

For this action FOX was awarded the Meritorious Unit Citation. On the 24th, FOX and BUCK left Da Nang for the North SAR
station where we relieved USS KING, DLG-10, off PIRAZ duty.

Before our first tour on Yankee Station, we received onboard a
contingent of intelligence personnel. They had their own working
compartment and stayed to themselves all the time they were aboard.
On 28 October, our air search radar detected an unknown, high-flying,
high-speed contact heading towards us from the northeast, from over
China. We went to GQ and attempted to identify this aircraft. When
we could not we locked on to it with our missile tracking and guidance radars. Just before the contact reached the "Fire" decision range,
the Intelligence Officer (IO), a lieutenant, walked in and told the Captain, "Don't fire." When the CO asked for clarification the IO only
replied, "I said, 'Don't fire.'" Then he turned and walked out. A short
time later the aircraft landed on the Yankee Station aircraft carrier.

On 7 November, we were visited by RADM Freeman,
COMCRUDESPAC. While out on PIRAZ we encountered a problem
in the missile system where every time we loaded a T-SAM on the
starboard launcher rail and assigned the launcher, the computer-
generated missile orders would go haywire. After troubleshooting the
problem, we determined the problem had to be in the T-SAM, but had
no way to prove it as our magazines were fully loaded and we could
not swap T-SAMS. On 12 November, a young civilian engineer from
the company that made the missile simulator visited FOX to assist in
solving this problem, but he was of no assistance and left. I came up
with what I considered a foolproof plan, sold it to LT Carter, the Firecontrol Officer, then to LCDR Todaro, the Weapons Officer, and finally to Captain Welander who was sitting in his chair on the bridge.

212

M from Miss. Fox's father wanting to know what
daughter. I told him that I did not know where she
was sure she was in good hands. Eventually the sailor
d as the date returned to Australia and married Miss.
Fox.

The next day I had the chance to go into town with another chief. We met some people and were invited to an American expatriates club where we played darts and, in general had a great time.

On the 29th, we left Sydney with a course set for Wellington, New Zealand. Three of our shipmates were absent, having gone having missed movement. As we left port we fired a 21-round salute.

Wilmington, New Zealand

We arrived at Wellington on 2 December, and fired a 21-gun salute. While temporally anchored out, we had to contend with small boats carrying protesters who believed that we had nuclear weapons aboard. We had to constantly warn them away from the ship and occasionally had to use high-pressure fire hoses to keep them away. Eventually FOX moored in Berth One, Queen's Wharf. I had the duty on Saturday, but was able to go ashore on Sunday. While waiting for a bus to take us in to town another chief and myself were offered a ride by a couple of New Zealand Air Force personnel. They told us that we did not want to go into town since everything was closed on Sunday and offered to take us to their club on their air base. We had an enjoyable visit there, drinking, swapping war stories, and playing darts.

Right after we left Wellington on the 6th, two stowaway girls who came on board the last day in port, were discovered hiding beneath the deck plates in an air-conditioning machinery room. FOX was clear of the port, with a course set for Tonga, when they were discovered. We turned about, and were met by a Wellington pilot boat just outside of the harbor. Two New Zealand policemen came aboard and the girls were taken off and the sailors responsible got busted. One of the guys had been a first class petty officer when we left the states; he lost a stripe in the Philippines, and lost another before arriving in San Diego. He also had 60 days restriction, and was visited every night by his wife who stood by him. What a sea story he must have told her![8]

Tonga

When we arrived at Nuku'alofa, Tonga, on the 9th, we first presented a 21-gun salute, which was returned. We then anchored near the Queen Salote Wharf. It was the birthday of Queen Salote Tubou, III, so they put on a huge outdoor luau for us. I have never seen so many different kinds of fresh fruit and fish! We departed Tonga on the 11th, bound for Pago Pago, Tutuila Island, American Samoa.

Pago Pago, Tutuila Island, American Samoa

Enroute from Tonga to Pago Pago, the lookouts observed a small column of smoke on the horizon. Nothing could be detected on the surface search radar, so we attempted to identify a contact with the fire control radar, but without success. We evaluated this as a "possible volcano." Three days later a small island had emerged from the sea. After spending the day in Pago Pago, FOX sailed to return to our homeport of San Diego.

Miscellaneous Incidents Out of Time Sequence

Like in HARRY E. YARNELL, it was normal routine for us to run DSOT every morning before breakfast. These normally took about a half-hour to run after all stations were manned and ready. I had been training the junior Chief Firecontrolman off the experimental ship in the proper procedures for running the tests. One morning I finally left him in charge and went down to the Chief's Mess for morning coffee. When I walked in the other Chiefs were surprised to see me so early and wanted to know why I was not running my morning tests, so I explained. A few minutes later I heard the door open behind me and saw a questioning look on the other Chief's faces. When I turned around I saw the other FTC. He had encountered a problem in one of the elements of the system while running the test, and instead of bypassing the problem and continuing the test, he secured the crew! As soon as he secured them they all went off for breakfast and it was a hard task to get the stations remanned in order to complete the DSOT. In May, our Height Finding Radar Chief was advanced to Senior Chief; I missed quota, and therefore, was not advanced. As a result, I requested a transfer to another TERRIER ship; instead the new Senior Chief was transferred to shore duty.

One day the Carrier Air Group Commander (CAG) paid us a visit to observe our operations. As I toured him through the Weapons Control Area of CIC, he asked me what our main worry was on PIRAZ. I answered that it was friendly aircraft that return from in-country over North Vietnam without turning on their IFF (Identification Friend or Foe). He asked why and I told him that some day we might shoot down one of his aircraft. At that he informed me that his aircraft were not worried about our missiles. I knew they had missile detectors and could take evasive action if a missile was detected. I then let him know that procedure was to fire two missiles and that his aircraft could not maneuver fast enough to avoid the second. He promised that he would ensure the pilots were aware of this situation. Incidentally, firing two surface-to-air (SAM) missiles was also NVN protocol.

From 1967 to 1969, Bob Woodward served as the communications officer in FOX. Later he became an investigative reporter for the *Washington Post* where, teaming with Carl Bernstein, they first cracked the so-called "Watergate Scandal" that led to President Nixon's resignation in 1974. He later wrote the best-selling account of the Watergate break-in, *All the President's Men*.

San Diego Area 1968

After leaving Pago Pago, FOX steamed directly to San Diego where we arrived on 20 December. This return crossing was one of the smoothest that I have ever experienced. When we moored along-side PRAIRIE at the Naval Station, the three sailors who missed the ship in Sydney were returned.

On 26 January 1968, North Korean naval forces seized the USS Pueblo (AGER-2) on the high seas. The crew was held in captiv-ity in North Korea until December. The commanding officer was CDR Lloyd Bucher, USN. One sailor was killed and nine crewmen were injured including one marine.

FOX remained in port until 19 February, when we resumed underway training. As we got underway, we accidentally scraped the bow of USS COONTZ, DLG-10. Neither vessel sustained any seri-ous damage. Late in 1967, FOX had been selected as the test and evaluation ship for the Navy's upgraded, long-range Standard Missile (SM)^9 and an evaluation of new ECM capabilities. As a result, in January 1968, some senior FTs and I flew to Mare Island to learn the operation of the new ECM features. I had submitted an application for warrant officer (WO), and while at Mare Island, BuPers (the Bu-reau of Naval Personnel) requested that command interviews and rec-ommendations be expedited. The staff at Mare Island did not person-ally know me, therefore, all they could do is submit a neutral recom-mendation and I was not selected.

When we entered Anaheim Bay to load missiles at the NWS, Seal Beach on the 28th, there was a disagreement between Captain Welander and the Harbor Pilot with regard to the handling of the ship. The Pilot insisted he was quite capable of handling FOX and that he had the responsibility to do so. The Pilot had two tugs made up alongside: one on the port bow and the other on the port quarter. It turned out that he was not as capable as he thought as he buried the ship's bow about 12 to 15 feet into the reinforced concrete wharf. Captain Welander had taken the conn away from the Pilot and ordered

217

all engines back full, but it was too late—the ship had too much headway. This left a gaping hole in the pier that soon took on the unofficial name of "The FOX Hole."

Jackie had driven to the Weapons Station to pick me up for dinner. When she asked the gate guard where the FOX was berthed he replied, "*In* the pier." She then asked, "Don't you mean *at* the pier?" Again he told her, "No, *in* the pier."

Fortunately the damage was not as extensive as it could have been. The bulbous sonar dome under the bow was undamaged. Some of the shell plating was gashed in and some frames, webbing, and bulkheads were torn in the forward part of the ship. However, there was extensive damage to the side plating, the frames, webbing, and bulkheads in the bow. After off-loading ammunition, FOX proceeded to the LBNSY where we had temporary repairs made and our missile systems upgraded.

After temporary repairs were made to the bow, FOX left the LBNSY on the 4th and then spent several weeks in and out of San Diego and on the Pacific Missile Range test firing the new version Standard Missiles. Our missile systems were kept in perfect working order for the entire period of the tests. I have to give thanks to a hard working FT Gang for this accomplishment.

One evening in San Diego I was assisting NSMSES engineers to resolve a complex technical problem in a highly classified part of the missile system. At about 11 P.M. we decided we were not making any progress and resolved we would tackle the problem again in the morning. Due to the lateness of the hour, the NSMSES people decided the only place to get something to eat would be in Tijuana, Mexico and "convinced" me to go with them. While there, one of the engineers and I both had a simultaneous "Eureka" revelation pertaining to the cause of the problem. Of course, we could not discuss it in the bar, but we could draw cryptic diagrams and write notes on scraps of paper. The next day we tried our solution and it solved the problem.

While in port it was normal practice to stow the missile guidance radars oriented fore and aft and at about a 35-degree angle relative to the main deck. This provided a clean line from the main deck, up over the pilothouse and over the radar antennas. When we wanted to radiate we would turn the antenna on its back, pointing directly overhead so there was no threat from the high power radiation. For morning quarters, F-Division mustered on the starboard side of the forecastle. One morning the XO wanted an all-hands muster. However, we were getting ready to go to sea to fire missiles and the radar systems had to be checked out. I arranged with LT Carter to excuse a couple of FTs to work on the radar, contrary to the order for "all hands" muster. I told the FTs to leave the antenna in the stow position. As the XO was conducting Officer's Call on the port side, a sea gull apparently flew into the radar beam, was cooked like in a microwave, and fell at the XO's feet! Everyone knew our situation, so the circumstances surrounding the unfortunate demise of the seagull were discreetly ignored.

In 1967, I had received orders to report for instructor duty at the Guided Missile School, Mare Island, Vallejo, California. However, I asked LT Carter if there was anyway that I could get these orders changed to the U.S. Naval Ship Missile Systems Engineering Station (NSMSES), Port Hueneme, California. Captain Welander requested that I be retained onboard FOX for the duration of the standard missile tests and recommended that I then be transferred to NSMSES. CAPT Wayne. E. Meyer, Commanding Officer, NSMSES, endorsed my request and my orders were so changed.[10] In July, I was detached from FOX to report to NSMSES.

On 28 May, FOX's second anniversary, CAPT Marshall D. Ward relieved Captain Welander in San Diego. Captain Ward had destroyer experience in USS HOLDER, DD-819; on the staff of COMDESRON THIRTY; in USS NORFOLK, DL-1; and as commanding officer of USS JOSEPH K. TAUSSIG, DE-1030 and USS BARRY, DD-933. On 5 June, as we continued test firing missiles, a shipmate had to be airlifted off the ship by helo to go on emergency leave. Normally this action is only taken in the case of the death of a close family member.

While we were on the range conducting missile firings the exercises were frequently delayed due to unauthorized vessels, or aircraft, being in the restricted area. For example, on the 15th a merchant vessel, SS MANILLA, sailed into the missile firing path and the exercise was secured. FOX overtook her and, via bullhorn, told her to clear the area on course 160 at maximum speed for one hour. We also gave her a message that she was a "Master Menace to Navigation" and [would] be reported to [the] Maritime Commission and to the Philippine Consul General in Los Angeles. We received no reply to the message, but the vessel moved out of the area without incident. We completed test firings of the SM prior to July 4th.

Note

FOX continued to operate with the Pacific Fleet until she was decommissioned in 1994.

CHAPTER 18: USNSMES: Port Hueneme, California, 1968-'70

I reported on board U.S. Naval Ship Missile Systems Engineering Station (NSMSES) Port Hueneme, California in July 1968, and while there I served as TERRIER System Chief on the staff of CDR Bart Della Mura (Code 4400). At this time Jackie and I were still living in Long Beach. She had established her nursing career in a Long Beach hospital and, after some discussion, we decided it would be best if I obtained quarters in Port Hueneme and commuted to Long Beach when ever possible.

NSMSES was a tenant command aboard the Navy's Seabee Base at Port Hueneme and consequently did not have appropriate quarters for Chief Petty Officers. To accommodate us the Navy leased efficiency apartments in a local motel. We shared these units, two Chiefs to a unit. Shortly after moving in, I went out and bought myself a six-pack of 16-ounce beers. I drank one while watching the evening news on TV, then went to bed leaving the remaining five in the refrigerator. When I got up in the morning, all the cans were gone. That is when I realized that my roommate had a serious drinking problem. As it turned out he also had problems with the San Diego County Sheriff regarding his ex-wife. Shortly thereafter he was transferred.

My duties at NSMSES included providing technical assistance to the Weapons System Integration Division, providing interface support to the Ships Qualification Assistance Teams (SQAT), consulting with and advising the civilian system engineers, researching Discrepancy Action Reports, as well as normal staff duties.

During the spring and summer of 1969, I was assigned as assistant project officer, working with one of the civilian project engineers on an investigative project to improve the threat reaction time of missile ships.[1] This involved installing experimental equipment throughout the test ship, USS JOUETT, DLG-29, the ship to which I had been assigned prior to the change in my orders that directed me to FOX. My specific task was to ensure the ship's company had their missile systems functioning normally and ready to support the testing. One Monday, the civilian Project Engineer met me in Long Beach and we drove to San Diego where we boarded JOUETT for a week of testing. That Friday afternoon, after testing was completed, JOUETT put into Port Hueneme and the NSMSES Team left the ship. However, I had boarded in San Diego and when I turned in my expense report the computer system could not reconcile the fact my POV (privately owned automobile) was in San Diego. Eventually it took a senior manager to work out a solution.

On 2 June 1969, USS FRANK E. EVANS, DD-754, was cut in half by the Australian aircraft carrier MELBOURNE, R21, while participating in SEATO (South East Asia Treaty Organization) naval exercises in the South China Sea. FRANK E. EVANS lost 74 destroyermen.

On 5 June, Attorney General Robert F. Kennedy was assassinated in Los Angeles.

Retirement and College

In October 1969, Jackie and I bought a house in Huntington Beach, California and I would commute from there to Port Hueneme on Wednesdays and weekends. This was normally a two and one-half hour drive.

On 5 November1969, Richard M. Nixon was elected as the 37th president of the United States after campaigning on the theme of "Bring us together." Later in November he gave his so-called "Silent Majority" speech where he outlined his plan to get the Unites States out of Vietnam "with honor."

On 15 November, 250,000 people demonstrated in Washington, DC against the Vietnam War.

While at NSMSES, I started taking courses at Ventura College and put in my request for transfer to the Fleet Reserve. This was approved, so in November I interviewed for admission to California State College, Long Beach.[2] I guess I was somewhat naive—I went to the interview in uniform—and received many anti-military taunts from the students on campus. Clearly I must have impressed the counselor with my academic record as I was readily admitted with junior class status. However, I was advised to complete my California State core requirements at a junior college before matriculating at the four-year college.

Following the announcement of my pending retirement, I suddenly found out that I had more friends than I realized. From time to time the resident civilian contractor engineers would stop by my office and ask, "Are you free at noon? My boss is in town and we'd like to take you to lunch." During lunch there would be thinly veiled job offers—all of which I turned down. One day the head of the TERRIER Systems Division, made me a verbal offer of a GS-12 rating to work in his shop following my retirement. I thought this was acceptable and told him so. A few days later he told me that they could not offer me anything higher than GS-11 without a bachelor's degree. This reinforced my determination to attend school full-time. After consultation with Jackie, we agreed that I would do so. We agreed that with her nursing salary, my retirement and G.I. Bill payments, we could make our financial ends meet.

On 15 January 1970, I transferred to the Fleet Reserve, thus ending my 20-year cruise with the U.S. Navy. My retirement ceremony was a very emotional affair as I had quite a bit of anxiety about the future. The Navy had been the major part of my life ever since I was seventeen years old and now I felt like I was being cut adrift and I had little idea of what I would have to face in the future. Fortunately I had a loving, caring wife who would help me plot a safe course through the "mine fields" of civilian life that lay ahead.

The ceremonies started with an introduction of Jackie, who had come up from our new home in Huntington Beach. In addition to Jackie, there were many representatives of the civilian engineering staff present. First, CDR Dela Mura, Head of the TERRIER System Department (Code 4400) presented a review of my Navy career—the six ships I served in, the schools I attended, and my advancement to Senior Chief Petty Officer. He was followed by CAPT Meyer, Commanding Officer, NSMSES, offering his thanks for my contributions to the TERRIER Program.

After the talks by CDR Dela Mura and CAPT Meyer, I was presented with my final set of orders and a Certificate of Transfer to Navy Fleet Reserve. This was followed by a presentation by my fellow station CPOs of a desk pen set with a clock, a thermometer, and a statue of Neptunus Rex. The final event was the presentation of a United States flag in honor of my service and retirement.

When the ceremonies were completed, I requested permission to go ashore for the last time. CDR Dela Mura granted this, and I was piped-over-the-side by eight CPO side boys. We all adjourned to the CPO Club for a brief retirement luncheon. On the Monday following my retirement ceremony, I returned to college to finish my education and start a second career. The classes I had taken at Ventura College removed any fears I had about returning to school.

"Fair winds and following seas" to all ex-shipmates and to all future destroyermen.

EPILOGUE

After I transferred to the Fleet Reserve, I continued my college education, eventually receiving my BS in Electronics Technology, a MA in vocational Education, and a MS in Systems Management. While attending school I stayed active with the Navy League until the Long Beach Naval shipyard was shut down.

In the 30+ years since I retired, U.S. Navy destroyers have been sent in harms way and have been involved in many different operations and incidents in many different parts of the world, supporting national security policies and objectives. Here are but a few such occasions:

- On 17 September1970, USS INDEPENDENCE, CV-60, and six destroyers deployed off the coast of Lebanon after Jordanian troops attacked Palestinian guerrilla camps.

On 29 May 1972, President Richard M. Nixon and Soviet Premier Breznev signed an agreement outlining the "basic principles of détente," which relaxed the tensions between the world's major superpowers.

The national draft and mandatory registration of 18 year olds ended in 1973. However, registration was reinstated in 1980.

225

On 27 January 1973, at the Paris Accords, a practical settlement was reached and a cease fire was declared in Vietnam.

- On 24 October 1973, after a U. S. merchant ship was shot at, DDs commenced escorting U.S. merchant ships in the lower Red Sea. This escorting was to last for a month.

- On 12 May 1975, Cambodian Khmer Rouge patrol boats illegally seized the SS MAYAGUEZ. She was an American-flagged container ship operating in international waters in the gulf of Thailand.12 May 1975, when Cambodian patrol boats captured the ship claiming it was spying on Cambodia. President Ford ordered the ship be freed and the crew rescued. U.S. Marines performed this assignment. USS HENRY B. WILSON, DDG-7, and USS HENRY E. HOLT, FF-1074, assisted in the rescue operations.

- On 22 November 1975, USS BELKNAP, GC-26, collided with USS JOHN F. KENNEDY, CA-67, BELKNAP suffered severe damages and personnel casualties (8 crewmembers killed, 47 injured) mostly due to her aluminum superstructure. This event led to future ships being built with all steel superstructures.

- In June 1978, three U.S. Navy ships conducted operations in the Sea of Okhotsk to demonstrate the right of free navigation in international waters.

- On 4 November 1979, Iranian militants seized the U.S. Embassy in Teheran and took 63 Americans hostage. They would not be released until Ronald Reagan took office as President on 20 January 1981.

- From 23 October through 21 November 1983, U.S. forces were engaged in "Operation Urgent Fury," the invasion and freeing of Grenada, West Indies.

- On 11 April 1986, the U.S. launched air strikes against Libya in retaliation for Libyan terrorist acts.

- On 12 May 1986, USS DAVID R. RAY, DD-971, a SPRUANCE-class strike destroyer, deterred an Iranian Navy attempt to board a United States merchant ship, SS MC KINNLEY.

- On 17 May 1987, USS STARK, FFG-31, was struck by an Iraqi Exocet missile in the Persian Gulf, killing 37 destroyermen and wounding 21.

In 1987, President Ronald Reagan visited Berlin and demanded that Russian President Gorbachev remove the Berlin Wall.[1] This led to the opening of the Brandenburg Gate and other borders between East and West Germany on 9 November 1989, and to the eventual downfall of the Soviet Union. On 3 December 1989, President George H. Bush and Mikhail Gorbechev announced the official end of the Cold War. Then, on 25 December 1991, the Commonwealth of Independent States was created from the former Soviet Union.

- On 18 April 1988, USS SAMUEL B. ROBERTS, FFG-58, struck an Iranian mine while operating in the Persian Gulf. Ten crewmen were injured.

- On 3 July 1988, USS VINCENNES, CG-49, shot down an Iran Air commercial flight after mistaking the plane for an Iranian F-14 fighter.

- On 2 August 1990, Iraq invaded Kuwait leading to "Desert Shield" and "Desert Storm."

- During 1998, "Operation Southern Watch," enforcement of the extended "no-fly" zone in Iraq, and "Operation Desert Fox," air strikes that were launched after Iraq failed to comply with UN resolutions on weapons inspections took place. These are ongoing operations.

- On 12 October 2000, USS COLE, DDG-67, was attacked by two terrorists in a suicide boat while COLE was refueling during a scheduled port call at Adem, Yemen. Seventeen destroyermen were killed and 39 others were injured. The ship was severely damaged and was eventually returned to the United States for repairs.

- On 11 September 2001, terrorists hijacked four U.S. airlines over U.S. airspace. One crashed into the Pentagon in Washington, DC. Two were crashed into the Twin Towers of the World Trade Center in New York City destroying both towers. Passengers aboard the fourth overtook the hijackers and it crashe into a field in Pennsylvania. These events lead to Operation Enduring Freedom where U.S. forces went after the Taliban and Al Qaeda in Afghanistan.

In addition, over the past thirty-years, destroyers have supported many other operations all over the world. They have performed such tasks as making good-will visits; making port calls in support of diplomatic objectives; providing humanitarian assistance; showing the flag; conducting surveillance and intelligence gathering operations; screening Carrier Battle Groups (CVBG); and providing the President with a sea-based contingency response capability.

Fleet Admiral Chester W. Nimitz once stated that:

[O]f all the tools the Navy will employ to control the seas in future war, the most useful of the small types of combatant ships—the destroyer—will be sure to be there. Its appearance may be altered and it may even be called by another name, but no type, not even the carrier or submarine, has such an assured place in future navies."

(as quoted by J.J. Falk in *Out Navy*).

The Navy's newest destroyers of the ARLEIGH BURKE and the to-be-built ZUMWALT-classes will fulfill Fleet Admiral Nimitz's forecast well into the 21st century. Destroyers and destroyermen stand ready to "answer all bells" when called upon by the President, the CNO, or other leaders.

APPENDIX A

Destroyer Classes

APPENDIX A

<u>Summary of Destroyer Classes</u>

U.S. Navy ship "classes" are normally named after the first ship of the class to be commissioned. However, for a variety of reasons this doesn't always work out in practice. Destroyers are normally named after distinguished USN or USMC officers, enlisted men or other leaders (an exception is USS Winston S. Churchill, DDG-81). Ships that were originally designated as destroyers but later reclassified as guided missile cruisers are named after historical battles or distinguished Americans.

HULL NUMBER	CLASS NAME (#)	REMARKS
DD 1-5, 13	Bainbridge (6)	Bainbridge DD 1, was the first "torpedo boat destroyer." High-forecastle, four-pipers.
DD 6-7	Hopkins (2)	The first class to be called "destroyers." High-forecastle, four-pipers.
DD 8-9	Lawrence (2)	Flush deck, four-pipers.
DD 10-12	Paul Jones (3)	Also listed as Bainbridge-class. High-forecastle, four-pipers.
DD 14-16	Truxtun (3)	High-forecastle, four-pipers.
DD 17-19	Smith (3)	High-forecastle, four-pipers.
DD 20, 21	Flusser (2)	Also listed as Smith-class. High-forecastle, four-pipers.

DD 22-23, 26-31, 34-40	Paulding (21)	Flush deck, high-forecastle, Bath Iron Works (BIW). DDs 41 & 42 called Monaghan-class by BIW. DD 24, 25 & 32 called Roe-class by the Newport News Shipbuilding & Drydock Co.
DD 24, 25, 32, 33	Roe (3)	A sub-class of the Paulding class.
DD 41,42	Monaghan (2)	A sub-class of the Paulding class.
DD 43-46	Cassin (4)	First of two classes named Cassin. High-forecastle, four-pipers.
DD 47-50	Aylwin (4)	Cassin-class with different propulsion machinery arrangements.
DD 51-56	O'Brien (6)	High-forecastle, four-pipers. First U.S. DDs to carry 21" torpedoes.
DD 57-62	Tucker (6)	High-forecastle, four-pipers. Could carry and lay mines. The first of the class, DD-57, was commissioned in April 1916.
DD 63-68	Sampson (6)	High-forecastle, four-pipers. First U.S. DDs to carry antiaircraft guns. (four 4"/50 caliber). The first of the class, DD-65, was commissioned in June 1916.
DD 69-74	Caldwell (6)	High-forecastle, four-pipers. Fifty Caldwells, Wickes and Clemsons from the Reserve Fleet were given to the English Commonwealth at the start of WW II (1940). Britain renamed then as the Town Class. In return, the US received basing rights on Commonwealth territory.
DD 75-78, 93, 94, 113-118,126-156	Wickes (111)	This class was a mass-produced version of the Caldwell Class. Many of this class were converted to high-speed transports (APD). Others were converted to fast minesweepers (DMS) and still others to "miscellaneous auxiliary (AG).
DD 79-112, 161-179	Wickes/Little	A sub-class of the Wickes Class.
DD 119-124, 181-185	Wickes/Lambertson	A sub-class of the Wickes Class.
DD 125, 157-160	Wickes/Tattnall (5)	A sub-class of the Wickes Class. Commissioned in 1919.

DD 186-199 (200-205 canceled), 206-347	Clemson (154)	Last of the high-forecastle, four-pipers. First DDs with continuous sheer-lines. The first of the class, DD-186, was commissioned in 1919. First DDs to burn oil instead of coal. Built primarily for ASW. Many were converted to APD. The ships of Des-Ron 11 were Clemsons. USS Reuben James, DD-245, sunk by U-255 on 31 October 1941, was a Clemson-Class.
DD 348-355	Farragut (8)	First class of "modern" destroyers. The first of the class, DD-348, was commissioned in 1934. First to carry single, dual-purpose 5"/38 gun mounts.
DD 356-363	Porter (8)	Destroyer squadron leaders (for flush-deck DDs). First to carry double, dual-purpose 5"/38 gun mounts. Commissioned during 1936, '37. See Somers Class (below).
DD 364-371, 373-374, 376-379	Mahan (14)	Commissioned during 1936, '37.
DD 372, 375	Cassin (2)	Second class named Cassin. Modified Mahans.
DD 380, 382, 400-401	Gridley (4)	Commissioned during 1937, '38.
DD 381, 383, 394-396	Somers (5)	Second class of destroyer squadron leaders (for flush-deck DDs). Also carried double, dual-purpose 5"/38 gun mounts. Commissioned in the 1930s. See Porter Class (above).
DD 384-385	Dunlap (2)	Also called Fanning Class. Commissioned in 1937.
DD 386-393	Bagley (8)	Commissioned in 1937.
DD 397-399, 402-408	Benham (10)	Commissioned during 1939, '40.
DD 400, 401	McCall (2)	Sub-class of Benham class.
DD 409-420	Sims (12)	Based on the Benham Class only with enclosed gun mounts and the first Mk 37 gun director.

DD 421-422, 425-428, 459-460, 491-492, 598-617	Benson	Commissioned during 1940.
DD 423-424, 429-444	Benson/Gleaves (24)	Some were also called Livermore Class or Mayo Class. Commissioned during 1940, '41.
DD 453-458, 483-497, 598-628, 632-641 & 645-648	Bristol (72)	Improved Bensons. Built to fill the gap prior to the delivery of the Fletchers. Commissioned during 1940s.
DD 445-452, 498-502, 507-522, 526-541, 544-547, 550-570, 572-597, 629-631, 642-644, 649-691 & 792-804 (503-506, 523-525, 542, 543, 548, 549, 768, 769 canceled)	Fletcher (119)	Designed shortly after the start of the war in Europe. Larger than predecessor DDs. Some became known as La Vallette Class. Commissioned during 1942-45.
DD 482	Watson (1)	Modified Fletcher Class (canceled)
DD 692-709,, 723-741, 744-762, 770-781 781, & 857	Allen M. Sumner (70)	Fastest, longest range DDs built specifically as fast carrier escorts. Had improve/increased air defense capabilities over the Fletchers. Commissioned during 1944, '45.
DD 710-721, 742-743, 763-769, 782-791, 805-824, 826, 828-856 & 858-890	Gearing	Allen M. Sumner Class with 14-feet added mid-ships to increase fuel and stores capacity. Twenty-eight were converted to a DDR configuration starting in 1944. DD 712 was converted to DDG 1. DD 720, 721, 766 &767 were launched then canceled. DD 768 & 769 canceled. DD 741, 809-816, 854-856, 891-926: some were Classified as DDE (ASW escorts). Commissioned during 1944, '45.
DD 825, 827	Carpenter (2)	Modified Gearing Class (DDK & DDE)
DD 891-926	Unnamed	Canceled

236

DD 927-930	Mitscher (originally Gearings)	DD 927 7 928 were reclassified as DL. Later reclassified as DDG.
DD 931, 937, 940-951	Forrest Sherman	Last of the standard destroyers. Built on a post-WW II design primarily for ASW. The class was extensively modified in the 1960s and 1970s. Last of the Class was decommissioned in the 1890s.
DD 932-936, 938-939	Decatur (Mitscher)	Class reclassified as DDG. After gun mounts replaced with a Tarter missile launcher. From 1975-78, HULL, DD-945, had the forward 5" gun mount replaced with an experimental 8" gun.
DD 952-959	DDG	See Charles F. Adams Class (below). DD 955 was originally named Biddle. It was renamed and re-Classified Claude V. Ricketts, DDG-5.
DD 960-962		Foreign transfer (Japan)
DD 963-992 & 997	Spruance (31)	Built primarily as ASW ships. Powered by gas turbine engines.
DD 993-998	Kidd	Originally built for the Shah of Iran. DD 995 transferred to Greece. DD 993, 994 & 996 redesignated DDG 993, 994 & 996.
DD 999		
DDG 1	Gyatt (1)	Ex-DD 712, a Gearing class. Experimental ship for Terrier Missile System.
DDG 2-24	Charles F. Adams (23)	Essentially Forrest Sherman class with Mt. 51 replaced with a Tarter missile launcher.
DDG 25-DDG 30		Foreign transfer (DDG 25-27 to Australia; DDG 28-30 to Germany)
DDG 31-DDG 36	Decatur	Originally Forrest Sherman and Mitschner Class ships.
DDG 37-46	Farragut	Ex-DLG 6-15
DDG 47-50	Ticonderoga (4)	Later reclassified as Guided Missile Cruiser (CG)

DDG 51-98	Arleigh Burke (28)	Replacements for the Charles F. Adams & Farragut classes. Powered by gas turbine engines. Most powerful surface combatants ever put to sea. Features all-steel construction. USS Hopper, DDG-70, named after a female, Rear Admiral Grace M. Hopper.
DDG 79-113	Oscar Austin (29)	Flight IIA variants of Arleigh Burke class. DDG-81, USS Winston S. Churchill, is the only American naval ship not named after an American.
DL 1-5	Norfolk	Originally called Frigates. Later reclassified as DDG 37-46.
DLG 6-15	Coontz	Originally called Frigates. Later reclassified as DDG 40-49.
DLG 16-24	Leahy	Later reclassified as CG
DLGN 25	Bainbridge	First nuclear-powered destroyer-leader.
DLG 26-34	Belknap	Later reclassified as CG
DLGN 35	Truxtun	Later reclassified as CGN
DLGN 36 & 37	California	Later reclassified as CGN
DLGN 38-41	Virginia	Later reclassified as CGN
DDG-	Arleigh Burk, Flight I	
DDG-	Arleigh Burke, Flight IIA	
DD(X)	Zumwalt	Future multi-mission destroyers. Being designed for operations in the littoral regions. To be procured with all-electric drives. They will use "smart ship" technologies that will automate many of the current manual functions.

APPENDIX B

United States Navy Chief Petty Officer Creed

APPENDIX B

United States Navy Chief Petty Officer Creed

During the course of this day you have been caused to humbly accept challenge and face adversity. This you have accomplished with rare good grace. Pointless as some of these challenges may have seemed, there were valid, time-honored reasons behind each pointed barb. It was necessary to meet these hurdles with blind faith in the fellowship of Chief Petty Officers. The goal was to instill in you that trust is inherent with the donning of the uniform of a Chief. It was our intent to impress upon you that challenge is good; a great and necessary reality which cannot mar you - which, in fact, strengthens you. In your future as a Chief Petty Officer, you will be forced to endure adversity far beyond that imposed upon you today. You must face each challenge and adversity with the same dignity and good grace you demonstrated today. By experience, by performance, and by testing, you have been this day advanced to Chief Petty Officer. In the United States Navy - and only in the United States Navy - the rank of E7 carries with it United responsibilities and privileges you are now bound to observe and expected to fulfill. Your entire way of life is now changed. More will be expected of you; more will be demanded of you. Not because you are an E7 but because you are now a Chief Petty Officer. You have not merely been promoted one pay-grade, you have joined an exclusive fellowship and, as in all fellowships, you have a special responsibility to your comrades, even as they have a special responsibility to you. This is why we in the

United States Navy may maintain with pride our feelings of accomplishment once we have attained the position of Chief Petty Officer. Your new responsibilities and privileges do not appear in print. They have no official standing; they cannot be referred to by name, number, or file. They have existed for over 100 years; Chiefs before you have freely accepted responsibility beyond the call of printed assignment. Their actions and their performance demanded the respect of their seniors as well as their juniors. It is now required that you be the fountain of wisdom, the ambassador of good will, the authority in personal relations as well as in technical applications. "Ask the Chief" is a household phrase in and out of the Navy. You are now the Chief. The exalted position you have now achieved - and the word exalted is used advisedly - exists because of the attitude and performance of the Chiefs before you. It shall exist only as long as you and your fellow Chiefs maintain these standards. It was our intention that you never forget this day. It was our intention to test you, to try you, and to accept you. Your performance has assured us that you will wear "the hat" with the same pride as your comrades in arms before you. We take a deep and sincere pleasure in clasping your hand, and accepting you as a Chief Petty Officer in the United States Navy.

ACRONYMS AND ABBREVIATIONS

Abaft	Behind some reference point
ADIZ	Air Defense Identification Zone
ASW	Anti-Submarine Warfare.
BNSY	Boston Naval Shipyard
BBC	British Broadcasting Corporation
CDO	Command Duty Officer
CG	Cruiser, Guided Missile
CIC	Combat Information Center
CINCLANT/PAC	Commander in Chief Atlantic/Pacific Fleet
CNO	Chief of Naval Operations
CO	Commanding Officer
COD	Carrier on-Board Delivery
COMNAVFE	Commander, Naval Forces, Far East
COMSEVEN	Commander, Seventh Fleet
CV	Aircraft carrier
CVBG	Carrier Battle Group
DD/DDR/DL/DLG	Destroyer/Destroyer, Radar Picket/Destroyer Leader/Destroyer Leader, Missiles
DE/DER	Destroyer-Escort/Destroyer-Escort, Radar Picket
DesDiv/DesRon	Destroyer Division/Destroyer Squadron
DesLant/DesPac	Destroyers, Atlantic Fleet/Pacific Fleet
DMZ	Demilitarized Zone
DO	Disbursing Officer or Duty Officer

DRT	Dead Reckoning Tracer
DSOT	Daily System Operability Tests
ECM	Electronics Counter Measures
EM	Enlisted Man or Enlisted Men
FAAWTC	Fleet Anti-Air Warfare Training Center
FAT	Final Acceptance Trials
FO	Forward observer
GCI	Ground-controlled intercept
GQ	General Quarters
InSurv	Board of Inspection and Survey
LBNSY	Long Beach Naval Shipyard
LCM	Landing Craft; Medium
LT	Lieutenant
LTJG	Lieutenant, junior grade
MAA	Master-At-Arms
MiG	Mikoyan-Gurevich. Common name for Russian-built jet fighter aircraft.
MPC	Military Payment Certificate
NAD	Naval Ammunition Depot
NATO	North Atlantic Treaty Organization
NIS	Naval Investigative Service
NKPA	North Korean People's Army
NNSY	Norfolk Naval Shipyard
NOB	Naval Operating Base
NORAD	North American Radar Advisory Zone
NRT	Naval Reserve Training
NSFO	Navy Standard Fuel Oil
NSMSES	Naval Ship Missile Systems Engineering Station
NVN	North Vietnam
NWS	Naval Weapons Station
OBA	Oxygen Breathing Apparatus
OOD	Officer of the Deck
PAT	Preliminary Acceptance Trials
PIO	Public Information Officer
PIRAZ	Positive Identification and Radar Advisory Zone

PNSY	Philadelphia Naval Shipyard
RAS	Replenishment at Sea
Rate/Rating	A rate is a pay grade and a rating is a job classi- fication.
RDF	Radio Direction Finding
RecSta	Receiving Station
RF	Radio Frequency
RFA	Royal Fleet Auxiliary
R&R	Rest & Recreation
SAM	Surface-to-Air Missile
SAR	Search and Rescue
SFNSY	San Francisco Naval Shipyard
SOPA	Senior Officer Present Afloat
SQAT	Ship Qualification Assistance Team
SP	Shore Patrol
UCMJ	Uniform Code of Military Justice
USAFI	United States Armed Forces Institute
WestPac	Western Pacific (i.e., the Orient)
XO	Executive Officer

BIBLIOGRAPHY

_____. Booklet, "Glad to have You Aboard," USS CHAMBERS, DER-391.

_____. "The U.S. Navy's Korean War: Dull, Dirty, and They Die, Too." *Newsweek*, January 12, 1953, pp. 36-38.

_____. "Darkening shadows of crisis." *Newsweek*, March 9, 1959, pp. 29-30.

_____. "Text on Soviet ship and relevant laws," *New York Times*, March 27, 1959.

_____. "Visit and search," *Time*, March 9, 1959, pp. 14-15.

Alexander, B. *Korea: The First War We Lost*, NY: Hippocrene Books, 1986.

Alexander, J. E. *Inchon to Wonsan: From the Deck of a Destroyer in the Korean War*, Annapolis: Naval Institute Press, 1996.

Bonner, Kit, and Carolyn Bonner. *Cold War at Sea: An Illustrated History*. Osceola, WI: MBI Publishing Co., 2000.

Bosworth, Allan R. *My Love Affair with the Navy*. NY: W.W. Norton & Company, Inc., 1969. A non-technical history of the Navy from its inception through 1969.

Bouchard, Joseph F. "Guarding the Cold War Ramparts." Reproduced from the *Naval War College Review*, summer 1999. On the Internet at: http://www.fas.org/nuke/guide/usa/airdef/art5-su9.htm.

Carrison, Daniel J. *The United States Navy*. NY: Frederick A. Praeger, 1968, p. 107. Carrison discusses the provisioning problems destroyers face.

Coletta, Paolo E. "The Destroyer Tender," U.S. *Naval Institute Proceedings*, vol. 84, No. 5, May 1958, pp. 91-107.

Connolly, John B. *Underway: Tour of a Tin Can Sailor*, Baton Rouge: Author, 1990. My special thanks to Mr. Connolly for his permission to use his remembrances of life aboard a destroyer to refresh my memory of such a life.

Crew. *European Deployment: 1964-1965. USS HARRY E. YARNELL Cruise Book.*

Crew. *USS FOX 1967 Cruise Book.*

Crew. USS CASCADE, AD-16. *CASCADE in the Med—and Away We Go.* 1956 Cruise Book.

Cross, Richard F., III. "Destroyers." U.S. *Naval Institute Proceedings*, Vol. 97, No. 5, May 1971, pp. 244-273. This article is an analysis of destroyer development, and status, in the United Kingdom, France, the Soviet Union and the U.S.

Destroyer Escort Sailors Association. "The Destroyer Escort." On the Internet at <http://www.desausa.org/destroyer_escort.htm>.

Dudley, William S. (ed. *The Naval War of 1812: A Documentary History*, Vol. I. Washington: Naval Historical Center, 1985.

Falk, James J. "Destroyers—Backbone of the Fleet," *Our Navy*, January 1970, pp. 12-14.

Field, J. A., Jr. *History of United States Naval Operations: Korea*, Washington: U.S. Government Printing Office, 1962. An excellent high-level, historical overview of the Korean War, including the politics that were being played out amongst the civilian politicians and between military commanders. However, the book's main emphasis is on the roll of the aircraft carriers, the aircraft and the battleships and cruisers. Explanation of the role played by the destroyers is minimal and only ___ are included in the index.

Grove, Eric. *The Future of Seapower.* Annapolis: Naval Institute Press, 1990. In Part III, "The changing shape of naval war," Grove first addresses weapon systems and then platforms. This provides an excellent overview of weapons and ships of several navies up until the end of the Cold War.

Headland, E. Harvey. "Sitting Ducks: Leading the Inchon Invasion." On the Internet at: <http:www.usna.com/News_Pubs/ Publications/Shipmate/2000/2000_06/ducks.htm>. Captain (then commander) Headland was commanding officer of USS MANSFIELD and the senior captain present.

Isenberg, Michael T. *Shield of the Republic: The United States Navy in an era of Cold War and Violent Peace, 1945-1962*," Vol. I. New York: St. Martin's Press, 1993.

Jefferson, T. "First Annual Message to Congress," delivered December 8, 1801, *The Avalon Project at the Yale Law School.*

Johnson, Gregory G. "A testimony to the World: U.S. Sixth Fleet marks 200 years of Forward Presence." *Sea Power*, October 2001, pp. 51-53.

Johnson-Miles, Bill. "Fast ships in Harm's Way: 100 Years of 'Tin Cans' (Part 1 of a 3 part series). http://www.news.navy.mil/search/display.asp? story_id=3147.

Kalischer, P. "The Navy's girl in Hong Kong." *Colliers*, Vol. 134, October 1, 1956, pp. 60-61.

King, Ernest J., Jr. "First report to the Secretary of the Navy: Covering our Peacetime Navy and our Wartime Navy and including combat operations up to 1 March 1944." Issued 23 April 1944. Admiral King was Commander in Chief, United States Fleet, and Chief of Naval Operations.

Knox, Dudley W. *A History of the United States Navy.* NY: G. P. Putnam's Sons, 1948.

Lockee, G. E. "Red Crown"—an Unclassified Summary of PIRAZ (1968). Posted on the Internet. Captain Lockee is a former Commanding Officer, USS WAINWRIGHT, DLG-28.

Naval Historical Center. *Dictionary of American Naval Fighting Ships.* Washington, D.C.: U.S. Government Printing Office, 1968.

_____, Various Web pages at: <http:www.history.navy.mil/>. Washington, D.C.: Department of the Navy.

Morrison, Samuel E. *The Two-Ocean War: A Short History of the United States Navy in the Second World War.* Boston: Little Brown, 1963, pp. 584-85.

Nicholas, John B., and B. Tillman. *On Yankee Station: the Naval Air War over Vietnam.* Annapolis: Naval Institute Press, 1987. An excellent reference for the Naval Air War but no mention of any contributions of surface ships other than the aircraft carriers.

Parke, Everett A. "The unique and vital DER." U.S. *Naval Institute Proceedings*, Vol. 86, No. 2, February 1960, pp. 89-95.

Rees, David. *Korea: The Limited War.* NY: St. Martin's Press, 1964.

Reilly, John C., Jr. *United States Navy Destroyers of World War II.* Dorset, England: Blandford Press, 1983.

Roscoe, Theodore. *United States Destroyer Operations in World War II.* Annapolis: Naval Institute Press, 1953.

Sandler, Stanley. *The Korean War: No Victors, No Vanquished.* Lexington, KT: The University Press of Kentucky, 1999.

Sheehan, Neil. *The Arnheiter Affair.* NY: Random House, 1971.

Sumrall, R.F., *Summer-Gearing-Class Destroyers.* Annapolis, MD: Naval Institute Press, 1995.

Schofield, William G. *Destroyers - 60 Years.* NY: Rand McNally & Co., 1962. An excellent history of destroyers from *Bainbridge*, DD-1, to *Bainbridge*, DLGN-25.

Tilghman, William. "Doc" Tilghman provided information regarding his involvement in the unfortunate death of the commanding officer and the seaman who died after being washed under a gun mount. This information was provided in a series of e-mails during 2001 and 2002.

Tomajczyk, S. F. *Modern U.S. Navy Destroyers.* Oscola, WI: MBI Publishing Company, 2001.

Turbak, Gary. "USS WALKE: Navy's greatest combat loss." VFW magazine, March 2002, pp. 34-36.

USS SOUTHERLAND, DDR-743: Deck Logs 1950-1954. Reviewed at the National Archives II, College Park, MD.

USS WILLIAM T. POWELL, DER-213: Deck Log 1955. Reviewed at the National Archives II, College Park, MD.

USS CASCADE, AS-16: Deck Log 1956. Reviewed at the National Archives II, College Park, MD.

USS CHAMBERS, DER-391: Deck Logs 1956-1959. Reviewed at the National Archives II, College Park, MD.

USS HARRY E. YARNELL, DLG-17: Deck Logs 1963-1965. Reviewed at the National Archives II, College Park, MD.

USS FOX, DLG-33: Deck Logs 1966-1968. Reviewed at the National Archives II, College Park, MD.

Webster's Ninth New Collegiate Dictionary. Springfield, MA: Merriam-Webster, Inc., 1897.

Wilson, Jim. *Retreat Hell! We're Just Attacking in Another Direction*, NY: W. Morrow & Co., Inc., 1988.

Wyld, Lionel D. *The Navy in Newport.* Dover, NH: Arcadia Publishing, 1997.

Yates, Brock. *Destroyers and Destroyermen: The story of Our "Tin Can" Navy.* NY: Harper & Brothers, 1959. This is an easy-to-read, non-technical book suitable for anyone with an interest in destroyers and destroyermen.

Zumwalt, Elmo R. "A course for the destroyers." U.S. *Naval Institute Proceedings*, Vol. 88, No. 11, November 1962, pp. 28-39. This article was then-Captain (later CNO) Zumwalt's forecast of the role that destroyers would play 10-20 years later. This forecast is still applicable as evidenced by the requirements for the new DD (X) destroyer program.

NOTES

PROLOGUE

1 On 15 March 1943, Admiral Ernest J. King, serving in dual roles as Commander-in-Chief, U.S. Fleet and CNO, implemented a new standardized fleet numbering system to identify task organizations and their components. This numbering system (5th Fleet, 6th Fleet, 7th Fleet, etcetera) is still in use. The U.S. 7th Fleet is the largest forward-deployed U.S. fleet. It is stationed in the Western Pacific and directly supports the three principle elements of U.S. National Security Strategy: Deterrence, Forward Defense, and Alliance Solidarity. Its has several different elements the main one being the Fast Carried Task Force (TF) 77. *TF 77* consists of one or more aircraft carriers and supporting cruisers and destroyers. The 6th Fleet is stationed in Europe.

2 In order to be eligible to "ship out" with the Merchant Marine you had to qualify by a combination of: scores on a written test, educational background and veterans "preference points." WW II veterans earned these points for time in service and other criterion.

Chapter 1. MY FIRST ENLISTMENT: FEBRUARY 1950

1 In the Navy and Coast Guard, an enlisted sailor has two classifications: a rate (or rank) that is a pay grade, and a rating that is a job classification.

2 "Grinder" is a term used to describe a large, asphalt-covered drill field.

3 This strike lasted from 11 February until 5 March.

4 "Field day" refers to a period of time set aside for house-keeping, generally before an inspection.

5 The *Articles* were supplemented by *Regulations for the Government of the Navy*.

6 The UCMJ provides today's sailors with many of the constitutional rights and safeguards that pertain to their civilian counterparts.

7 Skivvies is the term the Navy uses for underwear.

8 Combat Information Center (CIC) is the space aboard ship where all radar, sonar, radio and lookout information is received, coordinated, evaluated and disseminated to the appropriate station. CIC is also responsible for controlling aircraft, when assigned, providing targeting information to weapons control and assisting in anti-submarine warfare. Its major role is to keep the ship's commanding officer and any embarked staff officers, advised of the tactical situation including identity of any and all friendly or hostile forces in the area.

9 The Radarman rating was later changed to Operations Specialist (OS).

10 USS SOUTHERLAND was a GEARING-class destroyer. GEARINGS were "stretch" versions of the ALLEN M. SUMNER class that superseded the FLETCHERS of WW II fame (see Appendix A). They had a 14-foot section added amidships designed to give them greater operating radius. SOUTHERLAND was a unit of Destroyer Division (DesDiv) 51 consisting of USS ROWAN DD-782, flagship; USS HENDERSON DD-785; and USS GURKE DD-783. At various times each of these ships was hit by North Korean shore batteries. DesDiv 51 was a division of Destroyer Squadron (DesRon) 5. A DesDiv usually consisted of four ships and a DesRon usually consisted of two or more DesDiv. Radar picket ships have extra powerful radars and serve as the long-range "eyes" of an aircraft carrier battle group.

11 In 1958 President Eisenhower declared USS ARIZONA a national memorial. It was dedicated as such on Memorial Day, 1962.

12 The formal name was Military Payment Certificate.

Chapter 2. A LEGACY OF DESTROYERS

1 As used herein, "destroyermen" or "destroyerman" refers to personnel of either sex.

2 Captain Arleigh Burke was the quintessential destroyerman—a destroyerman's destroyerman. He was the most famous DD squadron commander during WW II in the Pacific. As an admiral, Burke eventually served three two-year terms as Chief of Naval Operations, from August 1955 to August 1961.

3 Falk, J.J., "Destroyers—Backbone of the Fleet," *Our Navy*, January 1970, pp. 12-14.

4 The ships of Destroyer Squadron 8 were USS MCDOUGAL, DD-54; USS CONYNGHAM, DD-58; USS PORTER, DD-59; USS WADSWORTH, DD-60; USS WAINWRIGHT, DD-62; and USS DAVIS, DD-65.

5 Based, in part, on Chief Journalist Bill Johnson-Miles' "Fast Ships in Harm's Way: 100 Years of 'Tin Cans.'"

6 These destroyers were considered obsolete when they were built and many were converted to fast transports and mine sweepers. Appendix A contains a summary of destroyer classes.

7 USS EDSALL was sunk on 1 March 1942 by the Japanese battleships HIEE and KIRISHIMA during the evacuation of Java.

8 In action on 24 January 1942, FORD was damaged. POPE was sunk on 1 March 1942, by naval gunfire in the Java Sea after firing all of her torpedoes.

9 These other ships were: ENTERPRISE, CV-6; SALT LAKE CITY, CA-25; NORTHAMPTON, CA-26; VINCENNES, CA-44; NASHVILLE, CL-43; BALCH, DD-363; BENHAM, DD-397 (later sunk); ELLET, DD-398; FANNING, DD-385; GRAYSON, DD-435; GWIN, DD-433 (later sunk); MERIDITH, DD-434 (later sunk) and MONSEN, DD-436 (later sunk). LT COL Doolittle's task force (TF

16) was supported by two fleet oilers USS CIMMARRON, AO-22; and USS SABINE, AO-25.

10 These were: LAFFEY, DD-459; CUSHING, DD-376; BARTON, DD-599; AARON WARD, DD-483; MONSEN, DD-436 and GWIN, DD-433 that were sunk; and O'BANNON, DD-450, STARETT, DD-407 and FLETCHER, DD-445 that were damaged.

11 SOUTHERLAND was commissioned as a DD. I in 1949 she was converted to a radar picket destroyer, DDR.

12 For a full account of the action within Inchon Harbor see the article by Captain Harvey E. Headland. During the course of the Korean War there were 38 incidents of destroyer-type ships being hit or otherwise damaged by North Korean gunfire.

13 U.S. Navy shipboard guns are typically defined by their bore diameter, in inches, and their barrel length, in multiples of their bore diameter. Thus, a 5"/38 caliber gun has a bore that is 5-inches in diameter and a barrel length of 190" (5 x 38).

14 Under the 1930 *International Treaty for the Limitation and Reduction of Naval Armament,* the U.S. was limited to 29 light cruisers.

Chapter 3. USS SOUTHERLAND:WESTPAC CRUISE 1

1 As a point of interest, CIMMARRON was one of the two tankers that accompanied TF 16 on the "Doolittle Raid" on Tokyo in 1942.

2 A "highline" is a line rigged between the main deck of the oiler and the 01 deck, or the first deck above the main deck, of the receiving destroyer.

3 A breeches buoy is an apparatus used for transfers at sea, consisting of sturdy canvas breeches attached at the waist to a ring buoy that is suspended from a pulley running along a line stretched from ship to ship. Breeches buoys have since been replaced by an aluminum chair.

4 Navy ships operate under three material conditions: Condition X (Xray) is the normal inport condition when most doors and hatches can be opened. Condition Y (Yoke) is a normal steaming

condition where only those doors and hatches required for ease of passage are opened. Condition Z (Zebra) is a condition where all doors and hatches are closed and secured.

5 During general quarters all the ship's battle stations are manned, damage control teams are on station, and all non-essential openings to the outside of the ship are closed.

6 Early on in the Korean Conflict, the U.N. Forces had established control of the seas and the airspace above them. This same control would be established in the 1960-1970s in the seas around Vietnam.

7 My thanks to William "Bill" Tilghman, HM3, for providing details of this incident.

8 U.S. Navy destroyers that operated during WWII and during the Cold War period were steam-driven. They had four boilers that drove turbines that provided power to two shafts. With all four boilers in use (on-line) these ships could reach speeds of approximately 35 knots. With two boilers on-line they could reach approximately 27 knots and they could reach approximately 20 knots on one boiler. A speed of 16 knots was found to be most economical in terms of fuel usage.

9 When fully fueled, SOUTHERLAND carried 740 tons of Navy Standard Fuel Oil (NSFO). It was policy to keep the bunkers full as we never knew where we'd be tomorrow.

10 This interior fore and aft passageway was unique to Gearing class DDs.

11 On a ship, the MAA is the ship's policeman, responsible for good order and discipline.

12 This was in the time before e-mail, cell phones, or satellite TV.

13 Ropeyarn Sunday refers to early liberty or an early knock-off of ship's work. Refers to the days of sail, when Wednesday was generally a day for "make and mend" (i.e., personal administration rather than ship's work).

14 TACAN (Tactical Air Navigation) was an electronic system that would emit coded signals on different bearings. Pilots could then follow these codes in order to locate the ship.

15 In the Navy, a "striker" is a sailor who is serving an apprenticeship for a designated rating, e.g., radarman, radioman, machinist's mate, etc.

16 At various times aircraft carriers USS LEYTE, USS VALLEY FORGE, USS PHILIPPINE SEA, USS PRINCETON, USS BON HOMME RICHARD or USS BOXER formed the core of TF 77.

17 U.S. Navy ships normally operate under one of four conditions of readiness: Condition One or General Quarters (GQ), where all stations are manned; Condition Two, a relaxed GQ condition; Condition three where one-third of the stations are manned, and Condition Four where only essential stations are manned.

18 On 26 September 1950, USS BRUSH, DD-745, hit a mine off Tanchon. Nine destroyermen were killed and 10 others were wounded. On 30 September 1950, USS MANSFIELD, DD-728, hit a mine and 27 destroyermen were wounded and five more were missing. On 21 June 1951, USS WALKE, DD-723, struck a mine. Twenty- six destroyermen were killed and 35 more were wounded. On 7 October 1951, USS SMALL, DD-828, hit a mine and suffered extensive damage and 27 casualties. On 16 September 1952, USS BARTON, DD-722, struck a mine and suffered 11 casualties.

19 Ch'ongjin is located in the north-east corner of Korea, near where the Korean, Chinese and Russian borders meet.

20 *Abaft*: A Navy term meaning "aft of" or behind, a reference point.

21 The executive officer (XO) is responsible for the administrative functions of the ship (or station). His role is similar to that of a staff captain on a civilian cruise liner.

22 Task Force 95 (TF 95), the *United Nations Blockade and Escort Force* maintained a blockade along both the east and the west coasts of Korea. It consisted of two Task Groups (TG). TG 95.1, commanded by a British Rear Admiral, was responsible for the west coast and TG 95.2 was responsible for the east coast. There was also the Minesweeping Group, *TG 95.6*. The purpose was to deny the Communists any use of the coast railways or road networks. Due to the mountainous terrain of Korea these were the main supply routes.

23 My thanks to William "Bill" Tilghman, HM3, for providing details of this incident.

24 The "heavies" were: USS PRINCETON, CV-37; USS PHILIPPINE SEA, CV-47; USS VALLEY FORGE, CV-45; USS LEYTE, CV-32; USS BATAAN, CVE-29; USS MISSOURI, DD-63; USS MANCHESTER, CL-83; and USS JUNEAU, CLAA-119.

25 Destroyers typically loaded stores consisting of "thirty days fresh, ninety days dry," meaning that they could provide a well-balanced diet of fresh or frozen foods for a month and three months on dry staples and canned provisions.

26 A whaleboat was a 26-foot, double-ended, utility boat normally used to transport the crew to and from the ship when anchored.

27 Bum boat: a boat that brings provisions and commodities for sale to larger ships in port or offshore (Webster's).

28 Kalischer, P., "The Navy's girl in Hong Kong," *Collier's*, Vol. 139, October 1, 1954, pp. 60-61.

29 Gurkhas were soldiers from Nepal serving in the British Army.

30 Fortunately, this is one of the very few incidents that this author is aware of where the press divulged classified naval information during the Korean War.

31 A Dutch Catholic girl who was brought up by a Muslim family when her parents were interned during WW II married a Malay man. When the Court forced her to return to her Dutch parents after the war, riots broke out and lasted from 11to 13 December 1950.

32 Keelung is a port on the northern end of Taiwan and Kaosiung is a port on the southern end of the island.

33 Ships are assigned maintenance "availabilities' with the primary objective being the accomplishment of the maximum amount of maintenance, repair and overhaul of the ship. Work performed depends on workload, available funds and the relative operational and military need of various jobs. This type of maintenance normally occurs between regular overhauls

Chapter 4. USS SOUTHERLAND: SAM DIEGO AND HAWAII, 1951

1 When two or more ships moored alongside each other this grouping was called a "nest of ships." Generally one of the nested ships is designated as the nest duty ship and assumes all military responsibilities for the nested ships.

2 "Police duty" aboard ship would normally consist of cleaning less accessible spaces such as fan rooms.

3 For more details regarding this incident see: "USS WALKE: Navy's greatest combat loss," by Gary Turbak.

4 This was part of what is known as marlinspike seamanship: skill with rope, line and related topside gear.

5 Kahoolawe is located seven miles off the southeast coast of Maui. The Navy stopped using it for shore bombardment practice in 1990.

6 In September 1952, NOOTKA captured a North Korean minelayer. This was the only Communist warship captured during the Korean War (see Stanley Sandler, p. 185 and James A Fields, Jr., p. 444).

7 Squid was a British-made, three-barrel 12-inch ASW mortar with the mortars mounted in series, one behind the other. It was fired automatically from the sonar range recorder at the proper moment. The pattern formed a triangle about 40 yards on a side at a distance of 275 yards ahead of the ship.

8 The purpose of assigning an officer a lineal number is to establish seniority within the grade and corps.

9 CAPT Melgaard's Signal Number was 662. The commanding officer of BATAAN, CAPT W. Miller, Jr, had Signal Number 863 (from the Navy Register for 1952).

10 SOUTHERLAND's electronic countermeasures (ECM) equipment consisted of radio frequency (RF) receivers, RF signal analyzers and radio direction finding (RDF) equipment.

11 In all, during the Korean War there were 87 separate incidents where U.S. Navy ships either hit mines or were hit by North Korean gunfire

Chapter 5. USS SOUTHERLAND: SAN FRANCISCO AND SAN DIEGO, 1952

1 James A. Field, Jr., *United States Naval Operations: Korea*, pp. 374-5.

2 New radars included the AN/SPS-6, air search radar (replaced an SC) and the AN/SPS-10 surface search radar (replaced a model SG radar). Our 40-mm guns were replaced with 3"/50 caliber guns. These guns were controlled by a new Mark 56 Gun Fire control System, with Mark 35 radar.

3 Aluminum superstructures were found to be a major disadvantage when in 1973 USS WORDEN, DLG-18 was "attacked" by a Shrike ARM inadvertently released from a Navy Phantom jet. The most damage was caused by aluminum splinters and fragments from the superstructure. Then in 1975, USS BELKNAP CG-26, with an aluminum superstructure, collided with USS JOHN F. KENNEDY CV-67, and suffered severe damage and casualties. As a result of these incidents the Navy redesigned the superstructures of future ships to be made of steel.

4 When referring to Navy ships, sea-keeping is a ship's ability to safely execute a mission at sea or to successfully engage an enemy with gunfire, missiles, or other weapons despite adverse weather conditions.

5 This was the same type of aircraft that took off from USS HORNET, CV-8, on 18 April 1942, on a mission to bomb the Japanese mainland in retaliation for Japan's attack on Pearl Harbor on 7 December 1941.

6 The *Queen's Surf* is no longer there.

7 Normally an attempt would be made to return the remains home. However, this is not always possible due to the pace of military operations, lack of transport, or other reasons. Since the earliest times in the Royal Navy, when an officer or rating died while in service to the King (or Queen) at sea, the captain - priest, if one was aboard - of the vessel would be charged with the responsibility of administering the burial at sea of the fallen comrade. The same prayer

was always read, and it is quoted below in its entirety. The prayer appears in the Anglican *Book of Common Prayer*.

We therefore commit his body to the deep, to be turned into corruption,
Looking for the resurrection of the body when the sea shall give up her dead,
And the life of the world shall come through our Lord, Jesus Christ,
Who at His coming shall change our vile body that it may be like His glorious body,
According to the mighty working whereby He is able to subdue all things to Himself.
AMEN.

8 Interdiction fire is gunfire placed on an area or point to prevent the enemy from using the area or point. Additionally, it is fire to divert, disrupt, delay, or destroy the enemy surface military potential before it can be used effectively against friendly forces.

9 Normally, two-thirds of the crew would go on liberty at a time (three sections). During six section liberty, only one-sixth of the crew was allowed liberty at any given time.

10 At that time we carried 5-inch, 40-mm and 20-mm ammunition plus depth charges.

Chapter 6. A LEGACY OF DESTROYER ESCORTS

1 From ENGLAND'S *Presidential Unit Citation.*

2 Taffy III consisted of six CVE, three DD and four DE. They were backed up by TU 77.4.1, "Taffy 1," consisting of six CVE, three DD and four DE and TU 77.4.2, "Taffy II," consisting of six CVE, three DD and five DE.

3 For a full account of the "Arnheiter Affair," see the book by Neil Sheehan.

4 These were the EVERTS, the BUCKLEY, the CANNON, the EDSALL, the RUDDEROW and the JOHN C. BUTLER classes.

5 For the rational behind the change from DE to FF see Eric Grove's, *The Future of Seapower*, pp. 101-102.

Chapter 7. USS WILLIAM T. POWELL, DER-213

1 WILLIAM T. POWELL was a BUCKLEY class destroyer escort that was converted to a radar picket ship near the end of WW II. She was reclassified as DER on 18 March 1949. On 1 November 1965, she was struck from the Navy list.

2 The use of "Naval Districts" has since been discontinued.

3 On 10 December 1903, the U.S. signed a lease with the Cuban government for 45 square miles of land to be used as a naval base and a coaling station. This lease was to remain in effect unless both governments agreed to a cancellation. On 18 June 1952, the Naval Operating Base was changed to a Naval Base.

4 RIZZI was a reserve training ship operating out of New York.

5 BUCKLEY class DEs had a maximum speed of 24-knots when built. Changing screening stations frequently required speeds in excess of 30-knots.

6 Plebes are forth-class cadets.

7 When ships burn NSFO, soot accumulates on the boiler firewalls and in other areas of the steam producing system. Periodically this soot needs to be blown out of the system by high pressure steam. This soot is expelled through the ship's stacks. This process, called "blowing tubes," is normally performed at night with the wind blowing across the ship.

8 During the six months of an Antarctica winter the people who stay there are completely isolated from the outside world.

9 Firecontrol Technicians (FT) make major detailed casualty analyses, major repairs, and overhauls on fire-control equipment. They use all tools and electrical and mechanical measuring instruments necessary in maintenance and repair of firecontrol equipment, firecontrol radar, directors, and associated equipment. FTs read and work from mechanical drawings and wiring diagrams. They use boresights and align guns and directors. FTs also overhaul hydraulic

power drives and perform maintenance on optical firecontrol equipment.

Chapter 8. FIRCONTROL CONVERSION SCHOOL. ANACOSTA, VIRGINIA, 1955

1 These systems included the Mk. 37 Gun Fire Control System (GFCS), the Mk 56 GFCS and the Mk. 63 GFCS and their components.

2 The Warsaw Treaty included: the People's Republic of Albania, the People's Republic of Bulgaria, the Hungarian People's Republic, the German Democratic Republic (East Germany), the Polish People's Republic, the Rumanian Republic, the Union of Soviet Socialist Republics (USSR) and the Czechoslovak Republic.

3 WAVES stood for Women Accepted for Volunteer Emergency Service. This term has since been discontinued.

4 For additional information regarding this air show see: <http://www.ufx.org/russell/intro.htm>.

5 A CASCADE class destroyer tender (only ship of her class).

Chapter 9. USS CASCADE, AD-16: NEWPORT, RHODE ISLAND, 1956

1 The mission of the U.S. Sixth Fleet, created in 1948, was to counter the substantial Soviet threat to the Mediterranean region and to maintain peace and stability in regions surrounding the Med. At all times there was at least one carrier task force, an afloat Marine battalion, and various service and supply ships on duty in the Med. My thanks to Gregory Johnson for making me aware of this history.

2 For a good overview of the development and function of destroyer tenders see the article by Paolo E. Coletta, "The Destroyer Tender."

3 The Repair Department consisted of four "Repair Divisions," R-1, R-2, R-3 & R-4. R-1 was responsible for hull repair, R-2 was responsible for machinery repair, R-3 was responsible for electri-

cal repair and R-4 was responsible for ordnance repair. I was as-signed to R-4 and the Division Officer was CWO3 H.D. Christensen.

4 Med-moor is a method of mooring designed to save valuable wharf or pier space. The ship's stern is against the wharf or pier and anchors are out forward of the ship. Normal mooring is with one of the ship's sides against the wharf or pier.

5 This may have been USS PLYMOUTH ROCK, LSD-29.

6 An electromechanical machine made by Ford Instrument Co. This was before the age of digital computers. Ford Instrument co. is no longer in business.

7 According to Ford Instrument Company engineers at the time.

Chapter 10. USS CHAMBERS, DER-391

1 The DEW Line was a string of radar sites across Northern Alaska and Northern Canada with seaward extensions into both the Pacific and Atlantic Oceans. After the seaward extensions of the DEW line were discontinued, the DERs would be called upon to monitor the movement of junks during off-shore patrols around Viet-nam during "Operation Market Time." For an in-depth study of the Navy's role on the DEW Line see Captain James F. Bouchard's "Guarding the Cold War Ramparts."

2 Goat Island originally contained a Naval Torpedo Station. This station was commissioned in 1869 and deactivated in 1951.

3 A perpetual lease for a military base in Argentia was given to the United States in 1940 under the terms of the "Bases for Ships" agreement between England and the United States. Under this agree-ment, the United States transferred older destroyers to England in exchange for basing leases.

4 From the CHAMBERS' Deck Log for 13 May 1957.

5 The Oil King is responsible for the management of the ship's oil and water supplies.

6 A "dogging wrench" is a 1" steel pipe about 12" long used to tighten down the dogs (latches) on doors and hatches.

7 Storm threat Condition V is for normal conditions. Condition IV warns of a possible threat of destructive winds within 72 hours; Condition III warns of a possible threat of destructive winds within 48 hours; Condition II warns of a possible threat of destructive winds within 24 hours; and Condition I warns of a possible threat of destructive winds within 12 hours;

8 In the Barrel Method of transfer the goods to be transferred are placed in a water-tight barrel. This barrel is attached to a line that is sent to the receiving ship. The receiving ship's crew then pulls the barrel over and the goods are removed.

9 Aboard ship, "having the conn" is a legal *concept* denoting authority: the authority to issue steering and engine orders to the helmsman. The individual who "has the conn" is the only one who the helmsman will acknowledge. The conn can be assumed by a senior or passed to a junior.

10 From CHAMBERS' deck log for 25 August 1958.

11 This account of activity on the bridge was provided by. Elliott B. Simmons, who was OOD at the time

12 *The News — Newport, R.I.,* Saturday, November 8, 1958, p. 3.

13 Airborne Early Warning Squadrons 11, 13 and 15, flying WV-2 aircraft, comprised the Atlantic Early Warning Wing.

14 Before satellite communications the trans-Atlantic cable was the main means of voice communication between North America and Europe. It was first installed in 1858.

15 Grease ice is the second stage of ice formation. Its oily look gives it its name. Surface slush that agglomerates into rounded floating pads is referred to as "pancake ice." Growler ice refers to pieces of an iceberg that have broken off. They are typically less then three feet high and less than 16-feet long.

16 An automatic 292 cubic inch V-8.

17 My thanks to John Sheehan for reminding me of this incident and for providing the "story behind the story."

18 My thanks to John Sheehan for reminding me of this incident. LTJG Sheehan was OOD during this docking maneuver. I was in charge of the fantail detail at the time.

19 A forward firing anti-submarine weapon that has 48 spigots each holding a 7.2-inch rocket.

20 A remote station located just below the fantail where the ship could be steered manually, using an arrangement of block and tackle, in the event of a hydraulic failure.

21 A classified instrument (at that time) used to obtain temperature-depth profiles of the ocean.

22 The Army does an About Face maneuver on three counts, whereas the Navy does it on two counts.

23 My thanks to LTJG John Sheehan for contributing this poem.

Chapter 11. RECRUITING SCHOOL, BAINBRIDGE, Maryland, 1959

1 WAVES: Women's Auxiliary Volunteers for Emergency Service. This term is no longer used.

Chapter 12. RECRUITING DUTY, NEW YORK, 1960-'61

1 Butler buildings were large, Quonset hut-like, prefabricated buildings.

Chapter 14. MISSILE GUIDANCE RADAR SCHOOL, DAM NECK, VIRGINIA, 1962

1 The Terrier Guided Missile was part of the Navy's latest shipboard multi-function missile system. The AN/SPG-55 radar provided the missile with both a beam riding and an active homing capability.

2 This was when President Kennedy called the Russian's bluff and forced them to remove their offensive missiles from Cuba.

Chapter 15. USS HARRY E. YARNELL, DLG-17, 1962-'63

1 A LEAHY class (later re-designated as a guided missile cruiser, CG), named for Admiral Harry E. Yarnell, USN who was commander-in-chief of the Asiatic Fleet prior to WW II. For the rational behind the change from DLG to CG see Eric Grove's, *The Future of Seapower*, pp. 101-102.

2 So-called because it normally took about twelve years to make CPO and therefore, Chief's were considered by younger sailors to be "Old Goats".

3 The area is called the Tongue of the Ocean (TOTO) because it is bounded on the west by Andros Island, to the south and east by large areas of very shallow banks that are too shallow for boat navigation, and to the north by the Northwest Providence Channel. The basin floor is relatively smooth and soft, with very gradual depth changes. This unique geography results in very low boat traffic, minimal distant shipping noise, and the absence of large swells and sluggish currents. These factors make the TOTO location ideal for an undersea test facility (source: Naval Undersea Warfare Center).

4 Buckeley, and his PT Boats, took General MacArthur off the Philippine Islands in 1942.

5 This occasioned my initiation into the Royal Order of the Blue Nose.

6 See The *Illiad*, by Homer.

Chapter 17. USS FOX, DLG-33: 1966-'68

1 A BELKNAP class (later re-designated as a guided missile cruiser, CG), named for Gustavus Vasa Fox, Assistant Secretary of the Navy from 1861 to 1865. FOX was decommissioned and stricken from the Navy Register on 15 April 1994.

2 ADM Elmo R. Zumwalt later became Chief of Naval Operations (CNO).

3 J.B. Nichols and B. Tillman, p. 45.

4 "Yankee Station" was that area at the entrance to the Tonkin Gulf in which the carrier task force operated.

5 This fire started when an aircraft accidentally launched a missile while waiting on the flight deck. The errant missile caused a fire in another aircraft piloted by LCDR John S. Mc Cain. Mc Cain was later shoot down over NVN on 26 October 1967, and held captive until 1973. In 1981 he retired with the rank of captain. In 1982 he was elected to the House of Representative from Arizona. In 1895 he was elected as a senator from Arizona.

6 North Vietnam had Russian-built MiG 17s, MiG19s and MiG21s.

7 My thanks to LCDR William Lane for relating this story in an e-mail dated 23 May 2002.

8 My thanks to the shipmate who reminded me of this incident.

9 The Standard Missile was designed to replace the three shipboard missiles in use at that time: the short-range TARTER, the medium-range TERRIER and the long-range TALOS.

10 Captain Meyer was known as the "Father of Aegis." Aegis was an ancient type of cloak that was thought to possess supernatural powers. This type of cloak has generally been associated with Zeus, the King of the Gods. It is the name chosen for the Navy's newest radar/anti-air warfare system installed aboard destroyers and cruisers.

Chapter 18.   USNSMSES, PORT HUENEME, CALIFORNIA, 1968-'70

1 This followed the sinking of USS LIBERTY, AGTR-5, an American intelligence ship, during the Israeli-Egyptian war.

2 California State College, Long Beach, was later designated as California State University, Long Beach.

EPILOGUE

1 President Reagan's words were, "Mr. Gorbachev, tear down this wall."

ABOUT THE AUTHOR

The author holds a BS degree in Industrial Technology from California State University, Long Beach, CA, a MS in Systems Management from the University of Southern California and a MA in Vocational Education from California State University. He has taught in the extended education programs at the University of California, Irvine and at West Coast University. Mr. Chambers has published articles related to systems engineering and project management in the following:

- *Acquisition Review Quarterly, Defense Systems Management College*
- *Proceedings: ProjExpo '92*
- *1990 and 1992 Proceedings, National Council on Systems Engineering (NCoSE)*
- *Proceedings, 1990 IEEE International Conference on Systems, Man, and Cybernetics*
- *Project Management Journal*
- *Naval Engineer's Journal*
- *IEEE Transactions on Systems, Man, and Cybernetics*